First World War
and Army of Occupation
War Diary
France, Belgium and Germany

31 DIVISION
Divisional Troops
Divisional Trench Mortar Batteries
7 April 1916 - 28 February 1919

WO95/2351/2

The Naval & Military Press Ltd
www.nmarchive.com
Published in association with The National Archives

Published by

The Naval & Military Press Ltd

Unit 10 Ridgewood Industrial Park,

Uckfield, East Sussex,

TN22 5QE England

Tel: +44 (0) 1825 749494

www.naval-military-press.com

www.nmarchive.com

This diary has been reprinted in facsimile from the original. Any imperfections are inevitably reproduced and the quality may fall short of modern type and cartographic standards.

Contents

Document type	Place/Title	Date From	Date To
Heading	WO95/2351 Div. T.M. Batteries Apr 16-Feb 19		
Heading	31 Division Trench Mortar Batteries 1916 Apl-1919 Feb		
Heading	Confidential War Diary Of Z 31 Trench Mortar Battery. From 7th April 1916 To 31st May 1916		
War Diary	Colincamps (In The Field)	07/04/1916	26/04/1916
War Diary	Bus	27/04/1916	07/05/1916
War Diary	Colincamps (In The Field)	08/05/1916	31/05/1916
War Diary	Ref. Hebuterne Map 57 D. N.E.	01/06/1916	01/07/1916
Heading	31st Division. "X" 31. Medium Trench Howitzer Battery. 1st To 31st July 1916		
Heading	Confidential War Diary Of X 31 Trench Mortar Battery July 1916		
War Diary	Colincamp	01/07/1916	02/07/1916
War Diary	Bus	04/07/1916	04/07/1916
War Diary	Colincamps	04/07/1916	06/07/1916
War Diary	Bus	08/07/1916	08/07/1916
War Diary	Heuzecourt	09/07/1916	09/07/1916
War Diary	Frevent	10/07/1916	10/07/1916
War Diary	Steenbecque	15/07/1916	15/07/1916
War Diary	St Venant Laventie	15/07/1916	22/07/1916
War Diary	Left. Pacaut	28/07/1916	28/07/1916
War Diary	Richebourg	29/07/1916	31/07/1916
Heading	31st Division. "Y" 31. Medium Trench Mortar Battery 1st To 31st July 1916		
Heading	Confidential War Diary Of Y 31 Trench Mortar Battery July 1916. Vol 1		
War Diary	Colincamps	01/07/1916	23/07/1916
War Diary	Richebourg	28/07/1916	31/07/1916
Heading	31st Division. "Z" 31. Medium Trench Mortar Battery 1st To 28th July 1916		
Heading	Confidential War Diary Of Z 31 Trench Mortar Battery July 1916 Vol 4		
War Diary	Colincamps	01/07/1916	05/07/1916
War Diary	Bus	06/07/1916	06/07/1916
War Diary	Heuzecourt	08/07/1916	08/07/1916
War Diary	Conteville	09/07/1916	10/07/1916
War Diary	St Venant	10/07/1916	10/07/1916
War Diary	Laventie	15/07/1916	15/07/1916
War Diary	Pacaut	23/07/1916	23/07/1916
War Diary	Boutdeville	28/07/1916	28/07/1916
Heading	War Diary. Of Y/31 Medium Trench Mortar Battery. From August 1st, 1916 To August 31st, 1916 Volume II		
War Diary	Richebourgh	01/08/1916	31/08/1916
Heading	War Diary. Of Z/31 Medium Trench Mortar Battery. From August 1st, 1916 To August 31st, 1916. Volume II		
War Diary	Boutdeville	04/08/1916	31/08/1916
Heading	War Diary. Of X/31 Medium Trench Mortar Battery. From August 1st, 1916 To August 31st, 1916 Volume II		

War Diary	Richebourg St Vaast	01/08/1916	11/08/1916
War Diary	Bout De Ville	14/08/1916	14/08/1916
War Diary	Richebourg St. Vaast	15/08/1916	31/08/1916
Heading	War Diary Of V/31 Heavy Mortar Battery. From August 1st, 1916 To August 31st, 1916. Volume II		
War Diary	In The Field	01/08/1916	16/08/1916
War Diary	Lacouture	17/08/1916	31/08/1916
Heading	War Diary Of "V" Battery 31st Divn. Heavy Trench Mortar. From 1st September 1916 To 30th September 1916. Volume IX		
War Diary	In The Field	01/09/1916	30/09/1916
Heading	War Diary Of Y/31 Medium Trench Mortar Battery From 1st September 1916 To 30th September 1916 (Volume IX)		
War Diary		01/09/1916	30/09/1916
War Diary	Ferme Du Bois	02/09/1916	03/09/1916
War Diary	Neuve Chapelle	06/09/1916	19/09/1916
War Diary	Ferme Du Bois	13/09/1916	16/09/1916
War Diary	Givenchy	17/09/1916	30/09/1916
Heading	War Diary Of Z/31 Medium Trench Mortar Battery. From 1st September 1916 To 30th September 1916 (Volume IX)		
War Diary	Richebourg St. Vaast	01/09/1916	30/09/1916
Heading	War Diary Of V/31 Heavy Trench Mortar Battery. From 1st October 1916 To 31st October 1916		
War Diary	In The Field	01/10/1916	31/10/1916
War Diary	Givenchy	15/10/1916	15/10/1916
War Diary	Essars	17/10/1916	17/10/1916
War Diary	Hebuterne	18/10/1916	31/10/1916
Heading	War Diary Of Y/31 Medium Trench Mortar Battery. From October 1st 1916 To October 31st 1916. Volume X		
War Diary	Richebourg	01/10/1916	17/10/1916
War Diary	Hebuterne	18/10/1916	27/10/1916
Heading	War Diary Of X/311 Medium Trench Mortar Battery. From October 1st 1916 To October 31st 1916 Volume X		
War Diary	Ferme Du Bois	01/10/1916	17/10/1916
War Diary	Hebutern	18/10/1916	31/10/1916
Heading	War Diary Of "X" Medium Trench Mortar Battery. From 1st November 1916 To 30th November 1916 (Volume XI)		
War Diary	Hebuterne	01/11/1916	30/11/1916
Heading	War Diary Of "Y" Medium Trench Mortar Battery. From 1st November 1916 To 30th November 1916 (Volume XI)		
War Diary	Hebuterne	01/11/1916	29/11/1916
Heading	War Diary Of V/31 Heavy Trench Mortar Battery. From November 1st 1916 To November 30th 1916. (Volume XI)		
War Diary	Sailly-Au-Bois	14/11/1916	28/11/1916
War Diary	Hebuterne	29/11/1916	30/11/1916
Heading	War Diary Of "Z" Medium Trench Mortar Battery. From 1st November 1916 To 30th November 1916. (Volume XI)		
War Diary	Hebuterne	01/11/1916	13/11/1916

War Diary	In The Field	01/11/1916	30/11/1916
Heading	War Diary Of V/31 Heavy Trench Mortar Battery. From 1st December 1916 To 31st December 1916. Volume XII		
War Diary	In The Field	01/12/1916	31/12/1916
Heading	War Diary Of X/31 Medium Trench Mortar Battery. From 1st December 1916 To 31st December 1916 Volume		
War Diary	Sailly Au Bois	01/12/1916	05/12/1916
War Diary	Hebutern	06/12/1916	31/12/1916
Heading	War Diary Of Y/31 Medium Trench Mortar Battery. From 1st December 1916 To 31st December 1916. Volume XII		
War Diary	Hebuterne	12/12/1916	31/12/1916
Heading	War Diary Of Z/31 Medium Trench Mortar Battery. From 1st December 1916 To 31st December 1916. Volume XII		
War Diary	Hebuterne	01/12/1916	06/12/1916
War Diary	Sailly-Au-Bois	09/12/1916	19/12/1916
War Diary	Hebuterne	20/12/1916	27/12/1916
War Diary	Sailly-Au-Bois	27/12/1916	31/12/1916
Heading	War Diary Of Y/31 Medium Trench Mortar Battery. From 1st January 1917 To 31st January 1917. Volume XIII		
War Diary	Hebuterne	11/01/1917	12/01/1917
War Diary	Sailly Au Bois	13/01/1917	15/01/1917
War Diary	Hem	16/01/1917	31/01/1917
Heading	War Diary Of X/31 Medium Trench Mortar Battery. From 1st January 1917 To 31st January 1917. Volume XIII		
War Diary	Hebuterne	01/01/1917	01/02/1917
Heading	War Diary Of V/31 Heavy Trench Mortar Battery. From 1st January 1917 To 31st January 1917 Volume XIII		
War Diary	In The Field	01/01/1917	31/01/1917
Heading	War Diary Of Z/31 Medium Trench Mortar Battery. From 1st January 1917 To 31st January 1917 Volume XIII		
War Diary	Sailly Au Bois	01/01/1917	16/01/1917
War Diary	Hem	17/01/1917	01/02/1917
Heading	War Diary. Of Z/31 Medium Trench Mortar Battery. From 1st February 1917 To 28th February 1917. Volume XIV		
War Diary	Rederie Farm	01/02/1917	10/02/1917
War Diary	St Ouen	11/02/1917	11/02/1917
War Diary	Beauval	20/02/1917	25/02/1917
War Diary	Sailly	27/02/1917	28/02/1917
Heading	War Diary. Of X/31 Medium Trench Mortar Battery. From 1st February 1917 To 28th Feb. 1917. Volume XIV		
War Diary	Rederie Farm	11/02/1917	11/02/1917
War Diary	Stouen	11/02/1917	20/02/1917
War Diary	Beauval	20/02/1917	25/02/1917
War Diary	Sailly Au Bois	25/02/1917	26/02/1917
War Diary	Hebuterne	27/02/1917	28/02/1917
War Diary	St. Ouen	01/02/1917	20/02/1917

War Diary	Beauval	21/02/1917	25/02/1917
War Diary	Sailly Au Bois	27/02/1917	28/02/1917
Heading	War Diary Of V/31 Heavy Trench Battery. From 1st February 1917 To 28th February 1917. Volume XIV		
War Diary	In The Field	01/02/1917	28/02/1917
War Diary	Sailly-Au-Bois	01/03/1917	08/03/1917
War Diary	Bethune	10/03/1917	12/03/1917
War Diary	Givenchy	13/03/1917	31/03/1917
War Diary	Sailly Au Bois	01/03/1917	09/03/1917
War Diary	Bethune	10/03/1917	13/03/1917
War Diary	Annequin	14/03/1917	21/03/1917
War Diary	Cambrin Sector.	22/03/1917	31/03/1917
War Diary	Hebuterne	01/03/1917	06/03/1917
War Diary	Sally An Bois	07/03/1917	10/03/1917
War Diary	Bethune	11/03/1917	14/03/1917
War Diary	Cuinchy	15/02/1917	31/03/1917
War Diary	Hebuterne	01/03/1917	06/03/1917
War Diary	Sally An Bois	07/03/1917	10/03/1917
War Diary	Bethune	11/03/1917	14/03/1917
War Diary	Cuinchy	15/03/1917	31/03/1917
Heading	War Diary Of V/31 Heavy Mortar Battery From 1st March 1917 To 31st March 1917		
War Diary	In The Field	01/03/1917	31/03/1917
Heading	War Diary Of X/31 Medium Trench Mortar Battery. From 1st April 1917 To 30th April, 1917. Volume XVI		
War Diary	Cuinchy	01/04/1917	01/04/1917
War Diary	Annequin	02/04/1917	02/04/1917
War Diary	Petit Sains	03/04/1917	04/04/1917
War Diary	Souchez	05/04/1917	07/04/1917
War Diary	Petit Sains	08/04/1917	08/04/1917
War Diary	Calonne	09/04/1917	14/04/1917
War Diary	Petit Sains	15/04/1917	17/04/1917
War Diary	Maroeuil	18/04/1917	30/04/1917
Heading	War Diary Of V/31 Heavy Trench Mortar Battery. From 1st April 1917 To 30th April 1917. Volume X		
War Diary	In The Field	01/04/1917	30/04/1917
Heading	War Diary Of Y/31 Medium Trench Mortar Battery. From 1st April 1917 To 30th April 1917. Volume XVI		
War Diary	Vermelles Sector	01/04/1917	04/04/1917
War Diary	Annequin	05/04/1917	06/04/1917
War Diary	Sains En Gohelle	07/04/1917	16/04/1917
War Diary	Maroeuil.	17/04/1917	30/04/1917
War Diary	Givenchy	01/04/1917	04/04/1917
War Diary	Les Brebis	06/04/1917	06/04/1917
War Diary	Loos	09/04/1917	30/04/1917
Heading	War Diary Of Y/31 Medium Trench Mortar Battery From 1st May To 31st May 1917. Volume XVII		
War Diary	Maroeuil.	01/05/1917	31/05/1917
Heading	War Diary Of X/31 Medium Trench Mortar Battery From 1st May To 31st May 1917. Volume XVII		
War Diary	Maroeuil.	01/05/1917	03/05/1917
War Diary	Roclincourt	04/05/1917	31/05/1917
Heading	War Diary Of V/31 Heavy Trench Mortar Battery. From 1st May 1917 To 31st May 1917. Volume XVII		
War Diary	In The Field	01/05/1917	31/05/1917
War Diary	Maroeuil.	01/05/1917	03/05/1917

War Diary	Roclincourt	03/05/1917	31/05/1917
War Diary	Maroeuil	01/06/1917	06/06/1917
War Diary	In The Field	07/06/1917	30/06/1917
Heading	War Diary Of X/31 Medium Trench Mortar Battery. From 1st June 1917 To 30th June 1917. Volume XVIII		
War Diary	Maroeuil	01/06/1917	06/06/1917
War Diary	St. Nicholas	07/06/1917	08/06/1917
War Diary	Oppy	09/06/1917	30/06/1917
Heading	War Diary Of V/31 Heavy Trench Mortar Battery. From 1st June 1917 To 30th June 1917. Volume XVIII		
War Diary	In The Field	01/06/1917	30/06/1917
War Diary	Maison Blange.	01/06/1917	30/06/1917
Heading	War Diary Of Y/31 Medium Trench Mortar Battery. From 1st July To 31st July, 1917 Volume XIII		
War Diary	Maison Blanche Arras Sector.	07/07/1917	14/07/1917
War Diary	Armentiers	15/07/1917	31/07/1917
Miscellaneous	D.T.M. O.31 O/C Y M.T.M. B	18/09/1917	18/09/1917
Heading	War Diary Of V/31 Heavy Trench Mortar Battery. From 1st July To 31st July, 1917. Volume XIX		
War Diary	In The Field	01/07/1917	31/07/1917
War Diary	Oppy	01/07/1917	31/07/1917
Heading	War Diary Of Z/31 Medium Trench Mortar Battery. From 1st July To 31st July, 1917. Volume XIX		
War Diary	Maison Blange	01/07/1917	20/07/1917
War Diary	La Targette	22/07/1917	31/08/1917
War Diary	In The Field	01/08/1917	13/08/1917
War Diary	Arleux	22/08/1917	31/08/1917
Heading	War Diary Of V/31 Heavy Trench Mortar Battery. From 1st August To 31st August, 1917. Volume XX		
War Diary	Vimy	01/08/1917	31/08/1917
Heading	War Diary Of Z/31 Heavy Trench Mortar Battery. From 1st August To 31st August, 1917. Volume XX		
War Diary	Erquinghem	01/08/1917	31/08/1917
Heading	War Diary Of Y/31 Heavy Trench Mortar Battery. From 1st Sept. To 30th Sept. 1917 Volume XXI		
War Diary	In The Field	01/09/1917	30/09/1917
Miscellaneous	31 Div. 18G/	24/09/1917	24/09/1917
Heading	War Diary Of X/31 Trench Mortar Battery. From 1st Sept. To 30th Sept. 1917. Volume XXI		
War Diary		01/09/1917	30/09/1917
Heading	War Diary Of V/31 Heavy Trench Mortar Battery. From 1st Sept. To 30th Sept. 1917. Volume XXI.		
War Diary	Vimy	01/09/1917	06/09/1917
War Diary	Arleux	06/09/1917	30/09/1917
War Diary	War Diary Of Z/31 Medium Trench Mortar Battery. From 1st Sept. To 30th Sept. 1917. Volume XXI		
War Diary	Houplines	01/09/1917	25/09/1917
War Diary	Bac-St-Muir	26/09/1917	29/09/1917
War Diary	Roclincourt	27/09/1917	30/09/1917
Heading	War Diary Of Z/31 Medium Trench Mortar Battery. From 1st October To 31st October, 1917. Volume XXII		
War Diary	In The Field	01/10/1917	31/10/1917
Heading	War Diary Of X/31 Medium Trench Mortar Battery. From 1st October To 31st October, 1917. Volume XXII		
War Diary	Arleux Wood	01/10/1917	31/10/1917

Heading	War Diary Of V/31 Heavy Trench Mortar Battery. From 1st October To 31st October, 1917. Volume XXII		
War Diary	Arleux	01/10/1917	31/10/1917
War Diary	Rolincourt	01/10/1917	31/10/1917
Heading	War Diary Of Y/31 Heavy Trench Mortar Battery. From 1st November To 30th November, 1917. Volume XXIII		
War Diary	In The Field	01/11/1917	30/11/1917
Heading	War Diary Of X/31 Heavy Trench Mortar Battery. From 1st November To 30th November, 1917. Volume XXII		
War Diary	Arleux Wood	01/11/1917	30/11/1917
Heading	War Diary Of V/31 Heavy Trench Mortar Battery. From 1st November To 30th November, 1917. Volume XXIII		
War Diary	Arleux	01/11/1917	30/11/1917
Heading	War Diary Of Z/31 Medium Trench Mortar Battery. From 1st November To 30th November, 1917. Volume XXIII		
War Diary	Roclincourt	01/11/1917	30/11/1917
Heading	War Diary Of Y/31 Heavy Trench Mortar Battery. From 1st December To 31st December 1917. Volume XXIV		
War Diary	In The Field	01/12/1917	31/12/1917
War Diary	Arleux Wood	01/12/1917	31/12/1917
Heading	War Diary Of V/31 Heavy Trench Mortar Battery. From 1st December To 31st December 1917. Volume XXIV		
War Diary	Arleux	01/12/1917	31/12/1917
Heading	War Diary Of Z/31 Heavy Trench Mortar Battery. From 1st December To 31st December 1917. Volume XXIV		
War Diary	Roclincourt	01/12/1917	31/12/1917
Heading	War Diary Of Y/31 Heavy Trench Mortar Battery. From 1st January To 31st January, 1918. Volume XXV		
War Diary	In The Field	01/01/1918	31/01/1918
Heading	War Diary Of V/31 Medium Trench Mortar Battery. From 1st January To 31st January, 1918. Volume XXV		
War Diary	Arleux	01/01/1918	31/01/1918
Heading	War Diary Of X/31 Medium Trench Mortar Battery. From 1st January To 31st January, 1918. Volume XXV		
War Diary	Arleux Wood	01/01/1918	31/01/1918
Heading	War Diary Of Z/31 Medium Trench Mortar Battery. From 1st January To 31st January, 1918. Volume XXV		
War Diary	Roclincourt	01/01/1918	31/01/1918
Heading	War Diary Of Z/31 Medium Trench Mortar Battery. From 1st February To 28th February. 1918. Volume XXVI		
War Diary	Roclincourt	01/02/1918	13/02/1918
Heading	War Diary Of X/31 Medium Trench Mortar Battery. From 1st February To 28th February, 1918. Volume XXVI		
War Diary	Arleux Wood	01/02/1918	13/02/1918
War Diary	In The Field	14/02/1918	28/02/1918
Heading	War Diary Of Y/31 Medium Trench Mortar Battery. From 1st February To 28th February, 1918. Volume XXVI		

War Diary	In The Field	01/02/1918	28/02/1918
Heading	War Diary Of Y/31 Medium Trench Mortar Battery. From 1st March 1918 To 31st March 1918. Volume XXVI		
War Diary	In The Field	01/03/1918	31/03/1918
Heading	War Diary Of X/31 Medium Trench Mortar Battery From 1st March 1918 To 31st March 1918. Volume XXVII		
War Diary	Roclincourt	01/03/1918	05/03/1918
War Diary	Cambligneul	06/03/1918	22/03/1918
War Diary	Bavincourt	23/03/1918	26/03/1918
War Diary	Gaudiempre	27/03/1918	31/03/1918
Heading	War Diary Of Y/31 Medium Trench Mortar Battery From 1st April To 30th April, 1918. Volume XXVIII		
War Diary	Gaudiempre	01/04/1918	30/04/1918
Heading	31st Division X/31 Medium Trench Mortar Battery April 1918		
Heading	War Diary Of X/31 Medium Trench Mortar Battery From 1st April To 30th April, 1918. Volume XXVIII		
War Diary	Gaudiempre	01/04/1918	30/04/1918
Heading	War Diary Of Y/31 Medium Trench Mortar Battery. From 1st May To 31st May, 1918. Volume XXIX		
War Diary	Gaudiempre	01/05/1918	31/05/1918
Heading	War Diary Of X/31 Medium Trench Mortar Battery. From 1st May To 31st May, 1918. Volume XXIX		
War Diary	Gaudiempre	01/05/1918	31/05/1918
Heading	War Diary Of Y/31 Medium Trench Mortar Battery. From 1st June To 30th June, 1918. Volume XXX		
War Diary	Gaudiempre	01/06/1918	14/06/1918
War Diary	Monchy	15/06/1918	30/06/1918
Heading	War Diary Of X/31 Medium Trench Mortar Battery. From 1st June To 30th June, 1918. Volume XXX		
War Diary	Gaudiempre	01/06/1918	14/06/1918
War Diary	Monchy	15/06/1918	27/06/1918
War Diary	La Belle Hotesse	28/06/1918	03/07/1918
War Diary	Grand Hazards	04/07/1918	31/07/1918
Heading	War Diary Of X/31 Medium Trench Mortar Battery. From 1st July To 31st July, 1918. Volume. XXXI		
War Diary	La Belle Hotesse	01/07/1918	03/07/1918
War Diary	Grand Hazard	04/07/1918	31/07/1918
Heading	War Diary Of Y/31 Medium Trench Mortar Battery. From 1st August To 31st August, 1918. Volume XXXII		
War Diary	Nieppe Forest	01/08/1918	31/08/1918
Heading	War Diary Of X/31 Medium Trench Mortar Battery. From 1st August To 31st August, 1918. Volume XXVII		
War Diary	Grand Hazard	01/08/1918	08/08/1918
War Diary	Le Grand Hazard	09/08/1918	30/08/1918
Heading	War Diary Of Y/31 Medium Trench Mortar Battery. From 1st September To 30th September, 1918. Volume XXXIII		
War Diary	Nieppe Forest	01/09/1918	30/09/1918
Heading	War Diary Of X/31 Medium Trench Mortar Battery. From 1st September To 30th September, 1918. Volume XXXIII		
War Diary	Nieppe Forest	01/09/1918	19/09/1918
War Diary	Woesten	20/09/1918	29/09/1918

War Diary	Bailleul	30/09/1918	30/09/1918
Heading	War Diary Of Y/31 Medium Trench Mortar Battery. From 1st. October To 31st. October, 1918. Volume XXXIV		
War Diary	Caestre	01/10/1918	31/10/1918
Heading	War Diary Of X/31 Medium Trench Mortar Battery. From 1st. October To 31st. October, 1918. Volume XXXIV		
War Diary	Bailleul	01/10/1918	02/10/1918
War Diary	Caestre	03/10/1918	27/10/1918
War Diary	Heule	28/10/1918	30/10/1918
War Diary	Vichte	31/10/1918	31/10/1918
Heading	War Diary Of Y/31 Medium Trench Mortar Battery. From 1st November To 30th November, 1918. Volume XXXV		
War Diary		01/11/1918	30/11/1918
Heading	War Diary Of X/31 Medium Trench Mortar Battery. From 1st November To 30th November, 1918. Volume XXXV		
War Diary	Vichte	01/10/1918	02/10/1918
War Diary	Heule	03/10/1918	03/10/1918
War Diary	Bousbecque	04/10/1918	31/10/1918
Heading	War Diary Of Y/31 Medium Trench Mortar Battery. From 1st December To 31st December, 1918. Volume XXXVI		
War Diary	In The Field	01/12/1918	31/12/1918
Heading	War Diary Of X/31 Medium Trench Mortar Battery. From 1st January To 31st January, 1919. Volume XXXVII		
War Diary	Esquerdes	01/01/1919	31/01/1919
Heading	War Diary Of Y/31 Medium Trench Mortar Battery. From 1st January To 31st January, 1919. Volume XXXVII		
War Diary	Esquerdes	01/01/1919	31/01/1919
Heading	War Diary Of X/31 & Y/31 Medium Trench Mortar Batteries. From 1st February To 28th February, 1919. Volume XXXVIII		
War Diary	Esquerdes	01/02/1919	28/02/1919

WO 95/2351
Div. T. M. Batteries
Apr '16 - Feb '19

31 DIVISION

TRENCH MORTAR BATTERIES

1916 APL — 1919 FEB

XXXI

Vol 1 + 2

CONFIDENTIAL

War Diary

of

Z31 Trench Mortar Battery.

from 7th April 1916 to 31st May 1916.

Def '19

Instructions regarding War Diaries and Intelligence Summaries are contained in F. S. Regs., Part II. and the Staff Manual respectively. Title Pages will be prepared in manuscript.

WAR DIARY
or
INTELLIGENCE SUMMARY
(Erase heading not required.)

Army Form C. 2118

Place	Date	Hour	Summary of Events and Information	Remarks and references to Appendices
COLINCAMPS (In the Field)	7/4/16		Arrived here from 4th Army Trench Mortar School at VALHEUREUX having had a week's course of instruction on the 2" (Medium) Trench Mortars. Z 31 T.M. Battery consisting of 2 officers (Lt R.M. Alexander 13th (S) Bn East Yorkshire Regiment and 2nd Lt W Dann R.F.A 170th Bgde) + 23 other ranks (drawn from the 170th Bgde R.F.A) reported at the 31st Divisional Headquarters at BUS + were there told to report to the 94th Inf. Bgde HQ at COLINCAMPS - who were holding the front line. On arrival at COLINCAMPS I reported to HQ of the 94th Infantry Brigade + received orders from General Carter Campbell to reconnoitre the 31st Divisional front K23 D32 (JOHN COPSE) - K34 D9802 for suitable positions for the trench mortars.	Ref Trench Map HEBUTERNE 57D NE. 3+4
	8/4/16 to 26/4/16		During this period the men of the battery remained in billets in COLINCAMPS - dug-outs were made for the storage of ammunition etc close to the billets. The whole of the 31st Divisional front was carefully + thoroughly reconnoitred + as far as possible that of the enemy. Reports were sent in suggesting suitable positions for the mortars to the HQ of the Inf. Bgdes on the various dates + also to the T.M.O. of the division.	

R.M. Alexander Lt
O.C. Z 31 T.M. Batty

1875 Wt. W593/826 1,000,000 4/15 J.B.C. & A. A.D.S.S./Forms/C. 2118.

Instructions regarding War Diaries and Intelligence Summaries are contained in F. S. Regs., Part II. and the Staff Manual respectively. Title Pages will be prepared in manuscript.

WAR DIARY
or
INTELLIGENCE SUMMARY
(Erase heading not required.)

Army Form C. 2118

Place	Date	Hour	Summary of Events and Information	Remarks and references to Appendices
BUS.	27/4/16 to 7/5/16		Z31 Battery relieved by X31 T.M. Battery. During this period the Battery were occupied in felling timber & cutting it to the required lengths for the making of the gun emplacements.	
	29/4/16		2nd Lt W. Dann went on leave.	
	1/5/16		Lt R.M. Alexander went on leave.	
	7/5/16		2nd Lt W. Dann returned from leave	
COLINCAMPS (In the Field)	8/5/16		Z31 T.M. Battery returned & went into the trenches – one sub-section remaining in billets in COLINCAMPS.	
	14/5/16		Lt. R. M. Alexander returned from leave.	
	18/5/16		Six bombs were fired at the S side of the QUADRILATERAL with effect as results – bombs falling into the wire at K35-A45-35 ~~with~~ disastrous results for the wire – one degree more right was put on the gun with the result that a bomb fell into the enemy's trench at K35-A45 32 – it appeared to destroy the trench as we noticed large lumps of what appeared to be timber thrown high into the air – probably a "dug-out" was destroyed. Previous to firing the Company Commander of the troops in the front-line at this point had been warned – it was found that this is always advisable especially where	Ref. Trench Map HEBUTERNE 57D N.E. 3 & 4

1875 Wt. W593/826 1,000,000 4/15 J.B.C. & A. A.D.S.S./Forms/C. 2118.

Instructions regarding War Diaries and Intelligence Summaries are contained in F. S. Regs., Part II. and the Staff Manual respectively. Title Pages will be prepared in manuscript.

WAR DIARY
or
INTELLIGENCE SUMMARY
(Erase heading not required.)

Army Form C. 2118

Place	Date	Hour	Summary of Events and Information	Remarks and references to Appendices
COLINCAMPS (In the field)			the opposing lines are close together – as splinters from the bombs are liable to fall amongst our own troops – unless they are warned & the above happens it is liable to have a disconcerting effect on the men in the front-line. There was no retaliation from the enemy on this occasion.	
	20/5/16		A report was handed to us that the Enemy had a trench mortar position at K35 C3099. Seven bombs were fired at this point from an emplacement at K34 B45 with the result that four bombs were dropped into the Enemy trench at the desired point. The result of the shooting was reported to the Machine Gun Officer & he laid one of his guns on this point to prevent "working-parties" repairing the trench – very effective work can be done by the Machine Gun Company co-operating in this way with Trench Mortar Batteries	Ref Map as above.
	-31/5/16		Throughout the above period & until the end of the month – considerable work was done at preparing emplacements ~~for~~ so that all the guns of the three batteries could participate in a "Strafe" on the enemy's lines at PT 1200 opposite MATTHEW COPSE on June 3rd. Work was carried on at top pressure night & day – fresh emplacements being dug opposite the point	Ref Map as above.

1875 Wt. W593/826 1,000,000 4/15 J.B.C. & A. A.D.S.S./Forms/C. 2118.

Army Form C. 2118

Instructions regarding War Diaries and Intelligence Summaries are contained in F. S. Regs., Part II. and the Staff Manual respectively. Title Pages will be prepared in manuscript.

WAR DIARY
or
INTELLIGENCE SUMMARY
(Erase heading not required.)

Place	Date	Hour	Summary of Events and Information	Remarks and references to Appendices
			of entry of the "raiding party" & existing emplacements were strengthened in view of the probable heavy bombardment from the enemy guns. General LAMBERT C.B of the 31st Divisional Artillery personally inspected the positions day by day & ~~offered~~ gave valuable advise to the Battery Commanders. On one occasion the Artillery General of the VIII Army Corps visited the positions which were being made for the trench mortars & approved of their siting & construction	

[illegible signature]
O.C. Z31 T.M. Battery

1875 Wt. W593/826 1,000,000 4/15 J.B.C. & A. A.D.S.S./Forms/C. 2118.

Army Form C. 2118.

Instructions regarding War Diaries and Intelligence Summaries are contained in F. S. Regs., Part II. and the Staff Manual respectively. Title Pages will be prepared in manuscript.

WAR DIARY
or
INTELLIGENCE SUMMARY of Y. 31 Trench Mortar Bty.

(Erase heading not required.)

Place	Date	Hour	Summary of Events and Information	Remarks and references to Appendices
Ref: Hebuterne Map 57D.NE	1/6/16 to 2/6/16		Work was carried on in our positions in our 2nd Line trenches at K29c 2.4 and K29c 35,5	
	3/6/16		The Battery went into a temporary position in K29a 6.2 to take part in a small raid which was carried out on the enemies lines on the night of 3rd June.	
Ref Hebuterne Map 57D. N.E.	4/6/16 to 15/6/16		Work was resumed on our permanent positions at K29c 2.4 & K29c 35,5	
	16/6/16		2/Lt W. [illegible] was posted to the battery as Battery Commander.	
	16/6/16 to 21/6		Work carried on in our permanent positions. Ammunition was carried down and stored in the ammunition chambers. Gun platforms were put in and the mortar beds were placed in position	
	22/6		The four guns of the battery were each registered on the enemy front line wire	

2449 Wt. W14957/M90 750,000 1/16 J.B.C. & A. Forms/C.2118/12.

Instructions regarding War Diaries and Intelligence Summaries are contained in F. S. Regs., Part II. and the Staff Manual respectively. Title Pages will be prepared in manuscript.

WAR DIARY
or
INTELLIGENCE SUMMARY of Y.31 Trench Mortar Bty.

(Erase heading not required.)

Army Form C. 2118.

Vol 1

Place	Date	Hour	Summary of Events and Information	Remarks and references to Appendices
	23/6		The battery went into position in our permanent emplacements.	
	27/6 to 1/7/16		Battery took part in the operations which were carried out during this period. Each day the various enemy lines were shelled the barbed wire being destroyed and considerable damage was done to their trenches. The area covered by our four guns was from K29d 1.3 to K35a 85.85	

[signature] 2/Lt RFA
Y31 T.M. Bty

2449 Wt. W14957/M90 750,000 1/16 J.B.C. & A. Forms/C.2118/12.

31st Division.

WAR DIARY

"X" 31. MEDIUM TRENCH HOWITZER BATTERY.

1stb to 31st JULY 1916.

Confidential 31 Vol II

War Diary

of

X31 Trench Mortar Battery

July 1916.

X 31 Trench Mortar Battery
July 1916.

X/31 Trench Mortar Battery. Vol. I July 1916

Army Form C. 2118.

Instructions regarding War Diaries and Intelligence Summaries are contained in F. S. Regs., Part II. and the Staff Manual respectively. Title Pages will be prepared in manuscript.

WAR DIARY
or
~~INTELLIGENCE~~ SUMMARY
(Erase heading not required.)

Place	Date	Hour	Summary of Events and Information	Remarks and references to Appendices
Colincamps	1/7/16	6 am	Fired 10 bombs with remaining mortar at enemy trenches from position N of Matthew Copse	
		7.30	Ceased firing for infantry advance.	
		12 noon	Personnel left gun positions & proceeded to billets in Colincamps.	
"	3/7/16	10 am	Proceeded to rest billets in Bus-les-Artois.	
Bus	4/7/16	9	Returned to billets at Colincamps	
Colincamps	"	6 pm	Evacuated all mortars & stores from positions in the line.	
"	6/7/16	12 noon	Proceeded with stores & mortars to Bus	
Bus	8/7/16	8.30	Battery complete proceeded to Heuzecourt	
Heuzecourt	9/7/16	6 pm	" " " to Frevent for entrainment to Steenbecque	
Frevent	10/7/16	3.22 am	Proceeded by train to Steenbecque	
Steenbecque	"	11 am	Arrived in billets near St. Venant (Map Refce 36A P 7 b. 7. 9.)	
St Venant	15/7/16	"	Proceeded to Laventie & attached 61st Division.	
Laventie	"	11 pm	Inspected mortar opposite Sugar Loaf Salient.	
"	16/7/16	9 pm	Six casualties (2 NCOs & 4 gunners) of which 5 killed & 1 wounded by one H.E. shell, in front line.	
"	19/7/16	3 am	Two mortars ready for action.	
"	"	4 pm	Relieved by 5th Division T.M's & proceeded to billets Laventie.	
"	20/7/16	11 am	Evacuated mortars & stores from line.	
"	22/7/16	5 pm	Proceeded with battery complete to Le Grand Pacaut (Map Refce 36A. K 35. d. 5. 0.)	

X 31 Trench Mortar Batty.
July 1916 (contd)

Instructions regarding War Diaries and Intelligence Summaries are contained in F. S. Regs., Part II. and the Staff Manual respectively. Title Pages will be prepared in manuscript.

WAR DIARY
or
~~INTELLIGENCE SUMMARY~~
(Erase heading not required.)

Army Form C. 2118.

Place	Date	Hour	Summary of Events and Information	Remarks and references to Appendices
Left. Pacaut	28/7/16	1 pm	Proceeded to forward billet at Richebourg St. Vaast	
Richebourg	29/7/16		Took over existing emplacements between Vine St & Neuve Chapelle (S10 c.5.2 to M35.a.9.0)	
	30/7/16 31/7/16		Worked on existing & new positions in this sector.	
			Clinton 2/Lt R.F.A. O/C X31 T.M. Batty	

2449 Wt. W14957/M90 750,000 1/16 J.B.C. & A. Forms/C.2118/12.

31st Division.

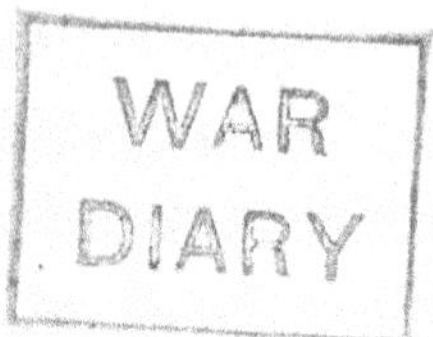

"Y" 31. MEDIUM TRENCH MORTAR BATTERY

1st to 31st JULY 1916.

31

First rec

Confidential

Vol I

War Diary

of

Y 31 Trench Mortar Battery

July 1916.

Y/31 Trench Mortar Battery Vol. I – July 1916

Army Form C. 2118.

Instructions regarding War Diaries and Intelligence Summaries are contained in F. S. Regs., Part II. and the Staff Manual respectively. Title Pages will be prepared in manuscript.

WAR DIARY
or
~~INTELLIGENCE SUMMARY~~ Y 31 T M BTY

(Erase heading not required.)

Place	Date	Hour	Summary of Events and Information	Remarks and references to Appendices
COLINCAMPS	1/7/16	*	Having finished our work as laid down in the programme given to us we were withdrawn from the line at K29c24 & K29c35.5, and the battery returned to COLINCAMPS.	Ref Hebuterne Map 57D NE
	2/7/16		The Battery went to BUS for a rest.	
	4/7/16		Battery returned to COLINCAMPS.	
	4/7/16 5/7/16		Battery carried out salvage work at each of its gun pits removing all mortars and equipment; it was impossible to remove these mortars and beds before as all four guns had been completely buried and they needed a considerable amount of labour & time spending on them to excavate them. The ammunition which remained in the pits was handed over to the D.T.M.O of the 48 DVN.	
	6/7/16		The battery left COLINCAMPS & proceeded by road to BUS.	
	8/7/16		The battery left BUS & proceeded by road to HEUZECOURT.	
	9/7/16		The battery left HEUZECOURT & went to AUXI-LE-CHATEAU where we entrained for THIENNES.	
	10.7.16		Battery arrived at THIENNES & proceeded by road to St. VENANT.	
	15.7.16		Battery engaged the period from 11.7.16 to 14.7.16 in cleaning up equipment &	

2449 Wt. W14957/M90 750,000 1/16 J.B.C. & A. Forms/C.2118/12.

Instructions regarding War Diaries and Intelligence Summaries are contained in F. S. Regs., Part II. and the Staff Manual respectively. Title Pages will be prepared in manuscript.

WAR DIARY
or
~~INTELLIGENCE SUMMARY~~

(Erase heading not required.)

Army Form C. 2118.

Y 31. T. M BATY.

Place	Date	Hour	Summary of Events and Information	Remarks and references to Appendices
			carrying out drills.	
	15.7.16		The Battery left St VENANT & went by road to LEVANTIE. As Battery Commander I went down to front line & chose positions for my four guns.	
	16.7.16		The battery proceeded to the front line with its mortars etc & proceeded to start on the positions chosen by me on the 15.7.16. On their way into the front line three men of the battery were killed & two were wounded. Having placed gun beds in position & started building emplacements, these together with all necessary gear for firing the mortars were handed over to the 61st DIVISION who carried out the programme [illegible] for 3" TM's in the operations on this front.	
	22.7.16		The battery removed all its mortars and equipment from the gun emplacements and returned to LAVENTIE	
	23.7.16		The Battery left LAVENTIE for PACAUT.	
[illegible]	28.7.16		The Battery left PACAUT & proceeded by road to forward billet at S8 a 7.9. The D.T.M.O. and myself had previously explored the right sector of the Divisional	Ref [illegible] Map 36 [illegible]

2449 Wt. W14957/M90 750,000 1/16 J.B.C. & A. Forms/C.2118/12.

Army Form C. 2118.

WAR DIARY
or
~~INTELLIGENCE SUMMARY~~

(*Erase heading not required.*)

Y 31 T.M. BTY.

Instructions regarding War Diaries and Intelligence Summaries are contained in F. S. Regs., Part II. and the Staff Manual respectively. Title Pages will be prepared in manuscript.

Place	Date	Hour	Summary of Events and Information	Remarks and references to Appendices
RICHEBOURG			Front and had noted all existing positions for 2" Trench Mortars and also selected a number of new ones extending over the whole sector.	
	20.7.16		Two mortars were taken down to the trenches and placed in position at S10c 2,1½. These emplacements were old positions and it was only necessary to drain the ground slightly and make new platforms for the beds. Twenty complete rounds were ready in these pits, so that these two guns were ready for firing by mid day on the 20th inst.	Ref. RICHEBOURG map 36 S.W. 3
	30.7.16 – 31.7.16		Another position was started at S16a ½ 7½ and the gun bed was placed in position.	[illegible]

W. Dann 2/Lt. R.F.A.
O/C Y. 31 T.M. Bty.

2449 Wt. W14957/M90 750,000 1/16 J.B.C. & A. Forms/C.2118/12.

31st Division.

"Z" 31. MEDIUM TRENCH MORTAR BATTERY

1st to 28th JULY 1916.

31/

Confidential

Vol 4 / I

June [illegible]

War Diary

of

Z 31 Trench Mortar Battery

July 1916.

JULY 1916.

Instructions regarding War Diaries and Intelligence Summaries are contained in F. S. Regs., Part II. and the Staff Manual respectively. Title Pages will be prepared in manuscript.

WAR DIARY ~~or~~ ~~INTELLIGENCE~~ SUMMARY

(Erase heading not required.) Z 31 TRENCH MORTAR BTTY.

Army Form C. 2118.

Vol. I. July 1916.

Place	Date	Hour	Summary of Events and Information	Remarks and references to Appendices
COLINCAMPS	1/7/16		Having completed the programme as laid down for the 2" Trench Mortars & the Infantry having commenced the assault ~~of~~ on SERRE – the Battery was withdrawn from the "Line" & returned to billets at COLINCAMPS.	
"	5/7/16		The Battery were taken into the "Line" to recover guns, tool boxes etc – All the guns with the exception of one (No 8) were recovered – the gun in Pit No 8 was completely buried – the head cover consisting of steel girders, sandbags, timber etc having been blown in by the concentrated fire of the enemy heavy artillery – this gun was however eventually recovered & is again in the possession of the Battery. The work of salving the guns, equipment etc was heavy as 3 out of the 4 guns were partly if not wholly buried – the ammunition & component parts ~~stored~~ left in the various gun positions were handed over to the D.T.M.O of the 48th DIVISION – the division which relieved the 31st. Throughout this bombardment the Trench Mortars were called upon to "carry out" a very heavy programme of firing & it was the experience of this Battery & it is believed of the other Batteries in action also, that the L.E. Rifle Mechanism as then fitted are very liable to get out of order – it is most important that the L.E. Mechanism supplied to 2" Trench Mortars should be in perfect condition & thoroughly	

2449 Wt. W14957/M90 750,000 1/16 J.B.C. & A. Forms/C.2118/12.

[illegible]

Army Form C. 2118.

Instructions regarding War Diaries and Intelligence Summaries are contained in F. S. Regs., Part II. and the Staff Manual respectively. Title Pages will be prepared in manuscript.

WAR DIARY
or
INTELLIGENCE SUMMARY

(Erase heading not required.)

Place	Date	Hour	Summary of Events and Information	Remarks and references to Appendices
			tested before being issued. The Mechanism of this Battery had to be ~~replaced time after~~ repaired time after time during the bombardment – during the bombardment on the day of the assault I had to personally repair the Mechanism of Gun No 6 after each shot – this meant the waste of valuable time as after each shot CPL JOHNSTONE or myself had to ~~un~~ unscrew the mechanism repair it & replace it – worn Mechanisms from old L-E rifles should not be issued as the springs & stocks very quickly give way under the strain of a sustained fire. It was also noticed that the effect of prolonged firing on the beds of the Mortars was to drive the front down – one bed which was taken up after 4 days firing & replaced was found to be at an angle of about 45° – the front of the bed should always be well supported – no "side-slipping" of the beds was noticed in any of the gun-pits.	
BUS	6/7/16		Battery went to BUS.	
HEUZECOURT	8/7/16		Battery marched to HEUZECOURT.	
CONTÉVILLE	9/7/16		Battery marched to CONTÉVILLE	
	10/7/16		Battery entrained for BERGUETTE.	

[illegible signature]

2449 Wt. W14957/M90 750,000 1/16 J.B.C. & A. Forms/C.2118/12.

Army Form C. 2118.

Instructions regarding War Diaries and Intelligence Summaries are contained in F. S. Regs., Part II. and the Staff Manual respectively. Title Pages will be prepared in manuscript.

WAR DIARY
or
INTELLIGENCE SUMMARY

(Erase heading not required.)

Place	Date	Hour	Summary of Events and Information	Remarks and references to Appendices
St VENANT	10/7/16		Battery in Billets at St VENANT – refitting.	
LAVENTIE	15/7/16		Battery reported to the D.T.M.O of the 61st DIVISION – certain sectors of the line in the TILLELOY sector were handed over to the three batteries of the 31st DIVISION – positions, as required, were made & guns put in – these positions were then handed over by the D.T.M.O of the 61st Division to the Trench Mortar Batteries of the 8th DIVISION. At the conclusion of the operations the Batteries of the 31st DIVISION salved their guns & other parts & then marched to rest billets in LE GRAND PACAUT	
PACAUT	23/7/16		Battery in Rest Billet refitting	
BOUT DEVILLE	28/7/16		Battery marched to BOUT DEVILLE & remained in reserve to X & Y Batteries who went into the Line & commenced on the work of making emplacements.	

[signature]

2449 Wt. W14957/M90 750,000 1/16 J.B.C. & A. Forms/C.2118/12.

Vol 2

CONFIDENTIAL.

WAR DIARY.

of

Y/31 MEDIUM TRENCH MORTAR BATTERY.

FROM AUGUST 1st, 1916 to AUGUST 31st, 1916.

VOLUME II

Instructions regarding War Diaries and Intelligence Summaries are contained in F. S. Regs., Part II. and the Staff Manual respectively. Title Pages will be prepared in manuscript.

WAR DIARY
or
~~INTELLIGENCE SUMMARY~~
(Erase heading not required.)

1st to 31st Augt 1916

Army Form C. 2118.

Y31 Med: T M. Bty

Vol II

Place	Date	Hour	Summary of Events and Information	Remarks and references to Appendices
Richebourg	1/8/16 to 4/8/16		The position at S16a ½ 7½, was carried on with and finished. Another emplacement was sited at S16a 1. 4½ and the building of the gun pit and ammunition store started. A platform for the mortar bed was also put in.	Ref Richebourgh Map 36 SW
	4/8/16		Y31 Med T.M.Bty was relieved by Z31 Med T.M.Bty who took over all existing positions. Y31 Med T.M.Bty withdrew mortars, etc from the line and became Battery in Reserve.	
	5/8/16 to 14/8/16		During this period the battery went into training, doing gun drill physical drill etc.	
	15/8/16		In company with the O.C. X31 T.M.B. I went over the Left Sector of the Divisional Front (S5b 3.9 to S10c 5.2) noting all existing emplacements and the proposed sites for new ones.	
	[illegible]/8/16		This battery relieved X31 Med T.M.Bty from the Left Sector and put 4 mortars in position at the following points (a) S10c 9½, 6½ (b) S10d 1,7 (c) S10d 3,8 (d) S10d 2½ 8½	

2449 Wt. W14957/M90 750,000 1/16 J.B.C. & A. Forms/C.2118/12.

Army Form C. 2118.

WAR DIARY
or
~~INTELLIGENCE SUMMARY~~ Y31 Med. T.M. Bty

(Erase heading not required.)

Instructions regarding War Diaries and Intelligence Summaries are contained in F. S. Regs., Part II. and the Staff Manual respectively. Title Pages will be prepared in manuscript.

Place	Date	Hour	Summary of Events and Information	Remarks and references to Appendices
Richebourg	11/8/16		I received orders that 3 emplacements had to be started at once, in order ~~that~~ to fire on to the enemy trenches etc from S22 c 7½ 9½ to S22 c 8½ 3 I chose 3 positions at (a) S21 b 9.1, (b) S21 d 9½ 8, (c) S21 d 9½ 9½.	Ref to Richebourg map SW 36.
	12/8/16 to 16/8/16		Platforms were laid in these three positions and gun pits & ammn chambers were completed. By 10 am 16/8/16 3 mortars were in position ready to fire with at least 20 complete rounds in each ammunition chamber.	
	16/8/16	8 pm.	In conjunction with 18 pdrs & 4.5 How we bombarded the enemies wire, front line & support trenches for ½ hr (8 pm to 8.30 pm.) The shooting of the mortars appeared to be very effective wire and parapets were badly damaged. Several dugouts seem to have been hit as large pieces of timber were thrown into the air, and also a fire was caused in the enemies lines. 48 bombs were fired from these three mortars during the half hour. During our firing, retaliation was practically nil, but about 5 minutes after we had finished he opened fire on our front line, support and communication trenches with 77's 4.2's and 5.9's which fire he kept up for about 5 mins. The damage done to our trenches was slight and our	

2449 Wt. W14957/M90 750,000 1/16 J.B.C. & A. Forms/C.2118/12.

Instructions regarding War Diaries and Intelligence Summaries are contained in F. S. Regs., Part II. and the Staff Manual respectively. Title Pages will be prepared in manuscript.

WAR DIARY
or
~~INTELLIGENCE SUMMARY~~

(Erase heading not required.)

Y31 Med T M Bty

Army Form C. 2118.

Place	Date	Hour	Summary of Events and Information	Remarks and references to Appendices
Richebourg			Casualties Nil.	
	18/8/16		From 4am to 4.20am we carried out another short bombardment of the enemy trenches from the same three positions. Owing to a very heavy mist, observation was impossible. On this occasion the enemy retaliated soon after we commenced firing and kept it up for about 1/2 hr. He used 77mm 4.2's & 5.9's. A few Trench Mortars were also used against us, but owing to the mist, it was impossible to observe where these were fired from. 45 rounds (both bombs) were fired from the three mortars. No damage was done to our positions and our casualties were Nil.	
	19/8/16		The three mortars were withdrawn from the positions at (a) S.21 c 9.1. (b) S.21 c 9½ 8 (c) S.21 c 9½ 9½	Richebourg 36
			and put into position in emplacements at (a) S.16 a 2½ 4 (b) S.16 a 2 4½ (c) S.16 a 1.4½	
			The fourth mortar was put into position at (d) S.16 a ½ 7½.	— do —

2449 Wt. W14957/M90 750,000 1/16 J.B.C. & A. Forms/C.2118/12.

Army Form C. 2118.

WAR DIARY
or
~~INTELLIGENCE SUMMARY~~
(Erase heading not required.)

Y. 31. MED. T. M. Bty.

Instructions regarding War Diaries and Intelligence Summaries are contained in F. S. Regs., Part II. and the Staff Manual respectively. Title Pages will be prepared in manuscript.

Place	Date	Hour	Summary of Events and Information	Remarks and references to Appendices
Richebourgh	19/8/16 to 23/8/16		During this period these four emplacements completed and 60 complete rounds were placed in each ammunition chamber. ~~The four mortars~~ Lines of fire were laid out for each mortar, onto the enemy's wire and trenches on the Boar's Head (S.16 a).	Richebourg map 36 S W
	23/8/16		The 92nd Inf Brigade had arranged a raid on the enemy's lines at about S16 a 7 8. The work of destroying the wire in front of this point was given to the three Med T M Bats of the 31st Division and one battery of 30 Div. This programme was carried out and after 20 mins shooting the wire was completely destroyed and the Raiding Party informed us they were ready to go in. The Trench Mortars then carried out the second part of their programme by switching on to communication & other trenches, in order to block these up. Whilst this was being done the ~~I~~ Infantry were able to enter the German trenches and carry out their part of the programme. It was afterwards reported that the Med T M's had completely destroyed the wire and front line trenches and had also been able to form a barrage on the communication trenches.	

2449 Wt. W14957/M90 750,000 1/16 J.B.C. & A. Forms/C.2118/12.

Instructions regarding War Diaries and Intelligence Summaries are contained in F. S. Regs., Part II. and the Staff Manual respectively. Title Pages will be prepared in manuscript.

WAR DIARY
or
~~INTELLIGENCE SUMMARY~~
(Erase heading not required.)

Y 31 MED. T M B'y.

Army Form C. 2118.

Place	Date	Hour	Summary of Events and Information	Remarks and references to Appendices
Richebourgh	23/8/16		The enemy's retaliation on our front line was moderate and several bays were damaged. Two of our 2 gun pits were hit ((a) + (b)) but not seriously damaged. We had no casualties.	
	25/8/16		X 31 T.M.B'y relieved Y 31 T.M.B'y from the line, taking over all emplacements etc. Y 31 T.M.B'y withdrew its four mortars from the line and became Battery in Reserve.	
	26/8/16 to 30/8/16		This period was used for gun drill and the calibrating of mortars.	
	31/8/16		Three new platforms were laid in the following positions (a) S10.6, 6, ½ (b) S10.6, 6½, 1 (c) S10.6, 6½, 2½.	Ref Richebourgh Map S.W.36

W. Dawes(?) Lt R.F.A.
OC Y31 Med. T.M.B.

2449 Wt. W14957/M90 750,000 1/16 J.B.C. & A. Forms/C.2118/12.

Vol 5

CONFIDENTIAL.

WAR DIARY.

of

Z/31 MEDIUM TRENCH MORTAR BATTERY.

FROM AUGUST 1st, 1916 to AUGUST 31st, 1916.

VOLUME II

1st to 31st Augt 1916

WAR DIARY
or
~~INTELLIGENCE SUMMARY~~
(Erase heading not required.)

Army Form C. 2118

Z 31. Med. T. M. Bty

Vol II

Instructions regarding War Diaries and Intelligence Summaries are contained in F. S. Regs., Part II. and the Staff Manual respectively. Title Pages will be prepared in manuscript.

Place	Date	Hour	Summary of Events and Information	Remarks and references to Appendices
BOUT-DE-VILLE	4/8/16	12 noon	Took over the Right Sector from Y31 T.M.B (S10c 5.1 – S11c 1.3)	RICHEBOURG 36 S.W. AWL
	5/8/16 to 15/8/16		Positions built & beds laid in Right Sector. During this period 7 casualties were inflicted by enemy rifle grenades & light aerial torpedos. Great difficulty was experienced in finding & constructing good "beds" owing to the ground being very swampy.	AWL
	16/8/16	8 pm	30 rounds fired into enemy front line at S11c 6.6½ – S11c 7.5½	AWL
		8.30 pm	30 rounds fired into enemy front line at S11c 6.6½ – S11c 7.5½	AWL
	18/8/16	4 am	Positions in support trench South of BOND ST consolidated & repaired	AWL
	19/8/16			
	21/8/16	6.5 pm	Registered No 4 gun (position S10c 2.1½) on enemy wire at S16a 7½ 8½	AWL
	22/8/16	5.50 pm	Registered No 3 gun (position S10c 2.1¼) on enemy wire at S16a 7½ 8½	AWL
	23/8/16	9.40 pm to 10.5 pm	In conjunction with artillery, wire was cut & trenches barraged round BOARS HEAD in preparation for an infantry raid. Two guns cut wire by searching & sweeping in front of enemy line expending 27 rounds, & enemy trenches blocked at S16a 7.5 & at S16a 9½ 3½ on which 35 rounds were expended. Wire was cut	AWL
	25/8/16	12 noon	Took over Left Sector from X31 T.M.B (S10c 5.1 – S5d ½-3). Fired 17 rounds into enemy front line at S11a 1½ 1 to S11a 4 1 (at 6.5 pm)	AWL
	28/8/16	5.50 pm to 6 [illegible] pm	66 rounds fired into enemy wire & communication trenches at S10d 5.6	AWL
	29/8/16	4 pm to 5.10 pm	44 rounds fired into enemy wire at S16a 7½ 9 to S16a 8½ 9½. Firing was stopped at 5.10 pm owing to the gun pits & amm. chambers being flooded by rain	AWL

Army Form C. 2118

Instructions regarding War Diaries and Intelligence Summaries are contained in F. S. Regs., Part II. and the Staff Manual respectively. Title Pages will be prepared in manuscript.

WAR DIARY
or
INTELLIGENCE SUMMARY
(Erase heading not required.)

Place	Date	Hour	Summary of Events and Information	Remarks and references to Appendices
31.8.16			2Lt. C.O.H. Clarke took over temporary command of Z31.	CoHC
31.8.16			In conjunction with artillery 12 Rds. were fired into enemy wire, and 16 Rds into his front line trench	CoHC
			[signature] 2/Lt R.F.A. OC Z 31st M.T.M. Bty	

1875 Wt. W593/826 1,000,000 4/15 J.B.C. & A. A.D.S.S./Forms/C. 2118.

Vol 3

C O N F I D E N T I A L.

W A R D I A R Y.

of

X/31 MEDIUM TRENCH MORTAR BATTERY.

FROM AUGUST 1st, 1916 to AUGUST 31st, 1916.

VOLUME II

Instructions regarding War Diaries and Intelligence Summaries are contained in F. S. Regs., Part II. and the Staff Manual respectively. Title Pages will be prepared in manuscript.

WAR DIARY
~~or~~
~~INTELLIGENCE~~ SUMMARY

(*Erase heading not required.*)

X31 T.M. Battery 1st – 31st AUGUST 1916. VOL II.

Army Form C. 2118.

Place	Date	Hour	Summary of Events and Information	Remarks and references to Appendices
Richebourg l'Avoué	Aug 1	9 am - 5 pm	Mortar emplacements proceeded with at S10d.1.9 and S5b.2½.9½. Ch.	All references to Maps refer to MAP France Bethune 1/10000.
"	2	"	Work on emplacements at S10d.1.7, S10d.3½.8½ and S5b 2½ 9½ Ch	
	3		New emplacements commenced at M35d.4.5 and S10b 7.1. Another position found at S10c.6.4. Ch.	
	4		Work proceeded with at S5b.2½ 9½ & S10b 7.1. Ch.	
	5		Mortar beds laid at S10c 5.3½ and S10c.6.4 Ch.	
	7		Work on positions at S10d.2½.8, S10c.5.7 & S10c 6.4. Ch	
	8	12 am - 4 am	Gun pits constructed with cover at S10c 5.7 and S10c 6.4 Ch	
	9	9 am - 5 pm	Platform bed laid at S10c.6.4. Position stated as S10c 5.7 should be stated as S10c 6.6½. Ch	
	10	7 pm - 7.30 pm	14 Rounds fired from position at S10b 7.1 at selected points in enemy trenches at S11a. (3 blinds). Ch	
	11		Work on position at S10d.3½ 8½	
		9.30 am	One man killed & three wounded by rifle grenade at S10d 1.9	
		1.30 pm	Battery proceeded to Pont de Ville (R24 a 5 8) MAP France Bethune combined sheet 1/40000 Ch.	
Pont de Ville	14	3.0 pm	Battery proceeded to billet at S8b 3 4 (MAP France Bethune combined sheet 1/40000.) Ch.	
Richebourg l'Avoué	15	9 am - 4 pm	Calibrated mortars on range at S8a 5 1 Ch.	

2449 Wt. W14957/M90 750,000 1/16 J.B.C. & A. Forms/C.2118/12.

Instructions regarding War Diaries and Intelligence Summaries are contained in F. S. Regs., Part II. and the Staff Manual respectively. Title Pages will be prepared in manuscript.

WAR DIARY
or
INTELLIGENCE SUMMARY
(Erase heading not required.)

Army Form C. 2118.

X31 T.M. Batty 1-31 AUG (contd) VOL II.

Place	Date	Hour	Summary of Events and Information	Remarks and references to Appendices
Richebourg St Vaast	Aug 16	6 pm -6.45 pm	Fired 49 rounds at enemy trenches at S10 d 6.6. Much damage to front line observed. Ch	All map references refer to France – Bethune 1/10000
	17	9 am - 5.30 pm	Work on position at S10 c 6 4, S10 d 3½ 8½ and S10 d. 0.6. Ch	
	18		As last Ch	
	19		As last Ch	
	20		as last Ch	
	21		as last Ch	
	22		as last ½ Round fired at S16.a 77 for registration Ch	
	23	9.40-10.0 pm		
	24	12.30 am -1.50 am	Fired 137 rounds with four mortars at wire & trenches in S16 a. in connection with raid on enemy trench. Ch	
	26	4.30 -5.0 pm	Fired 20 bombs with two mortars at enemy wire & trenches at S28. a. 8.8 and S22. d. 9.2 Ch	
	27	6.30- 7.0 pm	Fired 41 rounds at enemy wire & trenches at S22 c. 6 5 Ch	
	28	9 am -5 pm	Worked on position at S16 c. 3.8. Ch	
	29	4 pm -5 pm	Fired 17 rounds at enemy wire S16 a 7 3. to S16 a 7 6. owing to heavy thunderstorm pits were flooded, charges made damp & shooting was consequently erratic Ch	
	31	5 pm	Fired 7 rounds registration at enemy wire S22 c	

C. Chastey Lt. R.F.A.
Comm'd'g X31 Trench Howitzer Battery.
2.9.16

2449 Wt. W14957/M90 750,000 1/16 J.B.C. & A. Forms/C.2118/12.

Vol 1

C O N F I D E N T I A L.

W A R D I A R Y.

of

V/31 HEAVY TRENCH MORTAR BATTERY.

FROM AUGUST 1st, 1916 to AUGUST 31st, 1916.

VOLUME II

Instructions regarding War Diaries and Intelligence Summaries are contained in F. S. Regs., Part II. and the Staff Manual respectively. Title Pages will be prepared in manuscript.

WAR DIARY
or
~~INTELLIGENCE~~ SUMMARY
(Erase heading not required.)

V/31 HEAVY TRENCH MORTAR BATTERY
No. Vol 1.
Date 1.8.31.8.16

Army Form C. 2118.

V31 Heavy T. M. Bty

Place	Date	Hour	Summary of Events and Information	Remarks and references to Appendices
In the Field	1/8/16		Moved one Gun to Levante. One gun remained at Gorre	
			2nd Lieut L. A. De Jongh in charge at Levante. Capt F. J. Haney in charge at Gorre	
	2/8/16		Moved gun from Gorre to Givenchy. Choose positions at Levante	
	3/8/16		Choose position at Givenchy. Started on position at Levante	
	4/8/16		Started work on position at Givenchy	
	5/8/16 6/8/16 7/8/16	}	Working on positions	
	8/8/16		Right Section rejoined rest of Battery at Givenchy	
	8/8/16		Fired 20 rounds on Mine Shafts	
	10/8/16		Fired 7 Rounds on Mine Shafts. Enemy retaliated strongly	
	13/8/16		Fired 16 Rounds at Mine Shafts. Did great damage. Enemy retaliated strongly	
	14/8/16		Left Givenchy for Lacouture. Left one gun and 23 rounds Ammunition behind with 30th Division. Picked up a gun at Gorre for 61st Division, brought it to Lacouture. Rejoined 31st Division	
	15/8/16		Choose positions at Lacouture	
	16/8/16		Started work on positions. Sent gun picked up at Gorre, to 61st Division Levante	

Continued

2449 Wt. W14957/M90 750,000 1/16 J.B.C. & A. Forms/C.2118/12.

Instructions regarding War Diaries and Intelligence Summaries are contained in F. S. Regs., Part II. and the Staff Manual respectively. Title Pages will be prepared in manuscript.

WAR DIARY
or
INTELLIGENCE SUMMARY
(Erase heading not required.)

Army Form C. 2118.

V/31 HEAVY TRENCH MORTAR BATTERY
No. ....
Date ....

Place	Date	Hour	Summary of Events and Information	Remarks and references to Appendices
continued				
Lacouture	17/8/16		Carting material to positions. Capt F J Haney goes to hospital.	
	18/8/16		Working on positions	
	19/8/16		Working on positions. Received 120 rounds Ammunition	
	20/8/16		Finished Positions.	
	21/8/16		Moved gun into position, also took up 5 rounds Ammunition	
	22/8/16		Fired 4 rounds for registration	
	23/8/16		Fired 19 rounds as per programme. One premature. One dud.	
	24/8/16		Work on other positions	
	25/8/16		Work on positions. Took 10 rounds to position	
	26/27/8/16		Work on positions.	
	28/8/16		Finished another position. Fired 3 rounds at S11 a 5.3. Ammunition faulty. One round only went 20 yards in front of gun	
	29/8/16 30/8/16		Carting material to positions, and finishing same	
	31/8/16		Dismounted gun, and brought it to St Vaast dump, in readiness to move to another position	

G. P. [illegible]
2nd Lieut

2449 Wt. W14957/M90 750,000 1/16 J.B.C. & A. Forms/C.2118/12.

C O N F I D E N T I A L.

W A R D I A R Y

O F

"V" Battery 31st Divn. Heavy Trench Mortars.

From 1st September 1916 to 30th September 1916.

(V O L U M E IX)

1st to 30th Sept. 1916. VOL III

Army Form C. 2118.

Instructions regarding War Diaries and Intelligence Summaries are contained in F. S. Regs., Part II. and the Staff Manual respectively. Title Pages will be prepared in manuscript.

WAR DIARY
or
INTELLIGENCE SUMMARY

(Erase heading not required.)

V/31 Heavy Trench Mortar Battery

Place	Date	Hour	Summary of Events and Information	Remarks and references to Appendices
In the Field	1/9/16		Completed position. Took 20 rounds Ammunition to position in readiness to fire.	
	2/9/16.	11-30AM	Fired 6 rounds at S16 a 9½. 3½. One blind. Fired 5 rounds at 5 P.M at S10 d 0 ½. Enemy retaliated with 8 inch.	
	3/9/16		Fired 3 rounds at S10 d 2. 0. Started dug out for Ammunition at billet	
	4/9/16		Working on Ammunition pit, also started new positions.	
	5/9/16		Working for Mediums	
	6/9/16		- do -	
	7/9/16		- do -	
	8/9/16		- do -	
	9/9/16		- do -	
	10/9/16		- do -	
	11/9/16		Brought gun out of old position. Got everything in readiness to take to new position.	
	12/9/16		Got gun in position at S10 a 6½. 6½. Took 20 rounds Ammunition to gun position.	
	13/9/16		Finished gun position. Got gun ready for firing. Shoot postponed.	
	14/9/16		Fired 7 rounds at target S11 c 1½. 3½. Very good shoot. One blind.	
	15/9/16		Working on positions. Preparing to fire.	
	16/9/16		Received orders to cancell shoot. Work on positions	
	17/9/16		Working on positions. Orders received for one section to go to Givenchy	
	18/9/16		Right section sent to Givenchy. Took over one gun and 54 Rounds Ammunition.	

2449 Wt. W14957/M90 750,000 1/16 J.B.C. & A. Forms/C.2118/12.

Continued

Instructions regarding War Diaries and Intelligence Summaries are contained in F. S. Regs., Part II. and the Staff Manual respectively. Title Pages will be prepared in manuscript.

WAR DIARY
or
INTELLIGENCE SUMMARY
(Erase heading not required.)

Army Form C. 2118.

V/31. Heavy Trench Mortar Battery

Place	Date	Hour	Summary of Events and Information (continued)	Remarks and references to Appendices
In the Field	Sept 19		Working on positions, both sections	
	20		- do - -do-	
	21		Working on positions. Capt F. J. Haney rejoins.	
	22		Working on positions	
	23		Left Section complete position. Right Section fired 21 rounds at target A10c2.7 to A9b8½.2½. 15 rounds very good, 6 rounds short.	
	24		Right Section making new position. Left section fired 20 rounds at target S16a6.6. Very successful shoot as regards damage done to enemy. Range poor.	
	25		Shoot arranged for Left Section postponed. At work on positions received 60 rounds Ammunition from D.A.C.	
	26		Left section fired 12 rounds at target S16a9½.3½. Very successful shoot. Target hit 3 times. Enemy retaliated with 8 inch and 4.2	
	27		Working on positions. Choose new position	
	28		Send 12 men to R. E. to help construct positions for us	
	29		Working on position. Choose new position	
	30		Working on position. Orders received to bring Right Section and gun to their billet. Right Section and gun arrived	

F. J. Haney Capt R.F.A.

2449 Wt. W14957/M90 750,000 1/16 J.B.C. & A. Forms/C.2118/12.

C O N F I D E N T I A L.

W A R   D I A R Y

O F

Y/31 Medium Trench Mortar Battery

From 1st September 1916 to 30th September 1916.

(V O L U M E IX)

1st – 30th Sept 16.

WAR DIARY
or
~~INTELLIGENCE SUMMARY~~
(Erase heading not required.)

VOL III

Y 31. MED. T. M. BATY

Army Form C. 2118.

Instructions regarding War Diaries and Intelligence Summaries are contained in F. S. Regs., Part II. and the Staff Manual respectively. Title Pages will be prepared in manuscript.

Place	Date	Hour	Summary of Events and Information	Remarks and references to Appendices
	1/9/16 – 2/9/16.		Work on the positions in S10b. was continued.	Richebourg map. 36 S.W. 3.
	3/9/16 – 4/9/16.		Four new positions were started at the following places:– (a). S16c 3.8. (b). S16c 3.75. (c). S16c 3.5. (d). S16c 35.45. The guns being laid on enemy trenches between S16c 8.8 & S16c 8.4.	– do –
	5/9/16		From 10.30 a.m. to 11.0 a.m. we bombarded enemy's front line & wire at about S16c 8.8. to S16c 8.4. 59 rounds were fired & at least one good lane was cut through enemy's front line wire. Retaliation was practically nil.	– do –
	6/9/16		From 12.30 p.m. to 1.0 p.m. we again bombarded enemy's wire at above-mentioned points. His front line wire was completely destroyed for a distance of at least 30 & large gaps were made in his parapet.	– do –
	7/9/16		At 12.5 a.m. we fired a 4 gun Salvo into the Ferme du Bois (S16c 9.8)	– do –
	8/9/16		At 12.30 a.m. a raiding party of the 92nd Inf. Bde. entered the enemy's trenches at about S16c 8.5. The four guns of the Battery were laid on the Ferme du Bois ready to open fire in case of need. At about 12.45 a.m. we received a message from the raiding party to fire on Ferme du Bois & after the first 4 rounds the machine guns were silenced.	

2449 Wt. W14957/M90 750,000 1/16 J.B.C. & A. Forms/C.2118/12.

Army Form C. 2118.

WAR DIARY
or
~~INTELLIGENCE SUMMARY~~
(Erase heading not required.)

Y31 MED. T.M. BTY.

Instructions regarding War Diaries and Intelligence Summaries are contained in F. S. Regs., Part II. and the Staff Manual respectively. Title Pages will be prepared in manuscript.

Place	Date	Hour	Summary of Events and Information	Remarks and references to Appendices
	9/9/16 – 12/9/16.		Work was carried out, strengthening gun emplacements.	Richebourg map. 36S.W.3.
	12/9/16.		Our emplacement at 516c 3.5 received a direct hit from a hostile T.M. + was thereby totally wrecked. No casualties were caused.	
	17/9/16.		This battery took over all emplacements from 510c 2.54 to 510b 9.7.	-do-
	19/9/16 – 22/9/16.		During this period we fired on enemy's lines in 510d. in retaliation for hostile T.M. fire.	-do-
	24/9/16.		In conjunction with Heavy Artillery + Heavy T.Ms. we fired on enemy line between 510d 0.1 + 516a 7.8. Much damage was observed to be done to parapet + wire.	-do-
	26/9/16.		From 5.30 p.m. to 6.30 p.m. we carried out a shoot on enemy's lines at about 516a 5.7. Much damage was done to his front line, trench boards + revetment boards being thrown up.	-do-
	27/9/16 – 30/9/16		The battery remained in the line, in readiness to retaliate for any hostile T.M. fire.	-do-

H. Cretney 2/Lt.
for O.C. Y31 M.T.M.B.

2449 Wt. W14957/M90 750,000 1/16 J.B.C. & A. Forms/C.2118/12.

1st to 30th Sept 1916

WAR DIARY
or
INTELLIGENCE SUMMARY
(Erase heading not required.)

VOL III
Z 31 MED. T M B

Army Form C. 2118

Instructions regarding War Diaries and Intelligence Summaries are contained in F. S. Regs., Part II. and the Staff Manual respectively. Title Pages will be prepared in manuscript.

Place	Date	Hour	Summary of Events and Information	Remarks and references to Appendices
FERME DU BOIS	2.9.16	11.30am	14 Rounds fired into enemy wire at S10D 05.05.	C.M.T.C
	3.9.16	10.0am to 4.30pm	75 Rounds fired at trenches and M.G. Emplacements. Emplacment itself received 2 direct hits, at S16 B0080. S16 B0768. During this firing the enemy was exceedingly quiet, hardly retaliating at all.	C.M.T.C
NEUVE CHAPELLE	6.9.16	5.10pm	31 Rounds fired into wire and front line trench, making a lane at S11.2½.1½	C.M.T.C
			The enemy retaliated here by firing 5 M.T.Ms	
		9.0pm	3 Salvos (9 Rds.) fired into enemy front line, one round falling on a bomb store, explosions were heard for 2 minutes after the burst of the bomb, at S11 A 2½.2	C.M.T.C
	7.9.16	5pm.	~~65~~ 100 Rounds fired into enemy wire, making satisfactory lane, at* S11 2½.2	*C.M.T.C At this spot there was a lane made for the raiders of the Neuve Chapelle raid.
	8.9.16	6.10pm	59 Rounds fired into enemy wire & trenches, at S11 A 2½.2. This is the third time the 31st Divn have relied on the 2" T.Ms for making gaps & lanes in enemy wire preparatory to a raid. All interested units were very satisfied for the work done by the 2" T.Ms to such an extent, that they were mentioned in despatches and letters of appreciation were forthcoming from Divisional Commanders.	

1875 Wt. W593/826 1,000,000 4/15 J.B.C. & A. A.D.S.S./Forms/C. 2118.

Instructions regarding War Diaries and Intelligence Summaries are contained in F. S. Regs., Part II. and the Staff Manual respectively. Title Pages will be prepared in manuscript.

WAR DIARY
or
INTELLIGENCE SUMMARY
(Erase heading not required.)

Army Form C. 2118

Place	Date	Hour	Summary of Events and Information	Remarks and references to Appendices
NEUVE CHAPELLE	9.9.16	10.0am to 12.20pm	104 Rounds fired into wire at S11 A 2½. 2. 2 Complete gaps were cut for the raiders. The bursts had the effect of piling up the wire in heaps. These heaps could be seen at intervals all the way between S11 A 2½ 1½ and S11 d 4.3. The enemy front line was also flattened out in several places	CO RA
	10.9.16	1.30 am.	4 Rounds were fired to-gether at S11 A 5½. 1½. enemy support line. This salvo was a signal for infantry to enter enemy trenches.	CO RA
		1.50am to 3.0am	42 Rounds fired for the purpose of making a block in enemy's trenches on the right of the raiders	CO RA
		2.20am	+ ~~Round~~ Ordered by the infantry to open fire on M.G. emplacment at S11 A 1¼.1¼. This was done 1 round being fired. Afterwards found to have been a direct hit.	CO RA
FERME DU BOIS	13.9.16	2.50pm	12 Rounds fired in retaliation to enemy T.M's, map ref. target engaged S16 A 7.8.	CO RA
	14.9.16	3.0pm	53 Rounds fired on retaliation target at S10 D 2½. 2½ to S10 D 2.05 and S16 A 99.99	CO RA
	15.9.16	12.5am	23 Rounds fired on retaliation target at S16 B 15.65.	CO RA
		1.0pm	36 Rounds " " " " " S16 A 99.99. 10 Hostile H.T.M's were fired on to our front line to-day doing remarkably little damage.	CO RA

1875 Wt. W593/826 1,000,000 4/15 J.B.C. & A. A.D.S.S./Forms/C. 2118.

Instructions regarding War Diaries and Intelligence Summaries are contained in F. S. Regs., Part II. and the Staff Manual respectively. Title Pages will be prepared in manuscript.

WAR DIARY
or
INTELLIGENCE SUMMARY
(Erase heading not required.)

Army Form C. 2118

Place	Date	Hour	Summary of Events and Information	Remarks and references to Appendices
FERME DU BOIS.	16.9.16	9.55am	18 Rounds fired ~~in~~ retaliation on S16 A99.99.	[illegible]
	16/17.9.16		Received orders to move to the extended part of the Divisional Front (Givenchy Sector) removed our guns from the Neuve Chapelle Sector to the forward billett.	[illegible]
GIVENCHY	17.9.16		Moved to the Givenchy Sector to-day.	[illegible]
	18.9.16		Guns placed in positions in A9A in order to sweep enemy front line in rear of craters.	[illegible]
	19.9.16	8.0am	50 Rounds were fired for registration purposes on enemy front line in A9B	[illegible]
	20.9.16		Selected targets chosen for retaliation purposes. Junctions of enemy trenches and Sap-heads. 61 Rounds fired in retaliation to enemy T.M^s at A9B63.	[illegible]
	21.9.16	12.14am	28 Rounds fired at A9B3½.3. (Retaliation)	[illegible]
	22.9.16		Enemy very active throughout the day with their T.M^s and rifle grenades We fired 60 Rounds at intervals in retaliation to his T.M^s	[illegible]
	23.9.16		Enemy still more active, we retaliated by firing 123 rounds into one of his main communication trenches known as Prussian Way. We enfiladed this trench and absolutely demolished same. Our heavy T.M^s co-operated with us.	[illegible]

1875 Wt. W593/826 1,000,000 4/15 J.B.C. & A. A.D.S.S./Forms/C. 2118.

VOL III

Army Form C. 2118

Z 31 Med TM Bty

WAR DIARY
or
~~INTELLIGENCE SUMMARY~~
(Erase heading not required.)

Instructions regarding War Diaries and Intelligence Summaries are contained in F. S. Regs., Part II. and the Staff Manual respectively. Title Pages will be prepared in manuscript.

Place	Date	Hour	Summary of Events and Information	Remarks and references to Appendices
GIVENCHY	24.9.16		Enemy much quieter firing only 6 M.T.M.s We immediatly retaliated by firing 26 rounds on his front line. His T.M. emplacements were located and silenced by ours.	CO H C
	25.9.16		All quiet no firing.	CO H C
	26.9.16		35 Rounds fired in reply to enemy T.M.s on A9B33. B54. & B43.	CO H C
	27.9.16		88 Rounds fired in retaliation to enemy M.T.M.s Aerial Darts, and Rifle Grenades,	CO H C
	28.9.16	6.0pm 27th to 6.0pm 28th	90 Rounds fired on our retaliation targets in A9B & A9D, a large amount of new timber was thrown in the air, at all points. This shows the large amount of new work the enemy had done to their trenches	CO H C
	~~29.9.16~~			
	29.9.16		34 Rounds fired in retaliation on enemy front line at A16A. and A10E.	CO H C
	30.9.16		38 Rounds fired in retaliation on enemy front line at A10b ~~and~~	CO H C

Chas H Clarke
2/Lt R.F.A.
O.C. Z31 Med. T.M. B.

1875 Wt. W593/826 1,000,000 4/15 J.B.C. & A. A.D.S.S./Forms/C. 2118.

C O N F I D E N T I A L.

W A R D I A R Y

O F

Z/31 Medium Trench Mortar Battery

From 1st September 1916 to 30th September 1916.

(V O L U M E IX)

Trench Mortar Batteries Vol 21

C O N F I D E N T I A L.

W A R D I A R Y

O F

X/31 Medium Trench Mortar Battery

From 1st September 1916 to 30th September 1916.

(V O L U M E IX)

Instructions regarding War Diaries and Intelligence Summaries are contained in F. S. Regs., Part II. and the Staff Manual respectively. Title Pages will be prepared in manuscript.

WAR DIARY
~~or~~
~~INTELLIGENCE SUMMARY~~

(Erase heading not required.)

Army Form C. 2118.

X31 T.M. Battery

VOL. 3 1-30 Sept. 1916.

Place	Date 1916	Hour	Summary of Events and Information	Remarks and references to Appendices
Richebourg St. Vaast	Sept 1	2am - 2.28 am	Fired 63 Rounds with four mortars at enemy trenches & wire at S22.c. After firing 7 rounds one mortar & pit containing same was destroyed, probably by premature in bore. One officer 2 Lieut. J.J. Wilson, 6 Yorks Regt (attd. with T.M.B.) wounded, two other ranks killed and two other ranks wounded. Ck	All references to map sheet France Bethune 1/10,000.
"	2	11.30 am	Fired 9 rounds with one mortar at enemy emplacement S10d.05.05	
		5pm	Fired 17 rounds with two mortars at emplacement S10d 25.92 Ck	
"	3	10am	Fired 18 rounds with one mortar at emplacement at S16b.00.80	
		4.0pm	Fired 36 rounds with two mortars at emplacement S16b.07.68 Ck	
	9	3.0pm	Fired 33 rounds at trenches at S22c.6.7 Ck	
"	12	9am - 5pm	Work on emplacements at S22c. Ck	
"	13	"	do do. Ck	
	14	"	do do. Fired 6 rounds at trenches at S22c.7.7. Ck	
	15		do do. Fired 15 rounds at Germ periscope trenches at S22a 8.0. Ck	
	~~15~~	6pm	Emplacement & bomb store at S22a.[illegible] totally destroyed by enemy 10.5cm shell Ck	
	16	11.45 am	Fired [illegible] rounds with two mortars at Ferme du Bois trenches at S16c.[illegible].7 Ck	
			Worked on dugouts at S21a.9.3. Fired 24 rounds at trenches at S22c.7.6 in retaliation Ck	
	17	9.30am - 8pm	Battery took over Sector from S16a.2.5 to S22c.2.3.	
	18	12.0 mid	Stood by with three guns at S16a.6.1 and S16c.3.8 to give covering fire to four raiding parties. Raiders being successful, O/C raiders issued orders not to fire. Ck	

2449 Wt. W14957/M90 750,000 1/16 J.B.C. & A. Forms/C.2118/12.

Army Form C. 2118.

Instructions regarding War Diaries and Intelligence Summaries are contained in F. S. Regs., Part II. and the Staff Manual respectively. Title Pages will be prepared in manuscript.

WAR DIARY
or
~~INTELLIGENCE SUMMARY~~
(Erase heading not required.)

X 31 T.M. Batty
VOL. 3 (contd) 1–30 Sept. 1916.

Place	Date 1916	Hour	Summary of Events and Information	Remarks and references to Appendices
Richebourg St. Vaast	Sept. 20	5.10. 5.45 p.m.	In conjunction with Stokes mortars & 18 pdrs. fired 26 rounds at enemy trenches and piano periscope at S22a.8.1 & S22a.7.5. Enemy retaliated with about 25 7.7 cm shells at S22c.1.4. Ch.	All references to Maps refer to France Bethune 1/10000
	21	6.10 pm	Fired 9 rounds at trenches at S16c.8.5. Ch.	
			One section and one officer took up duty in trenches (H.Q. in Rope Trench S21a.8.5) Ch.	
	22	5.0 pm	Enemy artillery & mortars quiet. No retaliation necessary. Ch.	
	23	8.0 am - 6.0 pm	Fired 18 rounds at communicator at S22c.65.75. Stokes mortars cooperated. Ch.	
	24	9.10 pm 4.0 pm - 5.0 pm	Fired 70 rounds at Ferme du Bois & trench at S16c.80.50. Stokes mortars cooperated. Enemy retaliation exceptionally weak. Ch.	
		8.30 pm	Fired 10 rounds at enemy working party at S16a.65.65. Stokes cooperated. Ch.	
	25	5.40 pm - 6.35 pm	Fired 64 rounds at new trench at S16a.65.60 – S16a.65.68. Stokes cooperated. No retaliation observed. Ch.	
		7.55 pm	Fired 5 rounds at suspected M.G. Emp. at S22a.85.05. After 1st round M.G. ceased firing & did not fire again that night. Ch.	
	26	7.15 am	Fired 3 rounds at working party at S22c.65.80. Mist prevented observation. Ch.	
		5.0 pm	One section & one officer relieved other in trenches at S21a.8.5. Ch.	
	27	11.15 am	Fired 1 round at S22c.65.75. retaliation	
		5.20 pm	Fired 2 rounds at S22c.65.75 retaliation. Ch.	

Army Form C. 2118.

WAR DIARY
or
~~INTELLIGENCE SUMMARY~~
(Erase heading not required.)

Instructions regarding War Diaries and Intelligence Summaries are contained in F. S. Regs., Part II. and the Staff Manual respectively. Title Pages will be prepared in manuscript.

X 31 T.M. Battery
VOL 3 (contd) 1 - 30 Sept 1916

Place	Date	Hour	Summary of Events and Information	Remarks and references to Appendices
Richebourg St Vaast.	28/9/16	5 - 5.20pm	Fired 29 rounds into Enemy trench & wire S 22 c 6.6 to S 22 c 8.4. Preparation for Dummy Raid in the evening.	All Map references are to :- France 1/10.000 Map Béthune
	"	9.0 to 9-10 pm	Fired 11 rounds - repetition of above	
	"	9.15 to 9.17 pm	Fired 2 rounds - - ditto -	
	29/9/16	2-30pm	Fired 2 rounds - Retaliation - S.22 c 6.5	
	30/9/16	5.15pm	" 3 rounds. Retaliation - {Ferme Cour d'Avoué S.22 c 6.5	

[signature] Lt RFA
for OC X31 TMB
30/9/16

2449 Wt. W14957/M90 750,000 1/16 J.B.C. & A. Forms/C.2118/12.

Confidential

Vol 4

W A R   D I A R Y

O F

V/31 HEAVY TRENCH MORTAR BATTERY.

From 1st OCTOBER 1916 to 31st OCTOBER 1916.

V O L U M E X

October 1916

Army Form C. 2118.

Instructions regarding War Diaries and Intelligence Summaries are contained in F. S. Regs., Part II. and the Staff Manual respectively. Title Pages will be prepared in manuscript.

WAR DIARY
or
INTELLIGENCE SUMMARY
(Erase heading not required.)

V31 H. T. M. Bty

Vol. X

Place	Date	Hour	Summary of Events and Information	Remarks and references to Appendices
In the Field	Oct 1		Fired 20 Rounds at S11c50.30. Very successful shoot.	
	2		Received orders to stand by in readiness to move at any time	
	3		Straightening out at positions	
	4		- do -	
	5		- do -	
	6		Experimented with charge. Full report send to D A H 2	
			Received orders to fire. Everything in readiness, order cancelled at last minute	
	7		Received orders to move	
	8		Battery moved to Thrieves	
	9		Battery at Thrieves in Bivouacs	
	10		- do -	
	11		Left Thrieves for Collincamps	
	12		Battery working on Dug Out with 4 R. E. men attached	
	13			
	14		- do -	
	15			
	16		- do -	
	17		- do -	
	18			
	19		- do -	
	20		Fired 8 Rounds at Point 60: 2nd Lieut G. S. Farebrother and 2 O R wounded. Enemy shelled bivouacs.	

2449 Wt. W14957/M90 750,000 1/16 J.B.C. & A. Forms/C.2118/12.

Instructions regarding War Diaries and Intelligence Summaries are contained in F. S. Regs., Part II. and the Staff Manual respectively. Title Pages will be prepared in manuscript.

WAR DIARY
or
INTELLIGENCE SUMMARY
(Erase heading not required.)

Army Form C. 2118.

V31 H. T. M. Bty

Place	Date	Hour	Summary of Events and Information	Remarks and references to Appendices
In the Field	Oct 21		Battery moved to fresh quarters.	
	22		Fired 15 Rounds at Point 60. Very effective.	
	23		Fired 21 Rounds at Point 60. much damage done. Received 30 rounds from D. A. C.	
	24		Fired 40 Rounds at Point. much damage to same	
			Fired 19 Rounds at Point 60. - do -	
	25		Fired 11 Rounds at Point 60. - do -	
	26		Fired 33 Rounds at Point and Point 60. Very effective	
	27		No Firing	
	28 ~~29~~		Fired 40 Rounds between Point and Point 60. Charges not satisfactory.	
	29		Fired 12 Rounds at trench from Point 31 to North of Point 62. much damage done to trench etc. Heavy retaliation	
	30		No Firing	
	31		No Firing	

L. A. de [illegible]

Instructions regarding War Diaries and Intelligence Summaries are contained in F. S. Regs., Part II. and the Staff Manual respectively. Title Pages will be prepared in manuscript.

October 1916

WAR DIARY
or
INTELLIGENCE SUMMARY
(Erase heading not required.)

VOL X
Z 31 Med T M By

Army Form C. 2118

Place	Date	Hour	Summary of Events and Information	Remarks and references to Appendices
GIVENCHY	15.10.16	10pm	Handed over line to Y5 T.M.B. Withdrew all guns, stores, & personnel to ESSARS	AWR
ESSARS	17.10.16	10.30 am	Battery complete moved by motor lorries to Sailly-au-Bois Arrived Sailly-au-Bois 9pm. and billeted in that village	AWR
HEBUTERNE	18.10.16		Inspected gun positions and took over from the D.T.M.O 19th Divn	AWR
do	19.10.16		Improved pits & swung gun beds on to new lines of fire	AWR
do	20.10.16	3pm	50 rounds fired into enemy wire K17d 1½ 6½	AWR
do	21.10.16		60 " " " " " do	AWR
do	22.10.16		87 " " " " " do	AWR
do	23.10.16		134 " " " " " do	AWR
do	24.10.16		52 " " " " " do also at front line 5 " " " enemy front line & wire with Temple Silencer. This target was very difficult to observe, & shooting very erratic owing to wet component parts. Although components were immediately removed from the boxes & put in a dry place, they had already been affected by rain in transport from the dump through the trenches to the positions	AWR

1875 Wt. W593/826 1,000,000 4/15 J.B.C. & A. A.D.S.S./Forms/C. 2118.

Instructions regarding War Diaries and Intelligence Summaries are contained in F. S. Regs., Part II. and the Staff Manual respectively. Title Pages will be prepared in manuscript.

WAR DIARY
or
INTELLIGENCE SUMMARY
(Erase heading not required.)

Army Form C. 2118

Place	Date	Hour	Summary of Events and Information	Remarks and references to Appendices
HEBUTERNE	25-10-16		Platform had to be relayed	HWR
			12 rounds fired into enemy wire at K17d 1½.6	HWR
"	26-10-16	3pm to 4pm	39 rounds were fired into enemy wire at K17d 1½.3½ to broaden an existing gap in preparation for a raid	
		7.30pm to 8 pm	13 rounds fired into enemy front line + support line at K17d 2.4 (General bombardment)	HWR
		10pm to 1030pm	18 rounds fired into enemy front line + support line at K17d 2.4 (General Bombardment)	
"	29-10-16	10am	Battery moved into billets at HEBUTERNE.	
		5pm	Enemy shelled HEBUTERNE + set alight a billet jointly occupied by C + Z Batteries, destroying ~~much~~ many stores, etc, + a considerable quantity of clothing + equipment. Office papers were to a large extent burnt, but a large quantity saved. The fire was directly caused by a shell igniting a number of 4" Stokes T.M. Bombs which had been dumped temporarily in a room in the house.	HWR
"	30-10-16		New emplacements ~~are~~ commenced. Working party of 5th KOYL.I. Regt (Pioneer Battn) assisted. Owing to rain nearly all the work was destroyed by the earth slipping into holes already dug	HWR
	31-10-16		Work carried out on new emplacements	HWR

HW Ramsey Lt RA
O.C. Z31 TMB

1875 Wt. W593/826 1,000,000 4/15 J.B.C. & A. A.D.S.S./Forms/C. 2118.

Confidential.

W A R   D I A R Y

O F

Y/31 MEDIUM TRENCH MORTAR BATTERY.

From OCTOBER 1st 1916 to OCTOBER 31st 1916.

V O L U M E X

October 1916

WAR DIARY
or
~~INTELLIGENCE SUMMARY~~

(Erase heading not required.)

Vol X

Army Form C. 2118.

Instructions regarding War Diaries and Intelligence Summaries are contained in F. S. Regs., Part II. and the Staff Manual respectively. Title Pages will be prepared in manuscript.

Y31. Med. Trench Mortar Bty.

Place	Date	Hour	Summary of Events and Information	Remarks and references to Appendices
Richebourg	1/10/16		From 4·30pm to 5·30pm in conjunction with 18pdrs and 4·5 Hows? we fired on the enemy's front line wire & front line trenches at about S10d 5.5. In all 70 Rds were fired by this Battery, and good results were obtained. Considerable damage was done to the wire, a dug-out and a bomb store were also blown up. One German was blown about 30' into the air.	Richebourg Map 36 S.W. 3.
do	2/10/16	5pm to 5·15pm	7 Rds for registration purposes were fired on front line wire at S10d 5½ 6	— do —
do	2/10/16 to 11/10/16		2 Detachments remained in the line in readiness to retaliate for any hostile T.M. which fired	
do	11/10/16		This Battery came under the orders of the D.T.M.O. 61st Division. During the day 30 Rds were fired at the enemy's front line & front line wire at S10d 5½ 6. One lane was cut through the wire and several gaps were made in his parapet.	— do —
do	15/10/16		This Battery was relieved by 61st Div: T.M's. and moved into billets at Essars	Bethune Map 36a SE & 36 SW S25a

2449 Wt. W14957/M90 750,000 1/16 J.B.C. & A. Forms/C.2118/12.

Army Form C. 2118.

WAR DIARY
or
~~INTELLIGENCE SUMMARY~~
(Erase heading not required.)

Y. 31 MED TRENCH MORTAR BTY.

Instructions regarding War Diaries and Intelligence Summaries are contained in F. S. Regs., Part II. and the Staff Manual respectively. Title Pages will be prepared in manuscript.

Place	Date	Hour	Summary of Events and Information	Remarks and references to Appendices
	17/10/16		Battery went by road from Essars to Sailly au Bois.	
Hebuterne	18/10/16		Took over two positions at K17c 41,31.	Hebuterne Map 57d N.E.
	19/10/16 to 27/10/16		Daily shoots were carried out on enemy's front & support line wire at about K17d 1½ 2½. Front line wire for a distance of about 20x was completely destroyed. Both positions were frequently shelled with 77mm. 10cm & 15cm shells and considerable damage was done to both positions. One position was destroyed by a premature and it was then decided to make two new positions.	— do —
	25/10/16		~~Two positions~~ Positions for the two new emplacements were selected in the trench running from K17c 25,20 to K17c 3,2. and work was commenced on them.	— do —
	29/10/16 - 31/10/16		Work was continued on these positions, gun pits and ammunition recesses being constructed.	

2449 Wt. W14957/M90 750,000 1/16 J.B.C. & A. Forms/C.2118/12.

Army Form C. 2118.

Instructions regarding War Diaries and Intelligence Summaries are contained in F. S. Regs., Part II. and the Staff Manual respectively. Title Pages will be prepared in manuscript.

WAR DIARY
or
~~INTELLIGENCE SUMMARY~~

(Erase heading not required.)

Y. 31. MED TRENCH MORTAR BTY

Place	Date	Hour	Summary of Events and Information	Remarks and references to Appendices
HEBUTERNE	19/10/16 to 27/10/16		Owing to heavy rain and the difficulty experienced in keeping charges etc perfectly dry, it was found very difficult to obtain very accurate shooting in the daily shoots which were carried out during this period. However the front-line wire at about K17d 1½ 2½ had good lanes cut through it.	Hebuterne map 57D NE

W Dann Lt RGA
OC Y31 M.T.M.B.

2449 Wt. W14957/M90 750,000 1/16 J.B.C. & A. Forms/C.2118/12.

Confidential

W A R   D I A R Y

O F

X/31 MEDIUM TRENCH MORTAR BATTERY.

From OCTOBER 1st 1916 to OCTOBER 31st 1916.

V O L U M E X.

Instructions regarding War Diaries and Intelligence Summaries are contained in F. S. Regs., Part II. and the Staff Manual respectively. Title Pages will be prepared in manuscript.

October 1916

WAR DIARY
or
~~INTELLIGENCE~~ SUMMARY
(Erase heading not required.)

Army Form C. 2118

X31 T.M. Battery.
VOL X

Place	Date	Hour	Summary of Events and Information	Remarks and references to Appendices
Ferme du Bois	1/10/16	10.15 a.m.	Fired 2 rounds at enemy trenches at S22 c.60 50 in retaliation.	All map references refer to 1/10000 Trench Map
"	2/10/16	3.30 p.m.	Fired 2 rounds at enemy trenches at S22 a.90.10 in retaliation	
"	4/10/16	12.30 a.m. – 1.15 a.m.	Fired 21 rounds (percussion fuzes) at S22 a 80 20 & S22 a. 60.60. Premature at muzzle of one mortar. Gun pit destroyed, no casualties. Apparently a piece of debris from hostile 77 cm shell hit fuze as bomb was being fired.	
"	5/10/16	9.30 a.m.	Fired 2 bombs at S22 a 90 10 in retaliation	
		12.0 noon	Fired 2 bombs at S22 a 90 10 in retaliation	
"	6/10/16	10.30 a.m.	Fired 3 bombs on S22 a 90.10. } retaliation	
		12.15 a.m.	Fired 5 bombs at S22 a 90 10 } retaliation	
"	7/10/16	10.45 a.m.	Fired 5 bombs on S22 c 90.10 } retaliation	
		2.50 p.m.	Fired 2 bombs at S22 60.50 } retaliation	
		4.5 p.m.	Fired 2 bombs at S22 a. 90 10 } retaliation	
"	8/10/16	4.10 p.m.	Fired 2 bombs at S22 a 60.00. } retaliation	
			Fired 2 bombs at S22 c.60 50 } retaliation	
		5.10 p.m.	Fired 2 bombs at S22 a 80.20 } retaliation	
			Fired 2 bombs at S22 a. 90.60 } retaliation	

1875 Wt. W593/826 1,000,000 4/15 J.B.C. & A. A.D.S.S./Forms/C. 2118.

Army Form C. 2118

Instructions regarding War Diaries and Intelligence Summaries are contained in F. S. Regs., Part II. and the Staff Manual respectively. Title Pages will be prepared in manuscript.

WAR DIARY
or
INTELLIGENCE SUMMARY
(Erase heading not required.)

Place	Date	Hour	Summary of Events and Information	Remarks and references to Appendices

1375 Wt. W593/826 1,000,000 4/15 J.B.C. & A. A.D.S.S./Forms/C. 2118.

Instructions regarding War Diaries and Intelligence Summaries are contained in F. S. Regs., Part II. and the Staff Manual respectively. Title Pages will be prepared in manuscript.

WAR DIARY
or
INTELLIGENCE SUMMARY
(Erase heading not required.)

Army Form C. 2118

Place	Date	Hour	Summary of Events and Information	Remarks and references to Appendices
HEBUTERNE	26/10/16	6.0 am – 6.15 am	Fired 12 bombs at wire K17d.15.40 – K23b.05.80.	
		1.30 pm	Fired 17 bombs at wire —— do ——	
		3.0 pm	Fired 6 bombs at wire —— do —— Ch.	
"	27/10/16	2.30 pm – 3.30 pm	Fired 10 bombs at wire K17d.15.15. Ch.	
"	28/10/16	12.20 pm – 4.0 pm	Fired 45 bombs at wire K23b.05.80 – K17d.05.05. Further damage to wire observed.	
"		7.30 pm – 8.0 pm	Fired 4 bombs at trench K23b.15.90	
		10.4 – 10.30 pm	Fired 9 bombs at trench K23b.15.90 Ch.	
			Battery complete moved into billets at Hebuterne, vacated by 51st Trench [illegible]	
	27/10/16		Enemy shell hit battery billets & wounded a signaller. Ch.	
		3.15 pm – 3.25 pm	Fired 20 bombs at wire K17d 10.15. Fired 23 lethal bombs at K17d.20.10 [illegible] & K23b.20.80. One bomb failed to discharge gas owing to tail leaving bomb in the air & another dropped in front of mortar but failed to discharge gas. Enemy retaliated with guns of 15 cm & 10.5 cm & [illegible]. Ch.	
	29/10/16		Worked on new pits in KNOX Trench, the others having become untenable owing to damage caused by enemy shell fire. Ch.	
	30/10/16		Worked on new pits. Work difficult owing to bad weather conditions. Ch.	
	31/10/16		Worked on new pits. One mortar placed in action in pit at K23a.30.65. Ch.	

C. Carter Lt. R. [illegible]
O/C X31 T.M. Batty 1/11/16.

1875 Wt. W593/826 1,000,000 4/15 J.B.C. & A. A.D.S.S./Forms/C. 2118.

Vol 8

C O N F I D E N T I A L.

W A R D I A R Y.

O F

"X" MEDIUM TRENCH MORTAR BATTERY.

From 1st November 1916 to 30th November 1916.

(VOLUME XI)

Instructions regarding War Diaries and Intelligence Summaries are contained in F. S. Regs., Part II. and the Staff Manual respectively. Title Pages will be prepared in manuscript.

WAR DIARY
or
~~INTELLIGENCE~~ SUMMARY
(Erase heading not required.)

X31 T.M. Battery

November 1916

Army Form C. 2118

VOL. XI

Place	Date	Hour	Summary of Events and Information	Remarks and references to Appendices
Hebuterne	1/11/16	1.30p–3.45p	Fired 40 bombs at wire K17d.05.05. Shooting good. Wire at this point appears to be much damaged. Ck	
	2/11/16	3.15p–4.0p	Fired 20 bombs at wire K17d.05.05 Ck	
	3/11/16		Worked on positions at K23a.30.60, improving same. Old positions at K17c.45.05 evacuated definitely. Ck	
	4/11/16	2.30–4.0p	Fired 18 bombs at wire K17d.10.10. Eight bombs fell in wire. Reported a gap at this point after observation with field glasses Ck	
	5/11/16	2.0–3.0p	Fired 20 bombs at wire K17d.12.12 a gap being required here for raiding purposes. 12 bombs fell in wire. Reported a further small gap here Ck.	
	6/11/16		Worked on improving positions at K23a.30.60 Ck	
	7/11/16		Bad weather conditions. Trenches almost impassable. Raiding party which entered enemy trenches at gap K17d 12.12 (mentioned above) on night of 6/7 was successful capturing 4 prisoners. Ck	
	8/11/16		Bad weather continues. Work at positions impossible Ck	
	9/11/16		Weather fine but trenches waterlogged. At about 10.30pm enemy commenced shelling Sailly au Bois heavily with gas shells, continuing for about 3 hours. Ck	
	10/11/16	4 a.m.	Gas shell entered men's billet at Sailly au Bois. Five men gassed, two of which died a few hours afterwards at F.A. Men had been warned and were awake but appear to have been overcome by fumes before getting their helmets adjusted. Ck	

1875 Wt. W593/826 1,000,000 4/15 J.B.C. & A. A.D.S.S./Forms/C. 2118.

Instructions regarding War Diaries and Intelligence Summaries are contained in F. S. Regs., Part II. and the Staff Manual respectively. Title pages will be prepared in manuscript.

WAR DIARY
or
INTELLIGENCE SUMMARY.
(Erase heading not required.)

X 31 T.M. Bty.

November (continued)

Army Form C. 2118.

Place	Date	Hour	Summary of Events and Information	Remarks and references to Appendices
Hebuterne	10/11/16	4pm - 8pm	Worked on mortar positions & trench at K23a.40.70. Ch.	
"	11/11/16	10am - 12am	Carried material for positions to Brassaux Trench	
		8pm - 4.30am	Carried material over top from Brassaux to positions & constructed bomb store & improved positions Ch.	
"	12/11/16	6pm - 4am	Carried special & ordinary bombs over top from Brassaux to positions. Prepared all ammunition for firing. Ch.	
"	13/11/16	5.45am - 6.20am	Fired 60 special bombs at enemy trenches at K17d.15.10. Owing to excessive number of misfires amongst firing cartridges, it was found only possible to fire five ordinary (ammonal) bombs Ch.	
"		8.15am - 8.30am	Fired 5 ammonal bombs at enemy trenches K17d.15.00. Enemy retaliation with 77 mm & 10.5 cm shells on positions now heavy. Detachments were withdrawn as ordered. Ch.	
	15/11/16		Took over three positions from 33rd Divn. at K23a.50.30. Ch	
	16/11/16		Took over & inspected four positions, from 48th Divn. at K10d.90 20 Ch.	
	17/11/16 to 30/11/16		Guns out of action. Training and refitting & construction of elephant dugouts for new Ch.	

A5834 Wt. W4973/M687 750,000 8/16 D. D. & L. Ltd. Forms/C.2118/13.

C O N F I D E N T I A L.

W A R D I A R Y.

O F

"Y" MEDIUM TRENCH MORTAR BATTERY.

From 1st November 1916 to 30th November 1916.

(VOLUME XI)

80

Instructions regarding War Diaries and Intelligence Summaries are contained in F. S. Regs., Part II. and the Staff Manual respectively. Title Pages will be prepared in manuscript.

WAR DIARY
or
INTELLIGENCE SUMMARY
(Erase heading not required.)

Army Form C. 2118.

VOL XI

Y. 31 MED TRENCH MORTAR BTY

Place	Date	Hour	Summary of Events and Information	Remarks and references to Appendices
HEBUTERNE	1/11/16		23 Rounds were fired at front line wire about K17d, 1.2, which was badly damaged in several places	Hebuterne map 57d NE
do	2/11/16		17 Rds fired at front line wire at K17d 1.2. A clear gap of at least 10' was observed to be cut.	— do —
do	3/11/16 4/11/16		Work was continued on the two new positions at K17c, 3, 2	— do —
do.	5/11/16		43 Rds were fired at the front-line wire at K17d 12, 12. Accurate shooting was difficult, owing to a very strong wind. At least one lane was cut through the wire at this point. The enemy retaliated heavily with 5cm shells. One gun pit & dug out at K17c 41, 31, received several direct hits, obliterating the pit & putting the gun out of action.	— do — — do —
	6/11/16		Work was continued on the positions at K17c 3.2. I handed over the command of this Battery to 2nd Lieut C.O.H. Clarke, R.F.A.	— do —

W Dunn 2Lt R.F.A.

2449 Wt. W14957/M90 750,000 1/16 J.B.C. & A. Forms/C.2118/12.

"Y" / 31 Medium Trench Mortar Battery
1st to 30th Nov 16
Vol XI

Army Form C. 2118.

WAR DIARY
or
INTELLIGENCE SUMMARY.
(Erase heading not required.)

Instructions regarding War Diaries and Intelligence Summaries are contained in F. S. Regs., Part II. and the Staff Manual respectively. Title pages will be prepared in manuscript.

Place	Date	Hour	Summary of Events and Information	Remarks and references to Appendices
Hebuterne	13.11.16	5.45 AM	29 Rounds of 2" Gas Bombs were fired into German line at K.17 B. and D. after a lapse of half an hour 40 ordinary 60lb Bombs were fired on the same target.	Map Sheet France 57 D N.E
			The Battery after firing retired to Sailly-au-bois ~~where it~~ to go into billets there where it stayed until 20/11/16 during this time it was given every kind of necessary drilling for adding to the efficiency & appearance of the Battery.	
	20.11.16		We took over position from the 48th Div: T.M's at K 3 D 2.3	
	22.11.16		Guns were placed in Action for Retaliatory purposes only	
	23.11.16		Points of the enemy's front line were registered at K 3 D 6 K.7 8 K 3 D 8 3/4.5 1/4.	
	29.11.16		We were ~~relieved~~ relieved at this date by Z 31 M. T.M. B. We then returned to Sailly-au-bois as Battery in Reserve.	

Chas O H Clarke 2Lt R.F.A.
O.C. Y 31 Med T.M. Battery

A5834 Wt. W4973/M687 750,000 8/16 D. D. & L. Ltd. Forms/C.2118/13.

Vol

CONFIDENTIAL.

WAR DIARY

OF

V/31 HEAVY TRENCH MORTAR BATTERY.

From November 1st 1916 to November 30th 1916.

(VOLUME XI)

Instructions regarding War Diaries and Intelligence Summaries are contained in F. S. Regs., Part II. and the Staff Manual respectively. Title Pages will be prepared in manuscript.

WAR DIARY
or
INTELLIGENCE SUMMARY
(Erase heading not required.)

Army Form C. 2118

Place	Date	Hour	Summary of Events and Information	Remarks and references to Appendices
	Nov 1916			All Map references are to 1/10,000 Hebuterne 57D. NE Edition 3A
~~Hebuter~~ SAILLY-AU-BOIS	14th – 21st	–	Redrilling Re-inforcements – Overhauling Stores and building Winter Quarters	
"	22nd	–	2/Lt G.H. Dancocks R.F.A. attached to 'Y' Battery for duty.	
"	22nd – 26th	–	Redrilling Re-inforcements and building Winter Quarters	
"	26th	–	Lt H.W. Lacy vacated command of the Battery to assume Temp Command of the Divisional Trench Mortars, vice Capt H.B. Bates R.F.A.	
"	"	–	2/Lt R.N. Urquhart R.F.A. assumed Temp Command of the Battery vice Lt H.W. Lacy R.F.A.	
"	26th – 28th	–	Redrilling and building Winter Quarters	
HEBUTERNE	29th	–	Relieved 'Y31' Battery in the Line – Calvaire position	
"	30th	11.15am	Fired 7 rounds on registered zones about front line K3d – Retaliation	

R. Nicoll Urquhart 2/Lt R.F.A.
O.C. Z31 T.M.B.

1875 Wt. W593/826 1,000,000 4/15 J.B.C. & A. A.D.S.S./Forms/C. 2118.

C O N F I D E N T I A L.

W A R   D I A R Y.

O F

"Z" MEDIUM TRENCH MORTAR BATTERY.

From 1st November 1916 to 30th November 1916.

(VOLUME XI)

Instructions regarding War Diaries and Intelligence Summaries are contained in F. S. Regs., Part II. and the Staff Manual respectively. Title Pages will be prepared in manuscript.

WAR DIARY
or
INTELLIGENCE SUMMARY
(Erase heading not required.)

Z 31 MTM Bty
1st to 30th Nov 16
Vol XI

Army Form C. 2118

Place	Date	Hour	Summary of Events and Information	Remarks and references to Appendices
HEBUTERNE	1/11/16	11.30am	32 rounds fired into enemy wire at K17d 05.80.	All map references are to 1/10000 Hebuterne – 57D-NE – Edition 3A
HEBUTERNE	2/11/16	5pm	After having 11 casualties by enemy shelling billets, the battery returned to SAILLY-AU-BOIS to new billets.	
			Twenty rounds were fired into enemy wire at K17d 05.80 by one bombr. & 2 other ranks (the remaining effective strength of the battery with the exception of the battery Sergt & office clerk). On both the 1st & 2nd firing was very slow, as the bombs had to be stacked in a narrow trench (no amm. pits being available) & the process of cleaning each bomb ~~was~~ necessarily ~~[illegible]~~ caused a slow rate of fire.	
			Direct hit on one pit & shelled out both days of the other	
	3/4/5		Enemy continually shelled Ramb (main amm.) & rain caused land slips into work done	
	6 7th		Trenches impassable	
	8th		Attempt made to get dug out frames down to pos. 5 feet of water in [illegible] Abandoned	
	8	9 am	Took down frames. Baled out 2 existing pits & pumped water from Ramb Drains were also constructed	
	9	8.30pm	Constructing pits	
	10	8 pm	"	
	11	8pm	"	
	13	5.45am to 8.45am	Fired 32 gas bombs & 66 ordinary bombs into enemy line 92 Inf Bde attacked on our right the battery (in conjunction with 58th 2" M.T.M. Batty) [illegible] smoke [illegible] putting up a flank barrage)	

1875 Wt. W593/826 1,000,000 4/15 J.B.C. & A. A.D.S.S./Forms/C. 2118.

Instructions regarding War Diaries and Intelligence Summaries are contained in F. S. Regs., Part II. and the Staff Manual respectively. Title Pages will be prepared in manuscript.

WAR DIARY
or
INTELLIGENCE SUMMARY
(Erase heading not required.)

V 31 H.T.M. Batty

Army Form C. 2118.

VOL XI

Place	Date	Hour	Summary of Events and Information	Remarks and references to Appendices
In the Field	1916 Nov 1		No firing.	
	2		Fired 22 rounds at K23b6.0 to K23b6.4. Fired 6 rounds at K23b6-0 to K23b8.4 Fired 3 rounds at K23d9.7. Considerable damage done to enemy. Retaliation heavy. Enemy obtained direct hit on gun pit No 2. Gun buried and put out of action.	
	3		Clearing Gun Pits	
	4		do. No1 gun found not damaged. No2 gun found badly damaged.	
	5		Repairing gun pits & passages	
	6		do.	
	7		do Rain caused serious interference owing to sides of pit slipping	
	8		Work in Gun pits	
	9		do	
	10		do	
	11		do.	
	12		do. 4 reinforcements arrived from D.T.M.O & 13 from D.A.C.	
	13		do. Both pits again shelled - damages to passages. Withdrew detachments	
	14		Took over two guns & seven complete rounds of ammunition from 19th Division - also accessories.	

F.J. Harvey Capt R.F.A.
O.C. V.31 H.T.M.

2449 Wt. W14957/M90 750,000 1/16 J.B.C. & A. Forms/C.2118/12.

Instructions regarding War Diaries and Intelligence Summaries are contained in F. S. Regs., Part II. and the Staff Manual respectively. Title Pages will be prepared in manuscript.

WAR DIARY
or
INTELLIGENCE SUMMARY
(Erase heading not required.)

Army Form C. 2118.

V 31 H.T.M. Batt.

Place	Date	Hour	Summary of Events and Information	Remarks and references to Appendices
In the field	1916 Nov 15		Sent working detachments to new gun positions and to No 2 pit (old)	
	16		Working on gun positions. Received orders to take over 3 guns from 48th Divn.	
	17		do. Reconnoitred positions & billets of 48th Divn	
	18		do. Received orders to retain all guns & pits (seven).	
	19		do. 3 NCOs go on Refresher Course to T.M. School – Reconnoitred for suitable positions for gun emplacements. Further damage reported to gun position at Jean Bart. 2nd Lieut F.J. de [illegible] went on leave.	
	20		Work on gun positions. Enemy shelled billets – 2 O.R. killed, 3 wounded & 1 shell shock	
	21		Moved to Hebuterne. Took over from 48th Divn – 3 guns in position & 92 rounds of ammunition. Detachments withdrawn to billets.	
	22		Repairing positions. One O.R. wounded	
	23		do. 2nd Lieut R.Q. Bloor attached for duty	
	24		do	
	25		do.	
	26		do	
	27		do	
	28		do	
	29		Fired 9 rounds at K4c 80 70 & K4c 65.80	
	30		" 3 rounds from 11 to 11.30 AM at K3d 85 80. Fired 5 rounds from 2.30 to 3.15 pm at K5c. – 12.15.	

F.J. Haney Capt RFA
OC V 31 H.T.M.

2449 Wt. W14957/M90 750,000 1/16 J.B.C. & A. Forms/C.2118/12.

C O N F I D E N T I A L.

W A R   D I A R Y

O F

V/31 HEAVY TRENCH MORTAR BATTERY.

From 1st DECEMBER 1916 to 31st DECEMBER 1916.

VOLUME XII.

1st Dec 1916 to 31st Dec 1916

Volume XII

Army Form C. 2118.

Instructions regarding War Diaries and Intelligence Summaries are contained in F. S. Regs., Part II. and the Staff Manual respectively. Title Pages will be prepared in manuscript.

WAR DIARY or INTELLIGENCE SUMMARY

(Erase heading not required.)

V 31 H. T. M. Battery

Place	Date	Hour	Summary of Events and Information	Remarks and references to Appendices
In the Field	1916 Dec 1st		No Firing. At work on Gun Pits.	
	2		Fired 5 rounds - one at Sunken Road - two to register K5c. 12.15 and two at T.M located at K11a 25.78 - 1 dud and 1 air burst.	
	3		No Firing - work on gun pits & O. P's. Three N.C.O's returned from Refresher Course. Billets shelled, no damage.	
	4		Fired 8 rounds between 10 & 11.30 AM at EPTE. & FELON - much damage - all rounds very close to trenches. Work on Gun Pits	
	5		Fired 32 rounds - Two guns fired 18 rounds at Sunken Road, Bulow Trench and Trench K17b.00.50 to K11d.00.20 All in enemy lines - Enemy retaliated. 2.30 to 3.30 pm 14 rounds fired on Trench K4c 90.40 to K4d 15.50 & area about K4a 05.50. Direct hits on trenches - No retaliation. Work on gun pits.	
	6		Twelve reinforcements arrived from D.A.C. Fired 13 rounds at Trenches K5c.11. and K11a 90.35. Good Results. Enemy retaliated on No 4 & 5 guns.	
	7		Dismantling three guns to reconstruct beds. Work on Pits at Jean Bart & Baker.	
	8		Work on Gun Pits & beds - Taking stock at Jean Bart and Baker	
	9		Work on Gun beds. Nos 1, 2 & 3 finished ready for action - All pits ready for action	
	10		Fired 9 rounds - Lightest Charges used. Three shells in our lines - one in No Mans Land & 5 in German Line. all hit trenches	
	11		Repairing No 1 Pit Prepared to fire from 1 & 3 guns. Infantry unable to withdraw	

W. V. Grune Capt RFA. Tr. OC. V/31. HTMB

2449 Wt. W14957/M90 750,000 1/16 J.B.C. & A. Forms/C.2118/12.

Army Form C. 2118.

Instructions regarding War Diaries and Intelligence Summaries are contained in F. S. Regs., Part II. and the Staff Manual respectively. Title Pages will be prepared in manuscript.

WAR DIARY
or
INTELLIGENCE SUMMARY
(Erase heading not required.)

V31 H. T. M. Battery.

Place	Date	Hour	Summary of Events and Information	Remarks and references to Appendices
In the Field	1916 Dec 12		Fired 4 rounds at Trench K17a 00.65 Two hits. Handed over two guns stores &c and 34 rounds ammunition complete to 3rd Division - Positions at Caber & Jean Bart.	
	13		Fired 12 rounds around K4a 4.1. - eleven around target and 1 in No Mans Land - Cleaning guns and Pit handed over to 3rd Division.	
	14		Fired 6 rounds to register K11a 5.3 and Bock Graben - All hit Trenches.	
	15		Dismantling No 4 gun. making position & getting gun in position on Plain No firing	
	16		Completing Positions	
	17		do and carrying out tests.	
	18		do do	
	19		Completing positions. Billets heavily shelled. No casualties.	
	20		Repaired gun pits.	
	21		Mounted gun ready for action.	
	22		at work on new pits	
	23		do. 2nd Lieut Turner joined the Battery.	
	24		Working on positions	
	25		do.	
	26		Getting guns ready for action.	
	27		Fired 28 rounds from K4c 65.85 to K4c 80.60. Very successful.	
	28		Fired 17 rounds ~~from~~ about K4c 35.80. K4a 9.2 & K4b 50.00. Fog prevented — observation - All well in enemy lines.	
	29		No firing - Work on gun pits.	

W. V. Turner 2/Lt RFA.
for OC V31 HTMB

2449 Wt. W14957/M90 750,000 1/16 J.B.C. & A. Forms/C.2118/12.

Instructions regarding War Diaries and Intelligence Summaries are contained in F. S. Regs., Part II. and the Staff Manual respectively. Title Pages will be prepared in manuscript.

WAR DIARY
or
INTELLIGENCE SUMMARY
(Erase heading not required.)

V31 H.T.M. Battery.

Army Form C. 2118.

Place	Date	Hour	Summary of Events and Information	Remarks and references to Appendices
In the Field	1916 Dec 30		Fired 33 rounds at K4c 38.80, K4c 95.50 and K4d 25.50. effective.	
	31		Dismantling gun. Fired 15 rounds about K11c 55.90, K11a 70.10 and K11b 10.60. Considerable damage caused.	

W.W. [illegible] 2/Lt. RFA.
For OC V31. HTMB.

2449 Wt. W14957/M90 750,000 1/16 J.B.C. & A. Forms/C.2118/12.

Vol 9

C O N F I D E N T I A L.

W A R D I A R Y

O F

X/31 MEDIUM TRENCH MORTAR BATTERY.

From 1st DECEMBER 1916 to 31st DECEMBER 1916.

VOLUME ~~XII~~

Instructions regarding War Diaries and Intelligence Summaries are contained in F. S. Regs., Part II. and the Staff Manual respectively. Title pages will be prepared in manuscript.

WAR DIARY
or
INTELLIGENCE SUMMARY.
(Erase heading not required.)

Army Form C. 2118.

X 31 T.M. Battery
December 1916
VOL. XII

Place	Date	Hour	Summary of Events and Information	Remarks and references to Appendices
Sailly au Bois	1/12/16 – 5/12/16		Training & fatigues at Sailly au Bois	
Hebuterne	6/12/16	10 am	Took over from Z31 TM Battery four positions at K3d.22. and forward billet at K15d 99. Placed three mortars in action and a fourth mortar taken over from Z31 TMB. Ca.	
"	7/12/16		Improving positions & obtaining ammunition Ca	
"	8/12/16		do. do.	
"	9/12/16		do. do.	
"	10/12/16	1 am	Enemy did some damage at K3d.25 with about 20 medium Minenwerfer. We retaliated on K3d. 8.7 with 8 bombs (delay fuses). Ca	
"	11/12/16		Work on positions. Ca	
"	12/12/16		do. Ca.	
"	13/12/16	1 am	Fired 4 bombs at K3d. 7.7. for S.O.S. test.	
"		10.45 am – 11.30 am	Fired 13 bombs at K3d. 55.65 (Fourtree sap) with good results. Ca.	
		12 noon	Relieved from line by Y31 TM Batty for whom we left two mortars in action. Proceeded with Battery & two mortars to Sailly au Bois Ca	
	14/12/16 – 21/12/16		Training & rest. Ca.	
	22/12/16	7 am – 4.30 pm	Worked on elephant bomb store at K17d.25.20 Ca	

A5834 Wt. W4973/M687 750,000 8/16 D. D. & L. Ltd. Forms/C.2118/13.

Instructions regarding War Diaries and Intelligence Summaries are contained in F. S. Regs., Part II. and the Staff Manual respectively. Title pages will be prepared in manuscript.

WAR DIARY
or
INTELLIGENCE SUMMARY.
(Erase heading not required.)

Army Form C. 2118.

X31 T.M. Batty
December 1916 VOL VI (Contd)

Place	Date	Hour	Summary of Events and Information	Remarks and references to Appendices
Hebuterne	23/12/16	7am - 12 noon	Worked on elephant bomb store at K17 d. 25. 20 Ca	
"	27/12/16	9am - 12 noon	Took over four positions at K3d. 2 2. from Z31 T.M. Batty. Battery complete moved to Hebuterne, one Section at forward billet & one section at positions. Ca	
"	28/12/16	1am - 4am	Fired 5 rounds (delay fuse) using Temple Silencer at trenches K3d. 9 6.	
		11 30am - 12 noon	Fired 5 rounds (delay fuse) with Temple Silencer at trenches K3d. 85. 55 Ca.	
"	29/12/16		Bad weather conditions & visibility. Enemy quiet. Ca	
	30/12/16		Bad weather continues. Enemy mortars make no reply to our 9.45 Heavy T.M.'s which fired from 3 pm - 4 pm. Ca	
"	31/12/16	11.45 am	Fired 1 round with Silencer at K3d. 9 6	
		2.45 pm	Fired 4 rounds with Silencer at K3d. 9 6. No retaliation Ca.	

C.A. [illegible] Lt R.F.A.
O/C X31 T.M. Battery
1/1/17

A5834 Wt. W4973/M687 750,000 8/16 D. D. & L. Ltd. Forms/C.2118/13.

CONFIDENTIAL.

WAR DIARY

OF

Y/31 MEDIUM TRENCH MORTAR BATTERY.

From 1st DECEMBER 1916 to 31st DECEMBER 1916.

VOLUME XII.

1st to 31st Dec. 1916

Y 31 M/T. M. By

WAR DIARY
or
INTELLIGENCE SUMMARY.
(Erase heading not required.)

Army Form C. 2118.

Vol XII

Instructions regarding War Diaries and Intelligence Summaries are contained in F. S. Regs., Part II. and the Staff Manual respectively. Title pages will be prepared in manuscript.

Place	Date	Hour	Summary of Events and Information	Remarks and references to Appendices
HEBUTERNE	12.12.16	2-0PM	52 rounds were fired at Enemy's Saps + Front line on K 3 D.	Copy
"	15.12.16	7-45PM to 9-00PM	30 " " " " " " " " " and wire on K 3 D	
"	16.12.16	5-0PM	~~123~~ 23 " " " " " " " " " "	
"	17.12.16	1-0PM	30 " " " " " " " " " "	
"	18.12.16	11-0AM to 4-0PM	60 " " " " " " " " " "	
"	19.12.16	5-0PM to	27 " " " " " " " " " "	
"	20.12.16	5 AM		
"	21.12.16 to		Battery moved out of action back to Billets at Sailly-au-bois	
"	31.12.16		for Fatigue	

~~Preparatory~~ Preparation for Raid. Gaps were made in wire. Direct hits on 4 tree Sap + V Shaped Sap. Our infantry were able to easily get in Boche front line on 19/20 good. Gaps were made in Wire + enemy's front line + dugouts were all smashed in. Copy

Chas H Clarke Lt RFA
O.C. Y31 Medium Trench Mortar Battery.

A5834 Wt. W4973/M687 750,000 8/16 D. D. & L. Ltd. Forms/C.2118/13.

C O N F I D E N T I A L.

W A R   D I A R Y

O F

Z/31 MEDIUM TRENCH MORTAR BATTERY.

From 1st DECEMBER 1916 to 31st DECEMBER 1916.

VOLUME XII.

Instructions regarding War Diaries and Intelligence Summaries are contained in F. S. Regs., Part II. and the Staff Manual respectively. Title Pages will be prepared in manuscript.

1st Dec 1916 to 31st Dec 1916

WAR DIARY or INTELLIGENCE SUMMARY

(Erase heading not required.)

Z 31 Heavy T.M. Bty

Army Form C. 2118

Vol. XII

Place	Date Dec 1916	Hour	Summary of Events and Information	Remarks and references to Appendices
HEBUTERNE	1st to 5th		Strengthening CALVAIRE positions	
"	6th	9-0am.	Handed over to X31 TMB command of CALVAIRE positions – Battery returned to reserve billet SAILLY-AU-BOIS.	
SAILLY-AU-BOIS	9th	9-0am.	Lt H.W. LUCY RFA assumed command of the battery on completion of tour of duty as a/DTMO	
"	"		2/Lt R.H. URQUHART RFA granted leave of absence to UK 9/12/16 – 19/12/16	
"	9th to 19th		Redrilling, working parties etc	
HEBUTERNE	20th	12 noon	Relieved Y31 TMB at CALVAIRE Positions.	
"	26th	12 noon	Registered with 10 rounds on SE side of GOMMECOURT SALIENT K3d	
"	"	3-0pm	Fired 113 rounds into SE side of GOMMECOURT SALIENT K3d doing much damage to Enemy trench	
"	X 27th	11-0am	Relieved by X31 TMB at CALVAIRE positions & returned to reserve billet at SAILLY-AU-BOIS	X 27th – Lt H.W. LUCY RFA granted leave of absence & 2/Lt R.H. URQUHART RFA assumed command of the battery
SAILLY-AU-BOIS	27th to 31st		Redrilling	Map References 57D NE Issue Edition 3A

R.H. Urquhart 2/Lt RFA
OC Z31 TMB
31/12/16

1875 Wt. W593/826 1,000,000 4/15 J.B.C. & A. A.D.S.S./Forms/C. 2118.

C O N F I D E N T I A L.

W A R D I A R Y

O F

X/31 MEDIUM TRENCH MORTAR BATTERY.

FROM 1st JANUARY 1917 TO 31st JANUARY 1917.

V O L U M E XIII

Instructions regarding War Diaries and Intelligence Summaries are contained in F. S. Regs., Part II. and the Staff Manual respectively. Title pages will be prepared in manuscript.

WAR DIARY
or
INTELLIGENCE SUMMARY.
(Erase heading not required.)

1st January 1917 to 31st January 1917 VOL VII

Army Form C. 2118.

Y31. MED. TRENCH MORTAR BATTERY.

Place	Date	Hour	Summary of Events and Information	Remarks and references to Appendices
HÉBUTERNE	1/1/17	7am–7am	20 rounds fired in Salvos on K3 d + K4c. No retaliation from enemy.	
SAILLY AU BOIS	1/1/17		Battery returned to Sailly au Bois from Hébuterne.	
-do-	5/1/17		19th Divisional T.Ms. relieved 31st D. T.Ms. and on same day Battery proceeded to HEM on motor lorries.	
	5/1/17		O.C. Y Battery (Lieut Chas. O.H. Clarke) was taken to Hospital. [illegible] took over the command of Y Battery thenceforward.	
HEM	6/1/17 to 31/1/17		Battery training & recreational sports at HEM.	

[illegible]
Y31 M.T.M.B.

A5834 Wt. W4973/M687 750,000 8/16 D. D. & L. Ltd. Forms/C.2118/13.

Vol 10

CONFIDENTIAL.

WAR DIARY

OF

X/31 MEDIUM TRENCH MORTAR BATTERY.

FROM 1st JANUARY 1917 TO 31st JANUARY 1917.

VOLUME ~~XIII~~

Instructions regarding War Diaries and Intelligence Summaries are contained in F. S. Regs., Part II. and the Staff Manual respectively. Title pages will be prepared in manuscript.

WAR DIARY
or
INTELLIGENCE SUMMARY.
(Erase heading not required.)

Army Form C. 2118.

X31 T. M. Bty
January 1917 VOL VII

Place	Date	Hour	Summary of Events and Information	Remarks and references to Appendices
Hébuterne	1/1/17		Fired 10 rounds K 3d 86 + K 3d 77. Good results.	
"	2/1/17		Fired 1 round K 3d 657	
"	3/1/17		Fired 5 rounds K 3d 70 74 + K 3d 90 75. All fired with silence	
"	4/1/17 to 14/1/17		Fatigue parties + working parties on positions + bomb stores in Lene Road.	
	15/1/17		Battery moved by motor lorry to Hem for rest + training.	
	16/1/17 – 31/1/17		Training as per programme by D.T.M.O.	
	1/2/17		Battery moved by motor lorry to Radecie Farm, N.W. of St Omer (Somme)	
			[illegible] 2/Lt	

A5834 Wt. W4973/M687 750,000 8/16 D. D. & L. Ltd. Forms/C.2118/13.

C O N F I D E N T I A L.

W A R D I A R Y

O F

V/31 HEAVY TRENCH MORTAR BATTERY.

FROM 1st JANUARY 1917 TO 31st JANUARY 1917.

V O L U M E XIII

Army Form C. 2118.

VOL VIII

Instructions regarding War Diaries and Intelligence Summaries are contained in F. S. Regs., Part II. and the Staff Manual respectively. Title Pages will be prepared in manuscript.

1st January 1917 to 31st January 1917

WAR DIARY
or
INTELLIGENCE SUMMARY
(Erase heading not required.)

V 31. Heavy Trench Mortar Battery

Place	Date	Hour	Summary of Events and Information	Remarks and references to Appendices
In the Field	1917 1st Jan		Fired 9 rounds at K10b 90 85 & K5c 50 00 Damage to trench - Hit 3rd line - one round short. Billet shelled & damaged entrances - No casualties. Work on gun pits.	
	2		Fired 12 rounds K17b 00.80 to K17b 90 80 Trench around Sunken Road. Very effective - Heavy retaliation - Gun pit partly demolished.	
	3.		Fired 24 rounds at The Maze and trenches round. Great damage, explosion caused. Retaliation with 5.9" & 4.2 M.T.M's. Work on Gun Positions.	
	4.		Fired 23 rounds, 13 on trenches near Sunken Road & 10 on trenches near Point 61 back to 4th Line - Considerable damage done - Suspected O.P. & dug out blown up - Work on Gun Pits.	
	5.		Working on Gun Positions - repairing Pits.	
	6.		Do Do	
	7		Do Do 2nd Lieut. Bloor posted to this Battery.	
	8.		Do Do	
	9.		Fired 90 rounds at Sunken Road defences. Hair Alley junction, K4d 9.6 Bock Graben - K4c 2.9 to K4c 9.4 - K4a 31 to K4c 9.6 - 3rd Line - K4a 9.3 to K4d 1.9. Good results. accurate fire - one round short.	
	10		Fired 17 rounds on Sunken Road defences, Bock Graben, K4a 5.3 Communication Trench to K4d 9.6, K5c 0.1. Southern end Gommecourt Park. Pts 2nd Line trenches - Very effective fire - Heavy retaliation. Telephone wire.	

Army Form C. 2118.

Instructions regarding War Diaries and Intelligence Summaries are contained in F. S. Regs., Part II. and the Staff Manual respectively. Title Pages will be prepared in manuscript.

WAR DIARY
or
INTELLIGENCE SUMMARY

(Erase heading not required.)

V 31 H. T. M. Battery.

Place	Date	Hour	Summary of Events and Information	Remarks and references to Appendices
In the Field	1917 10 Jan		Wires broken all day by enemy fire.	
	11		Fired 20 rounds at K4a. 35 10 to K4c 9. 6. No accurate observation owing to mist - all in enemy lines - Heavy retaliation	
	12		Working on gun pits.	
	13		do	
	14		do	
	15		Handed over to relieving Division & moved to Sailly - Heavily shelled, no casualties.	
	16		Removed to Hardinval	
	17		Training & inspection	
	18		Do	
	19		Do	
	20		Do	
	21		Do	
	22		Winter training Programme	
	23		Do	
	24		Do	
	25		Do	
	26		Do . 2nd Lieut W. V. Turner posted to this unit	
	27		Do	
	28		Do	
	29		Do	
	30		Do	
	31		Do.	

R R Bloor
2/Lt R.F.A.

2449 Wt. W14957/M90 750,000 1/16 J.B.C. & A. Forms/C.2118/12.

C O N F I D E N T I A L.

W A R D I A R Y

O F

Z/31 MEDIUM TRENCH MORTAR BATTERY.

FROM 1st JANUARY 1917 TO 31st JANUARY 1917.

V O L U M E XIII

1st January 1917 to 31st January 1917

WAR DIARY
or
INTELLIGENCE SUMMARY
(Erase heading not required.)

Instructions regarding War Diaries and Intelligence Summaries are contained in F. S. Regs., Part II. and the Staff Manual respectively. Title Pages will be prepared in manuscript.

Army Form C. 2118

VOL VII
Z31 Medm T. M. Bty

Place	Date JAN 1917	Hour	Summary of Events and Information	Remarks and references to Appendices
SAILLY-AU-BOIS	1st and 2nd		Re-drilling	
"	3rd to 8th		Working on new positions etc.	
"	8th		2/Lt H W Lucy RFA returned from leave of absence to the UK	
"	"	12 midnight	One subsection complete went into reserve at HEBUTERNE	
"	9th	"	Two numbers I & four other gun numbers replaced casualties (shock) in Y31 Battery at ~~Hebuterne~~ HEBUTERNE	
	16th		The Battery came out into rest & were transported by Motor Lorries to the village of Hem.	
HEM.	17th – 31st		Carried out training & recreational sports	
"	24th		Lt H W. Lucy RFA went on a course to Valheureux understudying D.T.M.O.	
"	26th		2/Lt R R Whittall RFA was attached to the Battery from A/165 Bde RFA. as acting O.C.	
	1st Feb.		Battery moved in Motor Lorries to Ridouie Farm near St Omer	

R R Whittall 2/Lt R.F.A.
Acting O.C. Z31 M.T.M. Battery

1875 Wt. W593/826 1,000,000 4/15 J.B.C. & A. A.D.S.S./Forms/C. 2118.

C O N F I D E N T I A L.

W A R D I A R Y.

O F

Z/31 MEDIUM TRENCH MORTAR BATTERY.

From 1st February 1917 to 28th February 1917.

V O L U M E XIV

1st Feb 1917 to 28 Feb 1917. **WAR DIARY** *or* **INTELLIGENCE SUMMARY** *(Erase heading not required.)*

Army Form C. 2118

Instructions regarding War Diaries and Intelligence Summaries are contained in F. S. Regs., Part II. and the Staff Manual respectively. Title Pages will be prepared in manuscript.

Z 31 M. T. Mtby. Vol. XIV

Place	Date	Hour	Summary of Events and Information	Remarks and references to Appendices
Lidvrie Farm	1st to 10th	}	Carried out training & Recreational Sports	RHlo
St Ouen	11th		Battery moved down to St Ouen & continued training.	RHlo
Beauval	20th		Received orders to proceed back to Beauval & await orders from Div: Arty. Battery moved by Motor Lorries	RHlo
"	20th 25th	}	Awaiting orders at Beauval	RHlo
"	25th		Received orders to return to Sailly which move was carried out in Motor Lorries & the journey took over 12 hours owing to terrible state of the road.	RHlo
Sailly	27th		Battery worked on road branching off Serre - Hebuterne Road putting down two bridges & repairing road.	RHlo
"	28th		Assisted C/170 in building gun pits	RHlo

V H Whittall
2nd/Lt R.F.A.
a/ O.C. Z 31. M.T.M. Battery

1875 Wt. W593/826 1,000,000 4/15 J.B.C. & A. A.D.S.S./Forms/C. 2118.

C O N F I D E N T I A L.

W A R   D I A R Y.

O F

X/31 MEDIUM TRENCH MORTAR BATTERY.

From 1st February 1917 to 28th Feby. 1917.

V O L U M E XIV.

C O N F I D E N T I A L.

W A R D I A R Y

O F

Y/31 MEDIUM TRENCH MORTAR BATTERY.

From 1st February 1917 to 28th February 1917.

V O L U M E XIV.

1st Feb 1917 To 28th Feb 1917

Instructions regarding War Diaries and Intelligence Summaries are contained in F. S. Regs., Part II. and the Staff Manual respectively. Title pages will be prepared in manuscript.

WAR DIARY
or
~~INTELLIGENCE~~ SUMMARY.
(Erase heading not required.)

Y31 Med. T.M. Battery. Army Form C. 2118.

Vol XIV

Place	Date	Hour	Summary of Events and Information	Remarks and references to Appendices
Pedric Farm.	Feb 1st to Feb 11th/17.		Battery training + recreational sports at Pedric Farm NNW of St Ouen. H.C. 2/Lt	
	11 2/17		Battery moved into St. OUEN Transport: G.S. Wagons. H.C. 2/Lt	
St OUEN	11 2/17 to 20 2/17		Battery training + recreational Sports at St Ouen. H.C. 2/Lt	
	20 2/17		Battery moved into BEAUVAL by means of Motor Transport. H.C. 2/Lt	
BEAUVAL.	20 2/17 to 25 2/17		Battery training + re-equipping at BEAUVAL. H.C. 2/Lt	
SAILLY AU BOIS.	25/26/2/17		Battery moved into SAILLY AU BOIS by Motor Transport. H.C. 2/Lt	
	26 2/17		Battery took over Y19 billets in SAILLY AU BOIS. H.C. 2/Lt	
HÉBUTERNE	27 2/17		Battery helped to fill in trenches and wire which crossed SUNKEN ROAD at K16d 2.3. K22b 4.8.6. and K22b 5.7. H.C. 2/Lt	
	28 2/17		Battery helped to make temporary dugouts for C.B. Y170 Bat. in YELLOW LINE in K22a. H.C. 2/Lt	

H. Cretney 2/Lieut
O.C. Y31 Med T.M. Bty.

1st Feb 1917 to 28 Feb 1917

Instructions regarding War Diaries and Intelligence Summaries are contained in F. S. Regs., Part II. and the Staff Manual respectively. Title pages will be prepared in manuscript.

WAR DIARY
or
INTELLIGENCE SUMMARY.
(Erase heading not required.)

Army Form C. 2118.

X 31. Med. T. M. Bty

February. 1917. VOL XIV

Place	Date	Hour	Summary of Events and Information	Remarks and references to Appendices
ST. OUEN	1/2/17 to 11/2/17		Training & recreation at Redcroft Farm, N.W. of St. OUEN. Ca.	
"	11/2/17		Battery moved to billets in ST. OUEN Ca.	
	12/2/17 to 20/2/17		Continuation of training & recreation programme Ca.	
"	20/2/17		Battery moved to BEAUVAL Ca.	
BEAUVAL	21/2/17 to 23/2/17		Continuation of training & recreation programme Ca.	
	23/2/17		Battery moved to SAILLY AU BOIS, relieving X19 T.M. Batty & taking over billets	
SAILLY AU BOIS	27/2/17		Clearing barricades & laying artillery bridges on road from K.16 central to K22 b.6.2. Ca	
	28/2/17		Constructing gun positions for C/170 Brigade at approx. K22. b.0.9. Ca	

Clayton Lt R.F.A.
O/C X31 T.M. Batty
1/3/17

A5834 Wt. W4973/M687 750,000 8/16 D. D. & L. Ltd. Forms/C.2118/13.

Vol ~~II~~ 11

C O N F I D E N T I A L.

W A R D I A R Y.

O F.

V/31 HEAVY TRENCH MORTAR BATTERY.

From 1st February 1917 to 28th February 1917.

V O L U M E XIV

1st Feb 1917 To 28 Feb 1917.

Army Form C. 2118.

WAR DIARY
or
INTELLIGENCE SUMMARY
(Erase heading not required.)

VOL XIV

V31 H.T.M. Battery

Instructions regarding War Diaries and Intelligence Summaries are contained in F. S. Regs., Part II. and the Staff Manual respectively. Title Pages will be prepared in manuscript.

Place	Date	Hour	Summary of Events and Information	Remarks and references to Appendices
In the Field	1917 Feb 1		Removed to Saint Omer	[illegible]
	2–19		Divisional Winter Training Programme	[illegible]
	20		Removed to Beauval.	[illegible]
	21–24		Standing by for Removal Orders	[illegible]
	25		Removed to Hébuterne to take over	[illegible]

2449 Wt. W14957/M90 750,000 1/16 J.B.C. & A. Forms/C.2118/12.

over

Army Form C. 2118.

Instructions regarding War Diaries and Intelligence Summaries are contained in F. S. Regs., Part II. and the Staff Manual respectively. Title Pages will be prepared in manuscript.

WAR DIARY
or
INTELLIGENCE SUMMARY V31 Heavy Trench Mortar Battery

(Erase heading not required.)

Place	Date	Hour	Summary of Events and Information	Remarks and references to Appendices
In the Field	1917 Feb 26		Inspection of Gun Pits – Taking over 5 guns & 54 complete rounds of Ammunition. Casualties 2 O.R. admitted to Hospital – gassed.	F.J.H.
	27		Dismantling No 1 gun	
	28.		Fatigues for D 170. All guns out of action owing to enemy retirement	F.J.H.

F.J. Haney Capt R.W.A.
O.C.

V.31 HEAVY TRENCH MORTAR BATTERY
No. ....
Date 1st Mar. 1917

2449 Wt. W14957/M90 750,000 1/16 J.B.C. & A. Forms/C.2118/12.

Instructions regarding War Diaries and Intelligence Summaries are contained in F. S. Regs., Part II. and the Staff Manual respectively. Title Pages will be prepared in manuscript.

WAR DIARY
or
~~INTELLIGENCE~~ SUMMARY
(Erase heading not required.)

Army Form C. 2118

Z31 Medium Trench Mortar Bty
VOL. VIII

Place	Date	Hour	Summary of Events and Information	Remarks and references to Appendices
SAILLY-AU BOIS	1st to 7th		Worked on artillery roads, and gun positions in front of HEBUTERNE.	G.H.D
	7th		Received orders to move battery on the following day.	G.H.D
	8th		The battery moved from billets in SAILLY-AU-BOIS by D.A.C wagons to ACHEUX, where it entrained.	G.H.D
BETHUNE	10th		Battery arrived in BETHUNE and was quartered in MONTMORENCY BARRACKS, awaiting orders.	G.H.D
	12th		2/Lt G.H. Dancocks assumed command of the battery, vice: 2/Lt. P.N. Whittall transfered to Y31. M.T.M.B.	G.H.D
			The O.C. and N.C.Os inspected line, gun-positions, billets etc: at GIVENCHY.	
GIVENCHY	13th		The battery took over billets from Y5 M.T.M.B. at LE PREOL and 1 Section relieved Y5 in the line, taking over dug-outs, gun-positions and gun-beds.	G.H.D

1875 Wt. W593/826 1,000,000 4/15 J.B.C. & A. A.D.S.S./Forms/C. 2118.

Instructions regarding War Diaries and Intelligence Summaries are contained in F. S. Regs., Part II. and the Staff Manual respectively. Title Pages will be prepared in manuscript.

WAR DIARY
or
INTELLIGENCE SUMMARY
(Erase heading not required.)

Army Form C. 2118

Place	Date	Hour	Summary of Events and Information	Remarks and references to Appendices
GIVENCHY	14th	3.0pm	20 Rounds (Inst:) were fired on trenches in A9B	G.H.D
	16th		39 Rounds (Delay) were fired on trenches and dug-outs in A9B + A9D	G.H.D
	17th		37 do do do do do. A9B + A9D	G.H.D
	20th		22 do do do do do and sniper post in A9D	G.H.D
			2 Beds were laid in Farfar St. A27D95 40. and guns mounted by the Section out at rest, in readiness for a combined shoot by the 31st T.M.Bs	
	21st		48 Rounds (Delay) were fired on suspected mine-shaft in A9D.	G.H.D
	22nd		A pre-arranged shoot took place at 5.30am in the CAMBRIN Sector, J Bty. firing 22 Rounds (Delay) on to A28C.75 60, the infantry carrying party having failed to carry more bombs to the positions.	G.H.D
	[illegible]		On the GIVENCHY Sector 77 Rounds (Delay) were fired on to trenches and dug-outs etc in A9B and A9D.	

1875 Wt. W593/826 1,000,000 4/15 J.B.C. & A. A.D.S.S./Forms/C. 2118.

Instructions regarding War Diaries and Intelligence Summaries are contained in F. S. Regs., Part II. and the Staff Manual respectively. Title Pages will be prepared in manuscript.

WAR DIARY
or
INTELLIGENCE SUMMARY
(Erase heading not required.)

Army Form C. 2118

Vol ... 'Z' 31 Medium Trench Mortar Bty

Place	Date	Hour	Summary of Events and Information	Remarks and references to Appendices
GIVENCHY	23rd		22 Rounds (Delay) were fired in retaliation to 6 Minnies which the enemy fired on our front line.	G.H.D
	24th		38 Rounds (Delay) were fired in conjunction with Artillery on to enemy's front and support lines in A9B and A9D. The enemy's trenches in this part have been rendered very hard to locate	G.H.D
	25th		37 Rounds (Delay) were fired on A9D70.80	G.H.D
	26th		38 do do do do trenches in A9B and A9D	G.H.D
	27th		80 do do do do A9B60.40. and A9D70.80	G.H.D
	28th		33 do do do do A9B and A9D. At 9.45am a premature occured in the gun-pit in UPPER CUT, Bdr. Heyworth being wounded and the gun-pit destroyed. The gun and frame were recovered intact.	G.H.D
	29th		62 Rounds (Delay) were fired on dug-outs in A9B.	G.H.D
	30th		37 do do do do to trench junction at A9B55 15	G.H.D
	31st		42 do do do do A9D70. 80 and trenches in A9B.	G.H.D

G.H. Danvers 2/Lt. O.C. Z/31 T.M.B

1875 Wt. W593/826 1,000,000 4/15 J.B.C. & A. A.D.S.S./Forms/C. 2118.

VOL VIII

Army Form C. 2118.

WAR DIARY
or
INTELLIGENCE SUMMARY.
(Erase heading not required.)

Instructions regarding War Diaries and Intelligence Summaries are contained in F. S. Regs., Part II. and the Staff Manual respectively. Title pages will be prepared in manuscript.

Y31 M.T.M.B

Month Ending March 31st 1917

Place	Date	Hour	Summary of Events and Information	Remarks and references to Appendices
Sailly au Bois	1·3·17		Battery assisted to erect temporary shelters for gunners of 165th Bde R.F.A in their forward positions at K19a 5.0.	
" " "	2·3·17		Battery assisted to clear road + bridge trenches and craters on 16 Poplars Rd K19a 5.5	
" " "	3·3·17		Filling Shell holes and preparing road for Artillery Near La Louviere Farm.	RHG
" " "	4·3·17		Breaking down Barricades & Preparing road for Artillery at K17 B 5.9.	
" " "	5·3·17		Clearing Hébuterne – Puisieux Road for Transport.	5·3·17
" " "	6·3·17		Lieut Donsocks + two gunners went to take charge of Tramway system at Euston Dump, Battery Personnel roadmaking, and brought two H.T.M. guns out of action for V31.	
" " "	7·3·17		Battery preparing to move.	
" " "	8·3·17		Battery together with rest of Brigade marched to entraining point (Acheux) and entrained for Bethune	
	9·3·17		En Route.	RHG 13·3·17
Bethune	10·3·17		Arrived at Bethune. Personnel of Battery billeted in Montmorency Barracks.	
" "	11·3·17		2/Lieut Whittall ex Z31 to command of Battery V and inspected same during the morning. 2/Lt Donsocks appointed O/C Z31	
" "	12·3·17		O/C Battery + advanced Party proceeded to Cambrin Sector to take over from Z5.	
" "	13·3·17		Battery, provided with horse transport moved into rear billets at Annequin. Right section went into action fired 45 rounds with good effect on trench junction at A27 b 90-65. Material seen to be blown up.	
Annequin	14·3·17		Fired 39 rounds on different trench junctions slight retaliation. No casualties.	
" "	15·3·17		Fired 6 rounds in reply to S.O.S. 2½ minutes after signal was received. 49 Rounds on Trench Junction	M.B.E.
" "	16·3·17		Fired 36 rounds in conjunction with 18 pdrs and in reply to Enemy T.M. Fire. No retaliation	
" "	17·3·17		66 Rounds were fired in Retaliation to H.T.M. effects good	
" "	18·3·17		75 Rds. were fired. Offensive. Effects good. several 77mm received in Retaliation.	
" "	19·3·17		35 Rds. on M.G. emplacement & direct hits and trench in vicinity damaged. Retaliation slight	
" "	20·3·17		31 Rds in Retaliation for 3 H.T.M. (Enemy) which damaged Old Boots trench. Good Effect.	RHG
" "	21·3·17		106. Rds 94 of which were fired in an organized shoot. Effect good. Minenwerfer seen to be blown up in pieces. 12 in retaliation to 3 H.T.Ms which blew in a disused trench	21·3·17

A5834 Wt. W4973/M687 750,000 8/16 D. D. & L. Ltd. Forms/C.2118/13.

Army Form C. 2118.

Instructions regarding War Diaries and Intelligence Summaries are contained in F. S. Regs., Part II. and the Staff Manual respectively. Title pages will be prepared in manuscript.

WAR DIARY
or
INTELLIGENCE SUMMARY.
(Erase heading not required.)

Y 31

Month Ending March 31st 1917

Place	Date	Hour	Summary of Events and Information	Remarks and references to Appendices
Continuing Sector	22-3-17		Rounds fired 12. Offensive A22c 20/35. M.G. Emplacement. Hostile Fire destroyed many [illegible] for [illegible] Bomb Dump at [illegible] Chord A25b 90/40.	
" "	23-3-17		Trench Mortars in A22c 20.10 fairly active. We replied with 20 rounds which were effective in silencing them.	RHW 25.3.17
" "	24-3-17		No firing, shortage of Rifle Mechanisms. Worked on Reserve position & relaid gun Beds.	
" "	25-3-17		9 Rounds at request of Infantry to stop sniping. result. Sniping ceased.	
" "	26-3-17		Replied to S.O.S. no firing otherwise. Work carried on in gun Pits.	
" "	27-3-17		No firing. Rifle Mechanisms reserved for S.O.S. Shortage of Ammunition due to infantry carrying parties not turning up.	RHW 31.3.17
" "	28-3-17		6 Rounds A27b 70/50. [illegible] to S.O.S.	
" "	29-3-17		No firing on a/c of shortage of Rifle Mechanisms at the guns. A few 77 C.M.s fell in Maison Rouge Alley.	
" "	30-3-17		No firing. Selecting positions and exploring extension of Sector in G.4D 80.70.	
	31-3-17		Preparing positions in G.4D 30.70 and showing O/C 60 round positions. Two guns were fixed for firing.	

R H Whittall
2/Lt R.F.A.
O/c Y 31 M.T.M. Bty

A5834 Wt. W4973/M687 750,000 8/16 D. D. & L. Ltd. Forms/C.2118/13.

Instructions regarding War Diaries and Intelligence Summaries are contained in F. S. Regs., Part II. and the Staff Manual respectively. Title pages will be prepared in manuscript.

WAR DIARY
or
INTELLIGENCE SUMMARY.
(Erase heading not required.)

Army Form C. 2118.

X31 Med: T.M. Bty
March 1917.

VOL VIII

Place	Date	Hour	Summary of Events and Information	Remarks and references to Appendices
HEBUTERNE	1/3/17 to 6/3/17		Repairing roads for artillery purposes ~~at~~ near LA BOUTIERE FARM. Assisting field batteries to prepare positions. Ch.	
Sailly au Bois	7/3/17		Under orders to entrain at short notice Ch.	
do.	8/3/17	2 pm	Marched with Battery complete to Acheux and entrained there Ch	
	9/3/17 10/3/17		En route by rail via Abbeville to Bethune Ch	
BETHUNE	11/3/17 to 13/3/17		Billeted in Montmorency Barracks, Bethune awaiting orders Ch	
"	14/3/17	10 am	Proceeded to Annequin & took over CUINCHY Sector from X5 T.M.B. One Section took over billet in line at A21 a.75.75 and all positions. The other Section took over billets in Annequin. The Battery became attached to 3rd Div Artillery. Ch.	
CUINCHY	15/3/17	10 am	Fired 55 rounds at support trenches A22a and A22b. Ch	
		Midnight	Fired 8 rounds at Ducks Bill in connection with raid operations Ch	
"	16/3/17	6.0-12.0 pm	Fired 40 rounds at trenches A22a and A22b. Ch.	
"	17/3/17	5.15 pm	Fired 5 rounds retaliation at A10c 15.20	
		8.30 pm	Fired 30 rounds at support trenches in A22a Ch.	

A5834 Wt. W4973/M687 750,000 8/16 D. D. & L. Ltd. Forms/C.2118/13.

Army Form C. 2118.

WAR DIARY
or
INTELLIGENCE SUMMARY.
(Erase heading not required.)

Instructions regarding War Diaries and Intelligence Summaries are contained in F. S. Regs., Part II. and the Staff Manual respectively. Title pages will be prepared in manuscript.

X31 Med T.M. Batty.
March 1917 VOL VIII (continued)

Place	Date	Hour	Summary of Events and Information	Remarks and references to Appendices
CUINCHY	18/3/17	10.30 a.m.	Fired 25 rounds at support trenches in A22c.	
		2.15 p.m.	Fired 15 rounds at support trenches in A22a. Retaliation slight. Cle.	
"	19/3/17	11.30 a.m. – 2.15 p.m.	Fired 12 rounds on trenches in A22a & A22c. Cle.	
		8.30 p.m.	Fired 15 rounds at support trenches A22a – partly offensive & partly retaliation. Cle.	
		10.25 p.m.	Fired 25 rounds at trenches in A22a. Cle.	
	20/3/17	2 p.m.	No firing owing to clash of ammunition carrying parties. Cle.	
"	21/3/17	10.15 p.m.	Fired 12 rounds support trenches in A22a. – retaliation. Cle.	
	22/3/17	5.30 a.m.	Fired 51 rounds at support trenches A28a 25.00 – A22a 20.20 in a combined shoot with Y31 and Z31 T.M.B. & Heavy Artillery. Good results, much damage to enemy trenches. Cle.	
"	"	10 a.m. – 1 p.m.	Fired 25 rounds at support trenches in A22a. Cle.	
		5 p.m. – 11 p.m.	Fired 35 rounds at support trenches A22a. Cle.	
"	23/3/17	11 a.m.	Fired 8 rounds at trenches in A22c.	
		3 p.m.	Fired 12 rounds on same target, good results. } Cle.	
		8 p.m.	Fired 7 rounds at same target.	
"	24/3/17	2.30 p.m.	Fired 10 rounds at support trenches in A22a.	
		8 p.m.	Fired 15 rounds on same target, before which a premature then occurred in pit, one N.C.O. being killed & one man shell shocked. Mortar & bed damaged & pit rendered useless. A report of circumstances sent to D.T.M.O. Cle.	
		10 p.m.		

A5834 Wt. W4973/M687 750,000 8/16 D. D. & L. Ltd. Forms/C.2118/13.

Army Form C. 2118.

WAR DIARY
or
INTELLIGENCE SUMMARY.
(Erase heading not required.)

Instructions regarding War Diaries and Intelligence Summaries are contained in F. S. Regs., Part II. and the Staff Manual respectively. Title pages will be prepared in manuscript.

X31 Med T.M. Battery
March 1917 VOL. VIII (continued)

Place	Date	Hour	Summary of Events and Information	Remarks and references to Appendices
CUINCHY	25/3/17		No mortars in action owing to premature Cle	
"	26/3/17	9.0pm -11.0pm	Fired 25 rounds at support trenches in A22 b. Cle	
"	27/3/17	12.30pm -4.30pm	Fired 22 rounds at support trenches in A22 b. Cle Fired 7 rounds on trenches in A22 b. Offensive Cle	
"	28/3/17	9.0pm	Took over additional sector from La Bassee Rd. to Boyau 16 - A27 b 55.58 from Y31 T.M.B.	
"	28/3/17	8.0am 11.00am -2.0pm	Fired 24 rounds on trenches in A22 b. with good results.	
		2.15pm	Fired 9 rounds at Trench Junction A28 a.10.75	
		11.45pm	Fired 20 rounds at Trench Junction A22c.00.40 & A22c.00.25 also M.G. Empl. A22c.25.30. Cle	
"	29/3/17	12.0 noon	Fired 3 rounds at A27 b.75.55 registration	
		3.0pm -3.45pm	Fired 34 rounds at Sniper post. A21d.95.85 & A27 b.65.65 at request of Infantry Cle Fired 31 rounds at trenches A22a.05.20 - A21d.90.85	
"	30/3/17	11.30am 12.45pm	Fired 12 rounds at support trench A22c.00.20 - A22c.00.40 at request of Infantry Two officers and 21 O.R. of X66 TMB. reported at ANNEQUIN to be temporarily attached to Battery in accordance with instructions. Commenced renovating permanent reserve positions at A21c 55.65 - A21c.60.65	
		9.15pm -11.30pm	Fired 20 rounds at support trenches A22c.00.15 - A22c-00.40 Cle	
	31/3/17	—	Visited dumps & positions in sector with O/C X66 T.M. Batty	
		30-5.30 pm	Fired 55 rounds at support trenches in A22c. & Trench Junction A28 a.10.75 Cle	

C.A. Carter? for R.A. O/C X31 T.M. Battery 1/4/17.

A5834 Wt. W4973/M687 750,000 8/16 D. D. & L. Ltd. Forms/C.2118/13.

Army Form C. 2118.

864

WAR DIARY
or
INTELLIGENCE SUMMARY.
(Erase heading not required.)

Instructions regarding War Diaries and Intelligence Summaries are contained in F. S. Regs., Part II. and the Staff Manual respectively. Title pages will be prepared in manuscript.

X.31 Med: T.M. Bty

March 1917.

VIII

Place	Date	Hour	Summary of Events and Information	Remarks and references to Appendices
HEBUTERNE	1/3/17 to 6/3/17		Preparing roads for artillery purposes at / Assisting field batteries to prepare positions. Ch.	
Sailly au Bois	7/3/17		Under orders to entrain at short notice Ch.	
do.	8/3/17	2pm	Marched with Battery complete to [illegible] and entrained there Ch.	
	9/3/17 to 10/3/17		En route by rail via Abbeville to Bethune Ch.	
BETHUNE	11/3/17 to 13/3/17		Billeted in Montmorency Barracks Bethune awaiting orders Ch.	
"	14/3/17	10am	Proceeded to Annequin & took over CUINCHY Sector from X5 T.M.B. The one Section took over billet in line at A21c.15.75 and all positions. The other Section took over billet in Annequin. The Battery became attached to 2nd Div. Artillery. Ch.	
CUINCHY	15/3/17	10am	Fired 55 rounds at support trenches A22a and A22b. Ch	
		midnight	Fired 8 rounds at Duck's Bill in connection with raid operations Ch.	
"	16/3/17	6.0-10.0 pm	Fired 40 rounds at trenches A22a and A22b Ch.	
	17/3/17	5.15pm	Fired 5 rounds retaliation at A10c.15.30	
		8.30pm	Fired 30 rounds at support trenches in A22a Ch.	

A5834 Wt. W4973/M687 750,000 8/16 D. D. & L. Ltd. Forms/C.2118/13.

Army Form C. 2118.

Instructions regarding War Diaries and Intelligence Summaries are contained in F. S. Regs., Part II. and the Staff Manual respectively. Title pages will be prepared in manuscript.

WAR DIARY
or
INTELLIGENCE SUMMARY.
(Erase heading not required.)

X21 Mdm T.M. Batty 840
March 1917 VOL VIII (continued)

Place	Date	Hour	Summary of Events and Information	Remarks and references to Appendices
CUINCHY	18/3/17	10.20 a.m.	Fired 25 rounds at support trenches in A22c.	
		3.15 pm	Fired 15 rounds at support trenches in A22c. Retaliation [illegible]. Cb.	
"	19/3/17	11.30am–2.15pm	Fired 13 rounds at trenches in A22a & A22c. Cb.	
		9.30–10.30pm	Fired 19 rounds at support trenches A22a. partly offensive & partly retaliation. Cb.	
"	20/3/17	2pm	Fired 25 rounds at trenches in A22a. Cb.	
"	21/3/17		No firing owing to lack of ammunition carrying parties. Cb.	
"		10.15pm	Fired 15 at support trenches in A22c. – retaliation. Cb.	
"	22/3/17	5.30 a.m.	Fired 51 rounds at support trenches A28a.25.00 – A28a.20.20 in a combined shoot with V31 and Z31 T.M.B. & Heavy Artillery. Good results much damage to enemy trenches. Cb.	Cb.
"	"	10 a.m.–1.0pm	Fired 25 rounds at support trenches in A22a. Cb.	
		9.0–11.0pm	Fired 35 rounds at support trenches A22a. Cb.	
"	23/3/17	4.0 am	Fired 8 rounds at [illegible] in A22a.	
		3.15pm	Fired 12 rounds at same target. good results. Cb.	
		8.0pm	Fired 7 rounds at same target.	
"	24/3/17	3.45pm	Fired 10 rounds at support trenches in A22a.	
		8.0–10.0 pm	Fired 15 rounds at same target. Premature burst then occurred in pit, one NCO being killed & one man shell shocked. Mortar & bed damaged & [illegible] rendered useless. A report of circumstances sent to D.T.M.O. Cb.	

Army Form C. 2118.

Instructions regarding War Diaries and Intelligence Summaries are contained in F. S. Regs., Part II. and the Staff Manual respectively. Title pages will be prepared in manuscript.

WAR DIARY
or
INTELLIGENCE SUMMARY.
(*Erase heading not required.*)

X31 Med T.M. Battery
March 1917 VOL. VIII (continued)

Place	Date	Hour	Summary of Events and Information	Remarks and references to Appendices
CUINCHY	25/3/17		No mortars in action owing to [illegible] Ch.	
"	26/3/17	9.0pm – 11.0pm	Fired 25 rounds at support trenches in A22.b. Ch.	
"	27/3/17	12.30pm – 4.30pm	Fired 22 rounds at support trenches in A22.b. Ch.	
			Fired [illegible] rounds on trenches in A22.b. Afternoon Ch.	
"	28/3/17	3.0am	Took over additional area from La Bassee Rd to Boyau 15 – A27 d.55.58 from Y31 T.M.B.	
"	28/3/17	6.0am 11.0am – 2.0pm	Fired 24 rounds on trenches in A22.b. with good result.	
		2.15pm	Fired 9 rounds at Trench Junction A28 a.10.85	
		11.15pm	Fired 20 rounds at Trench junctions A22c.00.40 & A22c.00.25 also M.G. Empl. A22c.35.30. Ch.	
"	29/3/17	12.0 noon	Fired [illegible] rounds at A27 b.75.85 registration	
			Fired [illegible] rounds at sniper posts A21d.95.85 & A27b.65.65 at request of Infantry Ch.	
		3.0pm – 3.45pm	Fired 21 rounds at trenches A22c.05.30 – A21d.90.85	
"	30/3/17	11.30am	Fired 12 rounds at support trench A22c.05.30 – A22c.00.40 at request of Infantry	
		12.15pm	Two officers and 21 O.R. of X66 T.M.B. reported at ANNEQUIN to be temporarily attached to Battery in accordance with instructions.	
			Commenced [illegible] permanent [illegible] positions at A21c.55.65 – A21c.60.60	
		9.15 – 11.30pm	Fired 20 rounds at support trenches A22c.00.15 – A22c.00.40 Ch.	
			[illegible] with 9" X66 T.M. Batty.	
			[illegible] operations in [illegible] Trench junction A28 a.10.75 Ch.	
"	31/3/17	3.0 – 5.30pm	Fired 55 rounds at support trenches in A22c & Trench junction	

Chaterny[?] 2/Lt R.F.A.
O/C X31 T.M. Battery
1/4/17.

A5834 Wt. W4973/M687 750,000 8/16 D. D. & L. Ltd. Forms/C.2118/13.

C O N F I D E N T I A L.

W A R D I A R Y

O F

V/31 HEAVY TRENCH MORTAR BATTERY

From 1st MARCH 1917 to 31st MARCH 1917.

V O L U M E XV.

Vol 9

1st March 1917 To 31st March 1917

Instructions regarding War Diaries and Intelligence Summaries are contained in F. S. Regs., Part II and the Staff Manual respectively. Title Pages will be prepared in manuscript.

WAR DIARY
or
INTELLIGENCE SUMMARY
(Erase heading not required.)

Volume XV

Army Form C. 2118.

V31 Heavy Trench Mortar Battery

Place	Date	Hour	Summary of Events and Information	Remarks and references to Appendices
In the Field.	1917 Mar 1		Battery on Fatigues for D/170. Commenced construction of Gun Pit in forward position. Dismantled No 1 gun.	
	2		Completed Pit in forward position near Sunken Rd. one O.R. wounded.	
	3		Dismantled gun in Solferino and brought to billets. Fired 9 rounds at K6c.	
	4		Dismantled gun and moved forward.	
	5, 6		Taking gun and ammunition forward and digging new gun pit.	
	7		Bringing guns from pits to billets.	
	8		Taking Ammunition forward. Handed over four guns to D.T.M.O 31st Division	
	9		Taking up Ammunition	
	10		-do- 2 O R wounded.	
	11		Fired 25 rounds – 12 at Point 33 + 13 at Point 47. Good results.	
	12, 13		Taking up Ammunition. 1 O.R wounded.	
	14, 15		Fired 9 Rounds. 2 at L3c3.1. one at L3c2.2. Two at L2d4.7. Four at L2d3.3. Retaliation. one O R. wounded.	
	16		Fired 5 Rounds with good effect on point 47. Taking up remainder of ammunition to gun pit	
	17		Dismantling gun and taking same also ammunition into Bucquoy	
	18		Handed over gun and ammunition to 46th Division	
	19			
	20		Marched to St ~~Sulpice~~ Leger	
	21		-do- Hem	
	22		-do- Aubrometz	
	23		-do- Berguenuese.	

2449 Wt. W14957/M90 750,000 1/16 J.B.C. & A. Forms/C.2118/12.

Army Form C. 2118.

Instructions regarding War Diaries and Intelligence Summaries are contained in F. S. Regs., Part II. and the Staff Manual respectively. Title Pages will be prepared in manuscript.

WAR DIARY
or
INTELLIGENCE SUMMARY
(Erase heading not required.)

V31 Heavy Trench Mortar Battery

Place	Date 1917 Mar	Hour	Summary of Events and Information	Remarks and references to Appendices
In the Field	24		Resting at Berguenease	
	25		Marched to Camplain L'abbe	
	26		Resting at -do-	
	27		10 O R for fatigues at G.H.Q.	
	28		27 O R for fatigues, to 165th Bde. R F A	
	29		Capt Haney awarded Military Cross.	
			10 O R returned from 165th Bde	
	30 31		On fatigues.	

W. V. Sims 2/Lt RFA
For OC V31. HTMB.

2449 Wt. W14957/M90 750,000 1/16 J.B.C. & A. Forms/C.2118/12.

CONFIDENTIAL.

WAR DIARY

OF

X/31 MEDIUM TRENCH MORTAR BATTERY.

From 1st April 1917 to 30th April 1917.

VOLUME XVI

Instructions regarding War Diaries and Intelligence Summaries are contained in F. S. Regs., Part II. and the Staff Manual respectively. Title pages will be prepared in manuscript.

WAR DIARY
or
INTELLIGENCE SUMMARY.
(Erase heading not required.)

Army Form C. 2118.

X31. Med: T. M. Bty.
April 1917. VOL. 2/6

Place	Date	Hour	Summary of Events and Information	Remarks and references to Appendices
CUINCHY	1/4/17	12.30 am	Fired 10 rds. at A22c.00.15 – A22c.00.40 – retaliation	
	"	10.45 am	Fired 34 rds. at sniper post A21d.70.10 – post damaged.	
			Fired 4 rds. at A22c.00.40 retaliation	
		6 pm	Received orders to withdraw guns & personnel from the line to ANNEQUIN and await movement orders. Cle	
ANNEQUIN	2/4/17	9 am	Battery complete proceeded by motor lorry to PETIT SAINS and reported to S.C. 24th Div. Arty. Battery billeted in PETIT SAINS. Cle	
PETIT SAINS	3/4/17		O/C Batty. reported to D.T.M.O. 24th Divn. & proceeded with O/C Y24 T.M.B. to SOUCHEZ and inspected three mortar positions. Cle	
"	4/4/17		One officer and right section proceeded to mortar positions at SOUCHEZ and took over same from Y24 T.M.B. One position badly damaged. Cle	
SOUCHEZ	5/4/17 – 6/4/17		Worked on positions whenever possible. Cle	
	7/4/17	—	Owing to difficulties of ammunition supply & transport of guns & beds, received orders to withdraw right section to PETIT SAINS. Move was carried out with one casualty (1 O.R. wounded) Cle	
PETIT SAINS	8/4/17	8.30 am	O/C Batty and left section with three mortars proceeded to trenches at CALONNE and attached for tactical purposes to Y24 T.M.B. Placed three mortars in action. Cle	
CALONNE	9/4/17	11.30 am	Fired 24 rds. at M21a.15.65 – wire cutting Cle	
		4.0 pm	Fired 6 rds. at M20b.60.30 – retaliation to minenwerfer. Cle	

A5834 Wt. W4973/M687 750,000 8/16 D. D. & L. Ltd. Forms/C.2118/13.

Army Form C. 2118.

Instructions regarding War Diaries and Intelligence Summaries are contained in F. S. Regs., Part II. and the Staff Manual respectively. Title pages will be prepared in manuscript.

WAR DIARY
or
INTELLIGENCE SUMMARY.
(*Erase heading not required.*)

X31 T.M. Batty. 16
April 1917 VOL. [illegible] (contd)

Place	Date	Hour	Summary of Events and Information	Remarks and references to Appendices
CALONNE	10/4/17	2 am	4 rds at M 20 b. 60 30 retaliation to minenwerfer	
		11.0 am	23 rds at M 21 a. 15 65 - wire cutting } Good results	
		11 30 "	27 rds at M 20 b. 60 50 do. }	
		3 0 pm	23 rds at M 20 b. 35 30 do. } Cle	
"	11/4/17	6 am - 6 pm	9 rds at M 20 b. 60 35 retaliation Cle	
			Received one mortar from Ordnance and placed it in action making four mortars in action Cle	
"	12/4/17	11 15 am	12 rds at M 21 a. 50 70 - wire cutting } Cle	
		6 0 pm	12 rds at M 21 a. 50 70 - do. }	
"	13/4/17	10 45 am	32 rds at M 21 a. 50 70 - do. - Good results - two gaps observed Cle	
		2 30 pm	4 HE rds and 8 Thermit rds at M 20 b. 60 35 - ruined house smouldered for some time	
		4 30 pm	Infantry patrols entered enemy trenches and found them unoccupied. Enemy reported to be gradually withdrawing. Awaited orders. Cle	
"	14/4/17	11 am	Received orders from DTMO 4th Divn. to withdraw guns & personnel from the line to PETIT SAINS. Move completed by 7.0 pm Cle	
PETIT SAINS	15/4/17 16/4/17		Awaiting movement orders Cle	

A5834 Wt. W4973/M687 750,000 8/16 D. D. & L. Ltd. Forms/C.2118/13.

Army Form C. 2118.

Instructions regarding War Diaries and Intelligence Summaries are contained in F. S. Regs., Part II. and the Staff Manual respectively. Title pages will be prepared in manuscript.

WAR DIARY
or
INTELLIGENCE SUMMARY.

(Erase heading not required.)

X31 Med. T.M. Battery April 1917. VOL. ~~X~~ 16 (contd)

Place	Date	Hour	Summary of Events and Information	Remarks and references to Appendices
PETIT SAINS	17/4/17	10.30 am	Proceeded to MAROEUIL with battery complete and reported to 31st DAC H.Q. Billeted in the village Cl.	
MAROEUIL	18/4/17 to 20/4/17		Training, re-equipping and recreation in accordance with orders of DTMO 31st Divn. Cl.	

C Coatey [?] Lt R.A.
O/C X31 T.M. Batty
1/5/17.

A5834 Wt. W4973/M687 750,000 8/16 D. D. & L. Ltd. Forms/C.2118/13.

Vol 10

C O N F I D E N T I A L.

W A R D I A R Y

O F

V/31 HEAVY TRENCH MORTAR BATTERY.

From 1st April 1917 to 30th April 1917.

V O L U M E XVI

1st April to 30th April 1917

Instructions regarding War Diaries and Intelligence Summaries are contained in F. S. Regs., Part II. and the Staff Manual respectively. Title Pages will be prepared in manuscript.

WAR DIARY
or
INTELLIGENCE SUMMARY

(Erase heading not required.)

Army Form C. 2118.

V31 Heavy Trench Mortar Battery

Volume XVI

Place	Date April	Hour	Summary of Events and Information	Remarks and references to Appendices
In the Field	1		Battery on fatigues digging positions for 165th Brigade R.F.A.	
	2		Party sent to Houdain for Medium Trench Mortar. Capt Haney resumed command upon return from Hospital	
	3		Battery called up to join 1st Canadian Division. Total Strength 55 O R and 3 Officers. Commenced construction of position, also bringing up ammunition from dump to gun	
	4		Position completed and gun mounted for firing. 1 O R sniped whilst bringing up ammunition. Fired 8 rounds under great difficulties, owing to having no means of working gun; 5 Rounds fired at Trench Junction A 16 b 35.90 – 3 at Trench Junction A 16 b 40.25. – Gun temporary out of action owing to bending of elevation handle and faulty clamping gear. Started repairs right away.	
	5		Repairs completed. Fired 31 rounds: 10 at A 17 c 10.42. 5 at A 16 d 45.65. – 2 at A 16 b 40.25 – 5 at A 16 b 25.15. – 9 at Len Trench. Heavy retaliation, gunpit hit and partially demolished, gun piece destroyed.	
	6		New position in Trench almost completed, but work stopped, as no new gun piece could be obtained: 2nd Lieut Bloor granted leave	
	7		Working on billet making accommodation for men: 2nd Lieut Turner admitted to hospital sick	
	8		Working on billets	
	9		– do. Captain and 2 N.C.Os reconnoitring roads in captured area for Artillery	
	10		Working on billets. Captain and 4 O.R. reconnoitring roads in captured area for Artillery; 2nd Lieut Mills attached for duty	
	11 12 13 14 15 16 17		Repairing roads to enable Artillery to advance.	

F J Haney Capt RFA

2449 Wt. W14957/M90 750,000 1/16 J.B.C. & A. Forms/C.2118/12.

Instructions regarding War Diaries and Intelligence Summaries are contained in F. S. Regs., Part II. and the Staff Manual respectively. Title Pages will be prepared in manuscript.

WAR DIARY
or
INTELLIGENCE SUMMARY

(Erase heading not required.)

Army Form C. 2118.

Place	Date April	Hour	Summary of Events and Information	Remarks and references to Appendices
			Continued	
In the Field	18		Repairing Roads: party shelled	
	19		-do- -do-	
	20		-do- -do- 2nd Lieut Bloor returned from leave	
	21			
	22			
	23			
	24			
	25		Repairing roads	
	26			
	27			
	28			
	29			
	30			

F J Haney Capt RFA

V/31 HEAVY TRENCH MORTAR BATTERY
No. ....
Date 3-5-17

2449 Wt. W14957/M90 750,000 1/16 J.B.C. & A. Forms/C.2118/12.

C O N F I D E N T I A L.

W A R D I A R Y

O F

V/31 MEDIUM TRENCH MORTAR BATTERY.

From 1st April 1917 to 30th April 1917.

V O L U M E XVI

Instructions regarding War Diaries and Intelligence Summaries are contained in F. S. Regs., Part II. and the Staff Manual respectively. Title pages will be prepared in manuscript.

1st April 1917 To 30th April 1917

WAR DIARY or INTELLIGENCE SUMMARY. Y/31 M.T.M. Battery.

(Erase heading not required.)

Army Form C. 2118.

VOL 16

Place	Date	Hour	Summary of Events and Information	Remarks and references to Appendices
VERMELLES Sector	1/4/17		Fired 21 Rounds on Cross St and Hostile T.M.S. in retaliation for 4 Rds. M. Minenwerfer. Result good.	
do do	2/4/17		Fired 5 [illegible] in Retaliation to Hostile M.T.Ms. first round was a premature explosion causing 2 casualties.	KKG
do do	3/4/17		Enemy searched for positions in Boots Alley with 5.9 H.E & H.T.M.S. without result 24 Rounds effectively silenced them.	
do do	4/4/17		Work was done on new Positions renewing platforms. Handing over to new Division (T.M.C. of Y 66.	4/4/17
ANNEQUIN	5/4/17		Salving Mortar and preparing to leave. N.C.O. [illegible] buried in BETHUNE	
do do	6/4/17		Packing of stores preparing to leaving. Motor lorries arrived at 10AM to convoy Battery Stores & personnell to SAINS.EN.GOHELLE	
			Arrived at SAINS EN GOHELLE 2-15-P.M. where we were attached to 224 M.T.M.B.	
SAINS EN GOHELLE	7/4/17		Reconnoitred Positions in CALONNE Sector. and arranged for Positions in Pyrenees Trench, DORAN Alley & STUD Alley	KKG
" "	8/4/17		Personnell & guns removed to fine billets in CALONNE village leaving only one relief of S.E.N.G. to act as ration party. Placed three guns in action after relaying beds and fired five rounds in Retaliation to T.M. fire	
" "	9/4/17		Hostile fire very slight fired during an artillery strafe from 3 PM to 6-30 PM 170 Rounds as per programme. Enemy did not retaliate	10/4/17
" "	10/4/17		Enemy H.T.M. scored direct hit on ammunition recess in Stud alley position. No damage done, 15 rounds fired from position [illegible] silenced enemy T.M. 45 Rounds were fired from Doran Alley in retaliation.	
" "	11/4/17		Fired sixty rounds on Enemy Wire. Work very effectual no trace of wire could be seen when cease fire was ordered	
" "	12/4/17		Fired on Enemy Wire 60 Rounds. About 5 PM. Enemy was thought to have evacuated positions on our immediate front. This was found to be correct later.	
" "	13/4/17		Enemy having retired from front of Calonne Sector battery was withdrawn and personnell returned to rest billets leaving guns etc. [illegible] Forward Billets.	KKG
" "	14/4/17		Battery awaiting orders from C.R.A. 34 and cleaning up stores, equipment etc.	[illegible]/4/17
" "	15/4/17		Awaiting Orders, Overhauling Stores & cleaning guns.	

A5834 Wt. W4973/M687 750,000 8/16 D. D. & L. Ltd. Forms/C.2118/13.

Instructions regarding War Diaries and Intelligence Summaries are contained in F. S. Regs., Part II. and the Staff Manual respectively. Title pages will be prepared in manuscript.

Army Form C. 2118.

WAR DIARY
or
INTELLIGENCE SUMMARY.
(*Erase heading not required.*)

Y 31 M.T.M.B. 2nd Sheet for Month Ending 30-4-17.

Place	Date	Hour	Summary of Events and Information	Remarks and references to Appendices
SAINS-EN-GOHELLE.	16/4/17		Received orders to proceed to MAROEUIL and report to D.T.M.O. 31st Div. Motor transport was provided by 24th Division.	
MAROEUIL	17/4/17		Overhauling stores, Kits of Personell, and making billets habitable.	KHC 19/4/17
" "	18/4/17		Cleaning equipment & guns. Exercise & recreation for personell in afternoon. Instruction for Signallers	
" "	19/4/17		Re-equipping and thoroughly examining gun stores, cleaning guns & beds etc	
" "	20/4/17		~~[illegible]~~ Exercise, Rifle Drill, Gun Drill, & Recreation	KHC 22/4/17
" "	21/4/17		Lecture on Field Clinometer by O.C. N.C.O's. Practice on guns with the instrument. Options, Recreation	
" "	22/4/17		Personell attended Church Parade	
" "	23/4/17		Mortars Stores & Personell were inspected by D.T.M.O. 31.	
" "	24/4/17		Repairing billets, etc. & Inspecting thoroughly all technical stores.	KHC 25/4/17
" "	25/4/17		Morning Drill, Gun Drill, Physical Exercises, & Instruction in Telephony for Signallers.	
" "	26/4/17		Full Marching Order Parade & Inspection by D.T.M.O. Instruction for Signallers	
" "	27/4/17		Inspection of Technical stores, Rifles & Kit by O.C. Instruction for Signallers in visual signalling	KHC 30/4/17
" "	28/4/17		Physical Exercises, Route March in full marching order. Recreation	
" "	29/4/17		Church Parade	
" "	30/4/17		O.C.'s Parade. Rifle Drill & Musketry Drill. Instruction for Signallers, Recreation	

K H Chittell 2/Lt RFA.
OC Y 31 M.T.M. Bty

A5834 Wt. W4973/M687 750,000 8/16 D. D. & L. Ltd. Forms/C.2118/13.

1st April 1917 to 30th April 1917

WAR DIARY
or
INTELLIGENCE SUMMARY
(Erase heading not required.)

Z31 MTM Bty

Army Form C. 2118

Vol. ~~XV~~ 16

Instructions regarding War Diaries and Intelligence Summaries are contained in F. S. Regs., Part II. and the Staff Manual respectively. Title Pages will be prepared in manuscript.

Place	Date	Hour	Summary of Events and Information	Remarks and references to Appendices
GIVENCHY	1/4/17		47 Rounds (delay) were fired on trenches about A9B.5055.	R.H.D
	2/4/17		30 do do do do etc in A9B.	R.H.D
	3/4/17		31 do do do do do	R.H.D
	4/4/17		35 do do do do do	R.H.D
LES BREBIS	6/4/17		Ordered to proceed to LES BREBIS received. Move effected on this date, the Battery being attached to the 6th Divisional Trench Mortars.	R.H.D
LOOS	9/4/17		One detachment went into the line at LOOS.	R.H.D
	10/4/17		Z31 relieved Z6 in the line at LOOS. One other detachment of Z31 went into the line	R.H.D
	11/4/17		20 Rounds (delay) were fired on a M.G. emplacement in 14 BIS. direct hits being observed.	R.H.D
	13/4/17		30 Rounds (Inst.) were fired on to wire from temporary position by Hill 50	R.H.D
			35 Rounds (Inst.) were fired on to wire in front of 14 BIS	
	14/4/17		20 do do do do do do	R.H.D
	15/4/17		The Left Section relieved the Right Section in the line.	R.H.D

1875 Wt. W593/826 1,000,000 4/15 J.B.C. & A. A.D.S.S./Forms/C. 2118.

Army Form C. 2118.

Instructions regarding War Diaries and Intelligence Summaries are contained in F. S. Regs., Part II. and the Staff Manual respectively. Title pages will be prepared in manuscript.

WAR DIARY
or
INTELLIGENCE SUMMARY.

(Erase heading not required.)

Place	Date	Hour	Summary of Events and Information	Remarks and references to Appendices
LOOS	15/4/17		14 Rounds (Inst:) were fired on to trenches in 14 Bis.	G. H. D
	16/4/17		Orders received for the battery to withdraw from the line, This was effected on the evening of this date.	G. H. D
	17/4/17		Orders received for the battery to proceed to MAROEUIL. The move was carried out with 2 Motor Lorries on this date	G. H. D
	18/4/17 to 30/4/17		Battery occupied redrilling, overhauling stores and guns etc:	G. H. D

G. H. Dancocks 2/Lt
O.C. Z/31 T.M.B

A5834 Wt. W4973/M687 750,000 8/16 D. D. & L. Ltd. Forms/C.2118/13.

C O N F I D E N T I A L.

W A R D I A R Y

O F

V/31 MEDIUM TRENCH MORTAR BATTERY

From 1st May to 31st May 1917.

V O L U M E XVII

Instructions regarding War Diaries and Intelligence Summaries are contained in F. S. Regs., Part II. and the Staff Manual respectively. Title pages will be prepared in manuscript.

WAR DIARY

~~or~~

~~INTELLIGENCE SUMMARY.~~

(Erase heading not required.)

Y31 MED. T. M. Bty Army Form C. 2118.

May 1 - 31 1917 VOL. XVII

Place	Date	Hour	Summary of Events and Information	Remarks and references to Appendices
MARŒVIL	1/5/17		Battery personnel were drilled and had rifle exercises. Recreation in Afternoon	
" "	2/5/17		Battery personnel proceeded to A.R.P. at G9D09 (Sheet 51B. France) to staff of O/C Ammunition Dumps 31st Division	[illegible]
" "	3/5/17 to 30/5/17		Personnel still under control of O/C Ammunition Dumps, 31st Division at A.R.P. G.9D09 (Sheet 51B. France)	

[illegible signature]
2/Lt R.F.A.

A5834 Wt. W4973/M687 750,000 8/16 D. D. & L. Ltd. Forms/C.2118/13.

Vol XI

C O N F I D E N T I A L.

W A R D I A R Y

O F

X/31 MEDIUM TRENCH MORTAR BATTERY

From 1st May to 31st May 1917.

V O L U M E XVII

Instructions regarding War Diaries and Intelligence Summaries are contained in F. S. Regs., Part II. and the Staff Manual respectively. Title pages will be prepared in manuscript.

WAR DIARY
or
INTELLIGENCE SUMMARY.
(Erase heading not required.)

Army Form C. 2118.

X31 MED. T.M. BATTERY
May 1-31 1917 VOL. XVII

Place	Date	Hour	Summary of Events and Information	Remarks and references to Appendices
MAROEUIL	1917 May 1		Training & recreation in accordance with DTMO's programme. Three Signallers attached 31st DAHQ for temporary duty. Ch.	
"	2		Training & recreation. Four O.R. attached to 31st ARP for temporary duty. Ch.	
	3		Training & recreation Ch.	
ROCLINCOURT	4 to 31		Battery attached to A Batty 170th Brigade for accomodation and employed as working party. Ch.	

Chater
Lieut R.F.A.
O/C X31 T.M. Batty
31/5/17

C O N F I D E N T I A L.

W A R D I A R Y

O F

V/31 HEAVY TRENCH MORTAR BATTERY.

From 1st May 1917 to 31st May 1917.

V O L U M E XVII

Instructions regarding War Diaries and Intelligence Summaries are contained in F. S. Regs., Part II. and the Staff Manual respectively. Title Pages will be prepared in manuscript.

WAR DIARY
or
INTELLIGENCE SUMMARY
(Erase heading not required.)

V/31 HEAVY TRENCH MORTAR BATTERY
No............
Date............

Army Form C. 2118.

V31 Heavy T. M. Bty
VOL XI May 1-31 1917

Place	Date	Hour	Summary of Events and Information	Remarks and references to Appendices
In the Field	May 1		Assisting 12 inch Battery to make position for guns. (40 men)	
	2		Repairing forward roads for Artillery to advance (Party shelled)	
	3		- do - - do - - do -	
	4		Making positions for 165th Bde R F A	
	5		- do -	
	6		- do -	
	7		Received orders to take over 2 guns from V2 H T M Bty and go into action	
	8		Moved Battery to forward billet. Took over 2 guns from V2 H T M Bty commenced moving same to position. Received 8 Reinforcements.	
	9		Moved guns to position. Heavily shelled whilst doing so.	
	10		Received 25 rounds ammunition. Moved same to forward billet. Took them from there to position under very heavy shell fire: 2 O R wounded. Infantry ~~Co~~ Commander objected to position. Received orders to find new position	
	11		Moving guns to new position. Forward billet and wagon lines heavily shelled. No casualties	
	12		Mounting gun at new position very heavily shelled	
	13		Moving ammunition to new position very heavily shelled. 1. O R killed: 2. O R wounded: 1 O. R missing. Sent out search party for missing man, party returned unable to find any trace	
	14		Sent out party to search for missing man. No result. Received orders to evacuate position. Dismantled gun and brought in out under heavy shell fire. 3. O. R killed.	
	15		Brought guns from forward position to wagon lines. No casualties	
	16		Moved Battery from forward billet to wagon lines.	
	17, 18, 19		Constructing accommodation for men at wagon lines.	

2449 Wt. W14957/M90 750,000 1/16 J.B.C. & A. Forms/C.2118/12.

Instructions regarding War Diaries and Intelligence Summaries are contained in F. S. Regs., Part II. and the Staff Manual respectively. Title Pages will be prepared in manuscript.

WAR DIARY
or
INTELLIGENCE SUMMARY
(Erase heading not required.)

V/31 HEAVY TRENCH MORTAR BATTERY
No. ....
Date. ....

Army Form C. 2118.

Place	Date	Hour	Summary of Events and Information	Remarks and references to Appendices
In the Field	May 20		Constructing accommodation for men. Capt F J Haney goes on leave 2nd Lieut H. Mills in command	
	21		Constructing accommodation for men. Received orders to hand over guns.	
	22		Handed over 2 Guns, Stores, etc to 1st Army School of Instruction	
	23 24 25		Improving accommodation	
	26		Billets heavily shelled. No casualties. Decided to move to new billets	
	27		Reported removal to D T M O. who approved of action taken. Making new accommodation for men	
	28 29 30 31		Making accommodation for men at new billets.	

H Mills
2nd Lt RFA
For O/c V 31. H T M Bty
31. 5. 17.

2449 Wt. W14957/M90 750,000 1/16 J.B.C. & A. Forms/C.2118/12.

Instructions regarding War Diaries and Intelligence Summaries are contained in F. S. Regs., Part II. and the Staff Manual respectively. Title pages will be prepared in manuscript.

WAR DIARY
or
INTELLIGENCE SUMMARY.
(Erase heading not required.)

Army Form C. 2118.

231 Med: T.M. Bty

Vol XVII

May 1-31 1917

Place	Date	Hour	Summary of Events and Information	Remarks and references to Appendices
MAROEUIL	1/5/17 to 2/5/17		Battery re-drilling etc:	G. H. D
ROCLINCOURT	2/5/17		The Battery proceeded to A/170 Wagon lines at ROCLINCOURT where they bivouaced.	G. H. D
	3/5/17 to 31/5/17		Men engaged in fatigues, building gun positions etc: for 170 Brigade. During this period the Battery was split up amongst the various batteries in the Brigade	G. H. D

G. H. Damsacks 2Lt
O.C. Z/317 M. B

A5834 Wt. W4973/M687 750,000 8/16 D. D. & L. Ltd. Forms/C.2118/13.

1st to 30th June 1917. Volume XVIII

Army Form C. 2118.

Y 31 Medium Trench Mortar Batty

Instructions regarding War Diaries and Intelligence Summaries are contained in F. S. Regs., Part II. and the Staff Manual respectively. Title pages will be prepared in manuscript.

WAR DIARY
or
INTELLIGENCE SUMMARY.

(Erase heading not required.)

Place	Date	Hour	Summary of Events and Information	Remarks and references to Appendices
MARŒUIL	1-6-17 to 5-6-17		Personnel attd to O/C A.R.P.	} KHW
" "	6-6-17		Took over sites for two gun positions (No 1 & 2) at B.18-C65 Work commenced on same. Battery stores were moved to camp at B11 B6.2. Personnel having left A.R.P.	
4 [illegible]	7-6-17 to 14-6-17		Personnel Working in reliefs on gunpits and Sap Heads. Work well in hand. O/C took command of Left Group and also took over another gunpit at B18 67.55	KHW
" "	15-6-17 to 22-6-17		Work still proceeding at Gun Pits & Sap Heads	
	23-6-17		[illegible] to draw ammunition and stored same in line	KHW
	24-6-17		To date four steps in each Sap Head have been completed. Gun pits ready to receive guns.	
	25-6-17		Gun platforms [illegible] laid on following line No 1 True Bearing 75° No 2 69° No 3. 0°	
	26-6-17		Guns mounted and ready for action. To date six steps are completed in Sap Heads.	
	27-6-17		Work continued on Sap-heads. Enemy Medium [illegible] [illegible] in early morning	KHW
	28-6-17		[illegible] still in progress.	
	29-6-17 30-6-17		Work continued on Sap-heads. Eight steps completed in each Sap-head.	

K H Whittall
Lieut R.F.A.
O/C Y/31 M.T.M.B.

A5834 Wt. W4973/M687 750,000 8/16 D. D. & L. Ltd. Forms/C.2118/13.

CONFIDENTIAL.

WAR DIARY

OF

X/31 MEDIUM TRENCH MORTAR BATTERY.

From 1st June 1917 to 30th June 1917.

VOLUME XVIII

Instructions regarding War Diaries and Intelligence Summaries are contained in F. S. Regs., Part II. and the Staff Manual respectively. Title pages will be prepared in manuscript.

WAR DIARY
or
INTELLIGENCE SUMMARY.
(Erase heading not required.)

Army Form C. 2118.

X31. MED: T.M. BATTERY.
June 1st to 30th 1917. VOL. XVIII

Place	Date	Hour	Summary of Events and Information	Remarks and references to Appendices
MAROEUIL	1 June – 5		Personnel on detached duty with A.R.P. and with A Batty 170th Brigade and employed in working party. Ce.	
"	6	11.0 am	Battery collected and proceeded to camp at G 11 b. 8.4. (ST. NICHOLAS) Orders received from D.T.M.O. to prepare to go into the line in OPPY Sector. Ce	
	8	9 pm	Acting B.C. proceeded to line to select two positions and chose same at B 24 b. 3.4 and B 24 b. 3.5. Ce	
ST. NICHOLAS	7	9 pm	One section to selected positions and commenced night work. It was decided that for the present only night work was possible. Ce	
"	8	3.0 pm	One officer and one section proceeded to dug outs at B 21 c. 3.7 (Sunken Road) forward battery.	
		9 pm	Continued night on pits, camouflaging carefully. It was decided to carry out section reliefs every three days. Assistance in carrying material was received from V31 H.T.M.B. Ce	
OPPY	9-13		Continued night work on positions Ce	
"	14	3 am	Commenced deep dug out at B 24 b. 3.4. Decided to continue on dug out at position during early mornings. Ce	
"	15	9.30	During work positions were heavily shelled by hostile 5.9 Batty with aeroplane observation. Work healthy camouflaged but it appeared that position had also been seen from OPPY WOOD. Trench badly damaged but positions untouched. Ce	

A5834 Wt. W4973/M687 750,000 8/16 D. D. & L. Ltd. Forms/C.2118/13.

Instructions regarding War Diaries and Intelligence Summaries are contained in F. S. Regs., Part II. and the Staff Manual respectively. Title pages will be prepared in manuscript.

WAR DIARY
or
INTELLIGENCE SUMMARY.
(Erase heading not required.)

Army Form C. 2118.

X31. MED. T. M. BTY.

VOL XVIII CONTINUED.

Place	Date	Hour	Summary of Events and Information	Remarks and references to Appendices
OPPY	16 June		Received instructions from D.T.M.O. to carry on with night work only. Dug out to be proceeded with but positions to be left so as to appear abandoned. Ch.	
"	17 June to 24 June		Continued working on dug out in three eight hour shifts daily. Ch.	
"	25.		Constructed small bomb stores near pits with assistance of V31 HTMB carried 25 rounds complete to each store. Work on dug out continued. Ch.	
"	26.		Two mortars placed in action in pits. Ch.	
"	27.		Received instructions that only one mortar would be required to fire in operations on 28th inst, viz. that at B24 b.3.5. (No. 2 Pit) Ch.	
"	28.	7.10 pm	Fired two rounds at B24 b.50.90 a part of two minute barrage prior to Infantry attack Ch.	
"	29.		Continued work on dug out. Received instructions to dismount guns but hold them in readiness to be placed in action at short notice Ch.	
"	30.		Work on dug out continued Ch.	

Chesters Lt R.A.
O/C X31 T.M. Batty
1/7/17.

A5834 Wt. W4973/M687 750,000 8/16 D. D. & L. Ltd. Forms/C.2118/13.

Vol 12

C O N F I D E N T I A L.

W A R   D I A R Y

O F

V/31 HEAVY TRENCH MORTAR BATTERY.

From 1st June 1917 to 30th June 1917.

V O L U M E XVIII

1st June to 30th June 1917

Instructions regarding War Diaries and Intelligence Summaries are contained in F. S. Regs., Part II. and the Staff Manual respectively. Title Pages will be prepared in manuscript.

WAR DIARY or INTELLIGENCE SUMMARY

(Erase heading not required.)

V31 Heavy Trench Mortar Battery.

Army Form C. 2118.

Volume XVIII

Place	Date 1917 June	Hour	Summary of Events and Information	Remarks and references to Appendices
In the Field	1		Battery on fatigues for 165 Brigade R.F.A	
	2		- do - - do -	
	3		- do - - do - Capt F. J. Haney wounded by aeroplane shell splinter.	
	4		- do - - do -	
	5		- do - - do -	
	6		- do - - do -	
	7		Battery attached to Medium Trench Mortars to construct gun emplacements	
	8		- do - - do -	
	9			
	10		- do - - do -	
	11			
	12		- do - - do -	
	13			
	14		- do - - do -	
	15			
	16		- do - - do - - do - also salving ammunition	
	17			
	18		- do - - do - - do - - do -	
	19			
	20		- do - - do - - do - - do -	
	21		- do - - do - - do - - do -	
			2 O.R. wounded	
	22		Battery moved to forward position. Constructing emplacements - do - - do -	
	23		Constructing gun emplacements for Medium Batteries - do - - do -	
	24			
	25		- do - - do - - do - - do -	
	26		- do -	
	27			
	28		- do - - do - Capt F. J. Haney admitted - do -	
	29		- do - - do - hospital (sick) - do -	
	30		- do - - do - 2nd Lieut [illegible] Mills in command - do -	

[illegible] 2nd Lt. R.F.A. 1.7.17.

2449 Wt. W14957/M90 750,000 1/16 J.B.C. & A. Forms/C.2118/12.

1st June to 30th June 1917

WAR DIARY
or
INTELLIGENCE SUMMARY.
(*Erase heading not required.*)

Army Form C. 2118.

Instructions regarding War Diaries and Intelligence Summaries are contained in F. S. Regs., Part II. and the Staff Manual respectively. Title pages will be prepared in manuscript.

Vol. XVIII

Z31 Medium Trench Mortar Bty:

Place	Date	Hour	Summary of Events and Information	Remarks and references to Appendices
	1/6/17 to 5/6/17		The Battery still split up amongst the various Batteries in the 170 Bde. engaged on working parties etc:	G.H.D
MAISON BLANCHE.	5/6/17		Battery recalled and bivouaced at the A.R.P on the ARRAS-BAILLEUL road.	G.H.D
	6/6/17		Stores etc: brought from MARIDEVIL to A.R.P. Gun positions selected in the line at B.18.C.68.53. and B24 B3.5.	G.H.D
	7/6/17		Work commenced on these positions.	G.H.D
	8/6/17		2 Sub Sections moved to dug-outs in the SUNKEN RD.	G.H.D
	8/6/17 to 14/6/17		Work continued on positions and dug-outs.	G.H.D
	14/6/17		Gun position at B.18.C.68.53. handed over to Left Group under Y Bty. Gun position at B24 B3.5 handed over to Right Group under X Bty:	G.H.D
	15/6/17 to 28/6/17		Z31 Bty. works in conjunction with X and Y Btys in completing gun positions and dug-outs.	G.H.D
	29/6/17 to 30/6/17		Work continues on dug-out at B24 B3.5.	G.H.D

G.H. D[illegible]
[illegible] 2/Lt
O.C. Z31 M.T.M. Bty

A7092 Wt. W125.9/M1293 750,000. 1/17. D. D & L. Ltd. Forms/C2118/14.

CONFIDENTIAL.

WAR DIARY

OF

V/31 MEDIUM TRENCH MORTAR BATTERY.

From 1st July to 31st July, 1917.

VOLUME XIII

I.

Instructions regarding War Diaries and Intelligence Summaries are contained in F. S. Regs., Part II. and the Staff Manual respectively. Title pages will be prepared in manuscript.

WAR DIARY
~~or~~
~~INTELLIGENCE~~ SUMMARY.

(*Erase heading not required.*)

Y 31 Medium Trench Mortar Batty
for Month Ending July 31st

Army Form C. 2118.

VOL XIII

Place	Date	Hour	Summary of Events and Information	Remarks and references to Appendices
MAISON BLANCHE [illegible] SECTOR	July 1st to 7th		Battery Personnel were engaged in constructing M.T.M. positions in GPPY WOOD and vicinity	ref Diary for end of June
" "	July 8th to 12th		Work continued on positions as above. On 11th instructions were received to withdraw guns from line preparatory to move to another front	
" "	13th		Orders received to move to II Corps area. N.C.O's and men withdrawn from line	
"	14th		Personnel and battery stores were removed by Motor Transport to BAC-ST-MAUR. Reported to H.Q.R.A. 57th Division there and was instructed to take over billets at 25 Rue National ARMENTIERS. Region of billet heavily shelled this night	
ARMENTIERS	15th		Took eight M.T.M. positions over from Z 57 and explored HOUPLINES sector. This sector and positions were allotted to battery.	
"	16		Placed four [illegible] in defensive position in [illegible] trench and in offensive position in Pos. No 14 [illegible] Road (C.9 [illegible]) Infantry [illegible] [illegible] ammunition in these positions	
"	17		[illegible] from position No 14 [illegible] [illegible] Retaliation moderate. Enemy bombarded HOUPLINES [illegible] with new type of gas shell	
" "	18		Received orders to make temp. positions for four guns to support raid on [illegible] Trench (95 B).	
"	19 to 21st		Working on positions as above. All four positions in 2nd House Avenue	
" "	22nd		Ammunition placed in positions as above. 40 Rounds per gun	
" "	23rd		[illegible] from above positions, Zero Day.	
" "	24th		Zero [illegible] 2-30 am. Fired according to programme. Hostile fire of all Calibres very heavy. [illegible] were [illegible] fired 120 Rds. No casualties	
"	25th		[illegible] Enemy fire moderate mostly Medium Minen [illegible] 4.2 Shell [illegible] 9.10 am [illegible] Bland also wounded, all battery [illegible] taken to top story of a high building in Rue National. Enemy shelled ARMENTIERS very heavily with H.E. and Incendiary Shell. Many fires [illegible] and also a great many casualties among the civilian population. No 30 Rue National completely blown in. 12" Shells were used on battery at rear of billets.	
" "	26th		Battery [illegible] HOUPLINES under heavy barrage and fired 25 rds on NINA T.M. Position with good effect. Retaliation heavy. No casualties. Bombardment of ARMENTIERS continues. [illegible]	

A5834. Wt. W4973/M687 750,000 8/16 D. D. & L. Ltd. Forms/C.2118/13.

Sheet II

Instructions regarding War Diaries and Intelligence Summaries are contained in F. S. Regs., Part II. and the Staff Manual respectively. Title pages will be prepared in manuscript.

WAR DIARY
~~or~~
~~INTELLIGENCE SUMMARY.~~

(*Erase heading not required.*)

Army Form C. 2118.

Y3 Medium Trench Mortar Battery. Contd. for Month ending July 31st

Place	Date	Hour	Summary of Events and Information	Remarks and references to Appendices
ARMENTIERS	July 27		Fired 20 Rounds on 9 new Trench (95 B 30-40). Retaliation heavy. Effect Destructive. Enemy Bombarded ARMENTIERS with gas shell.	
"	July 28		Day was spent packing up stores preparing to leave billet. The town was bombarded heavily during the day with Shrapnel and H.E of all calibres. About 9 PM an intense hurricane bombardment of the town with gas shells was opened and several incendiary shells fell on the billet (25 Rue Nationale). All ranks became unconscious through the gas (yellow cross shell) and were admitted to hospital. The building and contained stores etc was thoroughly gutted by fire and nothing whatever was saved. 2 Officers and 25 O.R's became casualties. The bombardment was continued until about 6 AM on the morning of the 29 July.	
	29th		Battery Non effective	
	30 "		" "	
	31 "		" "	

[illegible]
Lt. R.G.A.

A5834 Wt. W4973/M687 750,000 8/16 D. D. & L. Ltd. Forms/C.2118/13.

T.M.O. 31 11 A.

O/C Y M.T.M.B.

Ref your L. of 17-9-17.

Herewith please find copy of War Diary, compiled from information at my disposal, for month of July. I would point out that during the month of August the battery was non-effective.

[signature] Lt. R.A.

O/C Y/31 M.T.M.B.

18-9-17.

Vol

C O N F I D E N T I A L.

W A R   D I A R Y

O F

V/31 HEAVY TRENCH MORTAR BATTERY.

From 1st July to 31st July, 1917.

V O L U M E   XIX.

Army Form C. 2118.

Instructions regarding War Diaries and Intelligence Summaries are contained in F. S. Regs., Part II. and the Staff Manual respectively. Title Pages will be prepared in manuscript.

1st July 1917 to 31st July 1917.

WAR DIARY
or
INTELLIGENCE SUMMARY

(Erase heading not required.)

V31. Heavy Trench Mortar Battery

VOL XIX

Place	Date 1917	Hour	Summary of Events and Information	Remarks and references to Appendices
In the Field	July 1		Battery on fatigues for Medium Trench Mortar Batteries.	
	2		-do- -do-	
	3		-do- -do-	
	4		-do- -do-	
	5		-do- -do- Capt F J Haney R.F.A. evacuated to England	
	6		-do- -do- Capt C Allen in Command	
	7		-do- -do- 1. O.R. accidentally wounded.	
	8		-do- -do-	
	9		-do- -do-	
	10		-do- -do-	
	11		-do- -do-	
	12		-do- -do-	
	13		-do- -do-	
	14		-do- -do-	
	15		-do- -do-	
	16		-do- -do-	
	17		-do- -do-	
	18		-do- -do- Men withdrawn from Forward Billet	
	19		-do- -do-	
	20		-do- -do-	
	21		-do- -do- Battery moved to new position. Erecting Shelters for men.	
	22		Battery assisting Medium Batteries in building position for Exhibition Shoot.	
	23		-do- -do-	
	24		-do- -do-	
	[illegible]		Party of 1 Officer & 17 men moved to Forward Position to assist Medium Batteries in erecting Gun positions. RMB.	

2449 Wt. W14957/M90 750,000 1/16 J.B.C. & A. Forms/C.2118/12.

Army Form C. 2118.

Instructions regarding War Diaries and Intelligence Summaries are contained in F. S. Regs., Part II. and the Staff Manual respectively. Title Pages will be prepared in manuscript.

WAR DIARY
or
INTELLIGENCE SUMMARY

(Erase heading not required.)

Place	Date	Hour	Summary of Events and Information	Remarks and references to Appendices
	1917		Continued	
In the Field	July 27		Battery on fatigues for Medium Trench Mortar Batteries	
	28		-do-	
	29		-do-	
	30		Party in forward position relieved, by one Officer and 18 men.	
	31		Battery on fatigues for Medium Trench Mortar Batteries	

R.P. Bloor
2/Lt R.F.A
for

V/31
HEAVY TRENCH
MORTAR BATTERY
No.
Date

2449 Wt. W14957/M90 750,000 1/16 J.B.C. & A. Forms/C.2118/12.

Army Form C. 2118.

Instructions regarding War Diaries and Intelligence Summaries are contained in F. S. Regs., Part II. and the Staff Manual respectively. Title pages will be prepared in manuscript.

WAR DIARY
or
INTELLIGENCE SUMMARY.
(Erase heading not required.)

X31. Med: T. M. Bty
July 1st to 31st 1917. VOL 19.

Place	Date	Hour	Summary of Events and Information	Remarks and references to Appendices
OPPY	1/7/17 to 14/7/17		Continued work on dugouts at B24 b.3.4. Clc	
"	15/7/17		Handed over dugout & one positions at B24 b.3.5 to Y63 T.M.B. Remaining position at B24 b.3.4 abandoned. Guns withdrawn to rear billet. Took over two positions in OPPY WOOD from Y31 TmB in course of construction Clc	
"	16/7/17 to 19/7/17		Worked on new positions in OPPY WOOD Clc	
"	20/7/17		Handed over these positions to X5 T.M.B & withdrew Battery personnel to rear billet Clc	
"	21/7/17		Battery training at rear billet. Lt. R.A. FRASER posted to command of Battery vice Lt. C. AXTEN transferred to Y31 HT.M.B. Clc	
	22/7/17		Battery moved by Motor Lorry in accordance with D.T.M.O's instructions from G11 b.8.4 St NICHOLAS to new rest billets at A8a 2.8. 1 Officer proceeded to forward with 1 Officer & 6 O.R. of Z31. T.M. Bty JRmw.	

A5834 Wt. W4973/M687 750,000 8/16 D. D. & L. Ltd. Forms/C.2118/13.

Army Form C. 2118.

Instructions regarding War Diaries and Intelligence Summaries are contained in F. S. Regs., Part II. and the Staff Manual respectively. Title pages will be prepared in manuscript.

WAR DIARY
or
INTELLIGENCE SUMMARY.
(Erase heading not required.)

X31. Med. T. M. Bty
July 1st to 31st 1917. VOL 19 (Continued)

Place	Date	Hour	Summary of Events and Information	Remarks and references to Appendices
	23/7/17 + 24/7/17		Work proceeded with on Range for Exhibition Shoot for Corps Commander with the assistance of V31. H.T.M. BTY. two positions made and two Guns complete with 100 rounds deposited at positions. JRMW	
	25/7/17		All available men proceeded to Range at 6-30am to prepare for Exhibition Shoot which took place at 10-0am 69 rounds were fired with satisfactory results. Guns etc withdrawn and taken back to rest billet. JRMW.	
	26/7/17		Battery relieved Z.31 M.T. M. Bty at forward billet. JRMW.	
	27/7/17 to 29/7/17		Work proceeded with in view of preparing two positions at T24. d. 04 Battery billeted at forward billet T25. d 39. relieved by Z 31. M.T M. Bty on the night of 29th JRMW	
	30/7/17 + 31/7/17		Usual parades + Training in accordance with D.T.M.O. programme JRMW	
			James R. M. Walker 2Lt I.F.R. for O/C X 31. M. T. M. Bty.	

A5834 Wt. W4973/M687 750,000 8/16 D. D. & L. Ltd. Forms/C.2118/13.

CONFIDENTIAL.

Vol

WAR DIARY

OF

Z/31 MEDIUM TRENCH MORTAR BATTERY.

From 1st July to 31st July, 1917.

VOLUME XIX.

1st July 1917 to 31st July 1917.

Army Form C. 2118.

WAR DIARY
or
INTELLIGENCE SUMMARY.
(Erase heading not required.)

Instructions regarding War Diaries and Intelligence Summaries are contained in F. S. Regs., Part II. and the Staff Manual respectively. Title pages will be prepared in manuscript.

231 Medium Trench Mortar Battery

VOL XIX

Place	Date	Hour	Summary of Events and Information	Remarks and references to Appendices
MAISON BLANGE.	1/7/17 to 20/7/17		Battery continued work on the dug-out at B24 B. 3. 5 and pits in the line	G.H.D
	20/7/17		Battery withdrew to rest billet at the A.R.P on the ARRAS-BAILLEUL road.	G.H.D
LA TARGETTE.	22/7/17		Battery moved to new billet at A8A2. 8. 1 Officer and 6 men proceeded to forward billet at VIMY.	G.H.D
	26/7/17		1 Officer and 6 men returned to rest billet	G.H.D
	29/7/17		Y Battery relieved X Battery at the forward billet	G.H.D
	30/7/17		Battery returned to rest billet, orders having been received to move to ERQUINGHEM. (31)	G.H.D
	31/7/17		Battery moved to ERQUINGHEM. guns stores etc. being left at rest billet at A8A2. 8.	G.H.D

G. Dancocks Lt R.G.A
O.C. Z 31, M.T.M.B

A7092 Wt. W12839/M1293 750,000. 1/17. D. D & L. Ltd. Forms/C2118/14.

Instructions regarding War Diaries and Intelligence Summaries are contained in F. S. Regs., Part II. and the Staff Manual respectively. Title pages will be prepared in manuscript.

1st Aug 17 – 31st Aug 17

WAR DIARY
or
INTELLIGENCE SUMMARY.

(Erase heading not required.)

Army Form C. 2118.

X 31 Med: T. M. Battery.

August 1st to 31st 1917. VOL 20

Place	Date	Hour	Summary of Events and Information	Remarks and references to Appendices
	1/8/17 to 31/8/17		Work continued with at T24. d. 04 with the assistance of V31 H. T. M. Bty in preparing 2 positions & Dug-Out ~~at~~ (three 8 hourly shifts daily.) RAF. Section reliefs take place every 6th night RAF.	
LA TARGETTE	1/8/17 to 31/8/17		Usual parades, Training & Fatigues carried out according to D. T. M. O's programme at rest billet. Also party of 1 N.C.O. & 4 men from men in rest billets employed daily under the Divisional Camouflage Officer for special work on Camouflage. RAF.	

R. A. Fraser
Lt E. Yorks Rgt
O/C X31

A5834 Wt. W4973/M687 750,000 8/16 D. D. & L. Ltd. Forms/C.2118/13.

Instructions regarding War Diaries and Intelligence Summaries are contained in F. S. Regs., Part II. and the Staff Manual respectively. Title pages will be prepared in manuscript.

Army Form C. 2118.

WAR DIARY
or
~~INTELLIGENCE~~ SUMMARY.
(Erase heading not required.)

Y31 M.T.M.B for Month ending Aug 31st 1917. Vol. XIV

Place	Date	Hour	Summary of Events and Information	Remarks and references to Appendices
In the Field	1/8/17 to 13/8/17		Owing to casualties caused by heavy gas shell bombardment of ARMENTIERS on July 29th the Battery was non-effective until 13-8-17 when Lieut Hill R.A. was posted as O.C. Posting ante-dated from 25-7-17. Personnel remaining (2 N.C.O.s 7 gunners) attd Z31	
	22/8/17		10 O.R. attached to Batty from D.A.C.	
ARLEUX	31/8/17		Personnel working on M.T.M. Positions at T24D04.	

Hill, R.A.
Lieut R.F.A.
O/C Y31 M.T.M.B.

(A7092). Wt. W12839/M1293. 750,000. 1/17. D. D. & L., Ltd. Forms/C.2118/14.

CONFIDENTIAL.

WAR DIARY

OF

V/31 HEAVY TRENCH MORTAR BATTERY.

From 1st August to 31st August, 1917.

VOLUME XX.

1st – 31st Aug 17

Instructions regarding War Diaries and Intelligence Summaries are contained in F. S. Regs., Part II. and the Staff Manual respectively. Title Pages will be prepared in manuscript.

WAR DIARY
or
~~INTELLIGENCE SUMMARY~~

(Erase heading not required.)

Army Form C. 2118.

V31. Heavy Trench Mortar Battery — VOL XX

Place	Date	Hour	Summary of Events and Information	Remarks and references to Appendices
~~In the Field~~ VIMY	1917 Aug 1st to 31st		Battery assisting Medium Batteries in work on two Gun pits and dug-outs at T24.d.04. Forward Billet located at T25.d.39. Rear billet located at A8a.2.8.	Ca.

[signature] Capt R.A.
O/C V31 H.T.M. Battery
2/9/17

2449 Wt. W14957/M90 750,000 1/16 J.B.C. & A. Forms/C.2118/12.

C O N F I D E N T I A L.

W A R   D I A R Y

O F

Z/31 MEDIUM TRENCH MORTAR BATTERY.

From 1st August to 31st August, 1917.

VOLUME XX .

1st Aug 917 – 31st Aug 917

Instructions regarding War Diaries and Intelligence Summaries are contained in F. S. Regs., Part II. and the Staff Manual respectively. Title pages will be prepared in manuscript.

WAR DIARY or INTELLIGENCE SUMMARY.

(Erase heading not required.)

Y31 Medium Trench Mortar Battery

Vol XX

Army Form C. 2118.

Place	Date	Hour	Summary of Events and Information	Remarks and references to Appendices
ERQUINGHEM	1/8/17		1 Officer and half the Battery, moved into dug-out at C28A 50 40.	G.H.D
	2/8/17		Received orders to salve stores left by Y31, and submit indents for deficiences.	G.H.D
			Took over from Z57 in the line	
	3/8/17 to 6/8/17		Inspected trenches, gun-pits ammunition stores etc: in the line.	G.H.D
	7/8/17		2Lt J.R.M. Walker admitted to hospital, suffering from gas.	G.H.D
	7/8/17 to 11/8/17		Preparing gun-pits for action, placing beds in position, etc.	G.H.D
	11/8/17		20 Rounds fired on German Support Line at C29 Central. Effect destructive.	G.H.D
	12/8/17		40 Rounds fired from two gun positions, on to German Trenches CENTAUR ROW & CENSUS SUPPORT	G.H.D
	13/8/17		Restocked 3 positions with bombs and placed Newton Bed in JAPAN TRENCH	G.H.D
	14/8/17		Fired 10 rounds on 15 D6.9. Medium Minenwerfer position. Effect destructive. Hostile fire on position heavy	G.H.D

A7092 Wt. W128 9/M1293 750,000. 1/17. D. D & L. Ltd. Forms/C2118/14.

Instructions regarding War Diaries and Intelligence Summaries are contained in F. S. Regs., Part II. and the Staff Manual respectively. Title pages will be prepared in manuscript.

2/

WAR DIARY
or
INTELLIGENCE SUMMARY.
(Erase heading not required.)

30th Medium Trench Mortar Battery

Army Form C. 2118.

Vol. XX.

Place	Date	Hour	Summary of Events and Information	Remarks and references to Appendices
ERQUINGHEM	13/8/17		Preparing positions for 3 gun shoot and registering offensive target from defensive position	G.H.D.
	15/8/17		Lt Evers H reported for duty.	G.H.D.
	16/8/17		Carried on sychonised shoot on German support line at C23 Central and enemy bomb store at C29 Central. 30 Rounds destructive fire, as a result of hostile retaliation, one pit was blown in.	G.H.D.
	17/8/17		5 Rounds fired on German support line at C29A.	G.H.D.
	18/8/17		Front line and support line at C23 C & D. 20 rounds destructive fire.	G.H.D.
	19/8/17		Cleaning up positions and guns	G.H.D.
	20/8/17		Relief carried out in line.	G.H.D.
	21/8/17		Orders received to place 4 guns in position to concentrate on CENSUS TRENCH from C23C to C29A.	G.H.D.
	22/8/17		Work carried out on above scheme, which was for the purpose of covering a raid. 1 gun detachment stood by all night.	G.H.D.

A7092 Wt. W125 g/M1293 750,000. 1/17. D. D & L. Ltd. Forms C2118/14.

3

Instructions regarding War Diaries and Intelligence Summaries are contained in F. S. Regs., Part II. and the Staff Manual respectively. Title pages will be prepared in manuscript.

WAR DIARY
or
INTELLIGENCE SUMMARY.
(Erase heading not required.)

Army Form C. 2118.

Z31 Medium Trench Mortar Battery.

Vol XX

Place	Date	Hour	Summary of Events and Information	Remarks and references to Appendices
ERQUINGHEM.	23/9/17		Standing by, raid postponed.	G.H.D
	24/8/17		Stood by, raid successfully carried out, but battery action was not required.	G.H.D
	25/8/17		Fired on CENSORS NOSE, CENSUS TRENCH, and CENSUS SUPPORT line. 36 rounds fired with destructive effect. Enemy retaliated with 5.9" HE and Heavy Minnenwerfer.	G.H.D
	26/8/17		Relief carried out.	
	27/8/17		Fired on CENSUS TRENCH, 10 rounds.	G.H.D
	28/8/17		Received orders for 3 guns to be placed in action in front line at I10B 80.20 and I10D 90.00 and I10D 60.50	G.H.D
	28/8/17		Placing beds in position, carrying ammunition etc.	G.H.D
	29/8/17		Working on above positions	G.H.D
	30/8/17		Still working on above positions, and preparing for Divisional shoot.	G.H.D
	31/8/17		Divisional shoot successfully carried out. G.H. Damant 2Lt. O.C. Z/31 T.M.B	G.H.D

A7092 Wt. W128.9/M1293 750,000. 1/17. D. D & L. Ltd. Forms/C2118/14.

Instructions regarding War Diaries and Intelligence Summaries are contained in F. S. Regs., Part II. and the Staff Manual respectively. Title pages will be prepared in manuscript.

WAR DIARY
or
INTELLIGENCE SUMMARY.
(Erase heading not required.)

Army Form C. 2118.

Place	Date	Hour	Summary of Events and Information	Remarks and references to Appendices
			C O N F I D E N T I A L.	
			W A R D I A R Y	
			O F	
			Y/31 MEDIUM TRENCH MORTAR BATTERY.	
			From 1st Sept. to 30th Sept. 1917.	
			V O L U M E XXI	

A5834 Wt. W4973/M657 750,000 8/16 D. D. & L. Ltd. Forms/C.2118/13.

Instructions regarding War Diaries and Intelligence Summaries are contained in F. S. Regs., Part II. and the Staff Manual respectively. Title pages will be prepared in manuscript.

WAR DIARY
or
~~INTELLIGENCE~~ SUMMARY. Y/31 M.T.M.B. for Month Ending Sept 30th 17

(*Erase heading not required.*)

Army Form C. 2118.

Vol XXI

Place	Date	Hour	Summary of Events and Information	Remarks and references to Appendices
In the Field	Sept 1 to Sept 7		Preparing position and digging dugouts in Alberta ~~Road~~ Road.	
" "	Sept 8 to Sept 15		Work continued as above.	
" "	Sept 16 to Sept 24		Positions in Alberta Road ready for action. Gun beds laid and ammunition stored. Dugout nearing completion.	
" "	Sept 25 to Sept 30		Work on dugout continued. Gallery of dugout opened up.	

H. Mills
Lieut R.F.A.
O/C Y/31 M.T.M.B.

(A7092). Wt. W12839/M1293 750,000. 1/17. D. D. & L., Ltd. Forms/C.2118/14.

31 Div.
180/

D. A. G.
G. H. Q. 3rd Echelon,
THE BASE.

Herewith War Diary for the months of JULY and AUGUST of Y/31 Medium T.M.B.

It is regretted that this was not forwarded before, and that the information contained therein is very scant, but during a gas shell bombardment on the night of July 28/29th, all the battery records were destroyed by fire, and the Diary has therefore had to be made from information supplied from other sources.

D. H. Q.
24.9.17.

Major-General
Commanding 31st Division.

Instructions regarding War Diaries and Intelligence Summaries are contained in F. S. Regs., Part II. and the Staff Manual respectively. Title pages will be prepared in manuscript.

WAR DIARY
or
INTELLIGENCE SUMMARY.
(Erase heading not required.)

Army Form C. 2118.

Place	Date	Hour	Summary of Events and Information	Remarks and references to Appendices
			C O N F I D E N T I A L.	
			W A R D I A R Y	
			O F	
			X/31 MEDIUM TRENCH MORTAR BATTERY.	
			From 1st Sept. to 30th Sept. 1917.	
			V O L U M E XXI.	

A5834 Wt. W4973/M687 750,000 8/16 D. D. & L. Ltd. Forms/C.2118/13.

Instructions regarding War Diaries and Intelligence Summaries are contained in F.S. Regs., Part II. and the Staff Manual respectively. Title pages will be prepared in manuscript.

Army Form C. 2118.

WAR DIARY or INTELLIGENCE SUMMARY.

(Erase heading not required.)

X.31 Med: T.M. Bty

Sept: 1st to 30th 1917 VOL 21.

Place	Date	Hour	Summary of Events and Information	Remarks and references to Appendices
	1.9.17 to 10		Half the Battery continued work at T.24.b.0.4 with the assistance of V.31 H.T.M. Bty preparing 2 positions & dug-out. (3. 8 hourly shifts daily) Half Battery at Rest Billet (LA TARGETTE A8.a.2.8) usual parades training, fatigues, & work on Camouflage for Div artillery.	
	5.9.17		then withdrawn from the line to Rest Billet	
	6.9.17 7.9.17		Battery moved in accordance with D.T.M.O's instructions to new Rest Billet at ROCLINCOURT WEST.	
	8.9.17 to 30.9.17		Relief proceeded to new forward Billet in TIRED ALLEY to continue work on positions at T.24.b.0.4. (Relief every 6 days)	
	16.9.17 to 20.9.17		Two 2" Mortars complete placed in position at T.24.b.0.4 ready for action. Three tubes placed in "Roving" positions at B6.c.5.2, B.6.c.2.4 & B6.c.4.0 ready for action	
	19.9.17		1 Officer & 10 O.R proceeded to ~~Farbus~~ FARBUS to work on artillery positions for Canadian Corps	
	24.9.17		9 O.R returned from FARBUS to Rest Billet	
	25.9.17 to 30.9.17		1 Officer & 20 O.R proceeded to forward billet in HART STREET to work on position vacated by V.31. H.T.M. Bty in Arleux Wood	

[illegible] Capt
O.C. X.31 M.T.M. Batty

A5834 Wt. W4973/M687 750,000 8/16 D. D. & L. Ltd Forms/C.2118/13.

Army Form C. 2118.

Instructions regarding War Diaries and Intelligence Summaries are contained in F. S. Regs., Part II. and the Staff Manual respectively. Title pages will be prepared in manuscript.

WAR DIARY
or
INTELLIGENCE SUMMARY.

(Erase heading not required.)

Vol 15

Place	Date	Hour	Summary of Events and Information	Remarks and references to Appendices
			C O N F I D E N T I A L. W A R D I A R Y O F V/31 HEAVY TRENCH MORTAR BATTERY. From 1st Sept. to 30th Sept. 1917. V O L U M E XXI.	

A5834 Wt. W4973/M687 750,000 8/16 D. D. & L. Ltd. Forms/C.2118/13.

Army Form C. 2118.

Instructions regarding War Diaries and Intelligence Summaries are contained in F. S. Regs., Part II. and the Staff Manual respectively. Title Pages will be prepared in manuscript.

1st Sept 1917 to 30th Sept 1915

WAR DIARY
or
~~INTELLIGENCE SUMMARY~~
(Erase heading not required.)

V.31. Heavy Trench Mortar Battery
Vol. 21.

Place	Date	Hour	Summary of Events and Information	Remarks and references to Appendices
	1917 Sept			
VIMY	1st to 6th		Battery assisting Medium Batteries in work on two Gun pits and dugouts at T24. d. 04. Ch	
ARLEUX	6th		1 Officer & 10 ORs. proceeded to Arleux and took over Heavy T. M. position in course of construction at B6. c. central from V5 H. T. M. Battery. Ch.	
"	7th		Battery moved rest billet to A28. b. 37. Ch.	
"	8th		Took over 1 Heavy Mortar from V5. H. T. M. Bty. Work on trench leading to gun position proceeded with. Ch.	
"	9th		5 ORs in addition to Arleux. Work on trench proceeded with. Ch	
"	10th		Work on trench carried on and completed. Ch	
	10th to 12th		Rest billet now at A28. b. 0. 3. Ch.	
"	11th		Commenced work on tunnel to Gun pit. Ch.	
"	12th		20. ORs. to forward billet as relief. Continued work on tunnel. Ch.	
"	13th to 18th		Continued work on tunnel and mens dugouts. Work in tunnel difficult. Air Pump applied for. Ch.	
"	19th		13. ORs detached for digging field Gun-pits in Canadian Area. Ch.	

2449 Wt. W14957/M90 750,000 1/16 J.B.C. & A. Forms/C.2118/12.

Army Form C. 2118.

Instructions regarding War Diaries and Intelligence Summaries are contained in F. S. Regs., Part II. and the Staff Manual respectively. Title pages will be prepared in manuscript.

WAR DIARY or INTELLIGENCE SUMMARY.

(Continued) V31. Heavy Trench Mortar Battery

(Erase heading not required.)

Vol 21

Place	Date	Hour	Summary of Events and Information	Remarks and references to Appendices
ARLEUX	1917 Sept 19th		Received notification from D.T.M.O that two 9.45 H.T.M's (Russian Gun) would be arriving shortly, and that positions must be chosen, and work commenced at once. Ca	
"	22nd		Sector reconnoitred, and two positions chosen at B5d.60.60	
			Decided to dig open pits (carefully camouflaged) and commence mining Ammunition recesses and dugouts immediately. Ca	
"	23rd		Work on position at B6.c. central discontinued. It was decided to hand this position to Medium Batteries. Ca	
			Work commenced on new positions. Ca	
"	24th		12 OR's on attached duty returned to Battery. Work continued on new positions. Ca	
"	25th		Work continued on new positions. Ca	
"	26th		1 Officer and 24 O.R's now at forward billet. Ca	
"	27th		Work continued on new positions. Ca	
"	28th		Work continued. 1 Officer and 31 O.R's now at forward billet. Ca	
"	29		Two pits dug for reception of guns.	
	30		Work continued on Ammunition recesses. Ca	

C. Carter Capt RGA
O/C V31 H.T.M. Batty
1/10/17

(A7092). Wt. W12839/M1293. 75,000. 1/17. D. D. & L., Ltd. Forms/C.2118/14.

Army Form C. 2118.

Instructions regarding War Diaries and Intelligence Summaries are contained in F. S. Regs., Part II. and the Staff Manual respectively. Title pages will be prepared in manuscript.

WAR DIARY
or
INTELLIGENCE SUMMARY.
(Erase heading not required.)

Place	Date	Hour	Summary of Events and Information	Remarks and references to Appendices
			C O N F I D E N T I A L.	
			W A R D I A R Y	
			O F	
			Z/31 MEDIUM TRENCH MORTAR BATTERY.	
			From 1st Sept. to 30th Sept. 1917.	
			V O L U M E XXI	

A5834 Wt. W4973/M687 750,000 8/16 D. D. & L. Ltd. Forms/C.2118/13.

Instructions regarding War Diaries and Intelligence Summaries are contained in F. S. Regs., Part II. and the Staff Manual respectively. Title pages will be prepared in manuscript.

WAR DIARY
or
INTELLIGENCE SUMMARY
(Erase heading not required.)

Army Form C. 2118.

1

X/37 Medium Trench Mortar Battery VOL XXI

Place	Date	Hour	Summary of Events and Information	Remarks and references to Appendices
HOUPLINES.	1/9/17		Fired 27 rounds on Trench Junction at C29 Central and 3 rounds at enemy minenwerfer at C29 A. 60. 40.	W.E.
	4/9/17		Fired 20 rounds on Trench Junction at C29 Central and enemy minnie at C29 A 60. 40. Much material was blown into the air.	W.E.
	5/9/17		Fired 25 rounds at enemy minenwerfer (medium) at C29 A. 60 70. and heavy minenwerfer at I 5 B. Results were good, a quantity of wood and material was blown into the air, an explosion was caused followed immediately by a fire.	W.E.
	6/9/17		Fired 15 rounds into trenches at CENSORS NOSE and 20 rounds at heavy minenwerfer at C29 C 30. 40. 5 rounds fell very near the target, which ceased fire. It is thought emplacement has been damaged.	W.E.
	7/9/17		Fired 30 rounds into trenches at CENSORS NOSE.	W.E.

Instructions regarding War Diaries and Intelligence Summaries are contained in F. S. Regs., Part II. and the Staff Manual respectively. Title pages will be prepared in manuscript.

2

WAR DIARY
or
INTELLIGENCE SUMMARY.
(Erase heading not required.)

Army Form C. 2118.

Medium Trench Mortar Battery

VOL XXI

Place	Date	Hour	Summary of Events and Information	Remarks and references to Appendices
HOUPLINES	8/9/17		Fired 25 rounds on CENTAUR SUPPORT.	[illegible]
	10/9/17		Fired 15 rounds on CENTRAL SUPPORT, several direct hits on trench were observed.	[illegible]
	12/9/17		Fired 10 rounds at wire at C29 C 4.7, several rounds were observed to fall into wire.	[illegible]
	13/9/17		Fired 25 rounds on CENTAUR LANE and CENTRAL SUPPORT.	[illegible]
	14/9/17 to 22/9/17		No firing owing to Divisional Relief. Battery employed in making temporary positions at C28 B 50. 65, C28 B 65. 60 and C28 B 50. 65. Defensive Emplacement at C28 B 27. 65. repaired on three occasions after direct hits from enemy shell.	[illegible]
	23/9/17		Fired 9 rounds at enemy front line at C29 A. 40. 20. and CENTRAL JUNCTION at C29 C 80. 75. Further shooting prevented by broken rifle mechanisms.	[illegible]
	24/9/17		Fired 6 rounds into CENTRAL AVENUE and CENTAUR LANE SUPPORT.	[illegible]
	25/9/17		Fired 8 rounds into CENTAUR LANE and CENTAUR TRENCH.	[illegible]

2

Army Form C. 2118.

* Instructions regarding War Diaries and Intelligence Summaries are contained in F. S. Regs., Part II. and the Staff Manual respectively. Title pages will be prepared in manuscript.

WAR DIARY
or
INTELLIGENCE SUMMARY.
(*Erase heading not required.*)

231 Medium Trench Mortar Battery

VOL XXI

Place	Date	Hour	Summary of Events and Information	Remarks and references to Appendices
HOUPLINES	25/9/17		Orders received to withdraw from the line, preparatory to transfer to XIII Corps. Battery moved to D.T.M.O's H.Q. at BAC · ST · MUIR	[initials]
BAC - ST - MUIR	26/9/17		Orders received to proceed to ROCLINCOURT to rejoin the 31st Division	[initials]
ROCLINCOURT.	27/9/17		Battery moved by moved by motor lorry to ROCLINCOURT.	[initials]
	28/9/17		1 Officer and 11 O.R. proceeded to forward dug-out in TIRED ALLEY.	[initials]
	29/9/17		Moved into dug-out in HART ST:	[initials]
	30/9/17		Working on 6" positions in the line.	[initials]

[signature] Lt.
for O.C. Z 31 M.T.M.B

A7092 Wt. W128 9/M1293 750,000. 1/17. D. D & L. Ltd. Forms/C2118/14.

Army Form C. 2118.

Instructions regarding War Diaries and Intelligence Summaries are contained in F. S. Regs., Part II. and the Staff Manual respectively. Title pages will be prepared in manuscript.

WAR DIARY
or
INTELLIGENCE SUMMARY.
(Erase heading not required.)

Place	Date	Hour	Summary of Events and Information	Remarks and references to Appendices
			C O N F I D E N T I A L.	
			W A R D I A R Y	
			O F	
			Z/31 MEDIUM TRENCH MORTAR BATTERY.	
			From 1st October to 31st October, 1917.	
			V O L U M E XXII	

A5834 Wt. W4973/M687 750,000 8/16 D. D. & L. Ltd. Forms/C.2118/13.

Army Form C. 2118.

Instructions regarding War Diaries and Intelligence Summaries are contained in F. S. Regs., Part II. and the Staff Manual respectively. Title pages will be prepared in manuscript.

WAR DIARY
or
INTELLIGENCE SUMMARY.

(Erase heading not required.)

Place	Date	Hour	Summary of Events and Information	Remarks and references to Appendices
			C O N F I D E N T I A L. W A R D I A R Y O F V/31 MEDIUM TRENCH MORTAR BATTERY. From 1st October to 31st October, 1917. V O L U M E XXII	

A5834 Wt. W4973/M687 750,000 8/16 D. D. & L. Ltd. Forms/C.2118/13.

Instructions regarding War Diaries and Intelligence Summaries are contained in F. S. Regs., Part II. and the Staff Manual respectively. Title pages will be prepared in manuscript.

WAR DIARY
or
INTELLIGENCE SUMMARY.
(Erase heading not required.)

Army Form C. 2118.

Y/31. T.M. Bty. Vol ~~16~~ 22

month ending 31st Oct 1917.

Place	Date 1917	Hour	Summary of Events and Information	Remarks and references to Appendices
In the field	1 Oct.		Battery completed at position in ALBERTA RD.	H.M.
	2 – 7		2nd beds taken out, 350 rounds of ammunit 6" taken to ALBERTA RD, rest of Battery assisting X 31 at position in ARLEUX.	H.M.
	8		Men returned from X 31, for work at ALBERTA RD; excavating new hut in trench. 2 6" Newton mortars taken over at Rest Billet, & cleaned.	H.M.
	9.		Cleaning out huts, storing ammunition, strengthening camouflage.	H.M.
	10.		2 cut beds for 6", completed, all Battery with the exception of 4 O.R. withdrawn to Rest Billet for instruction in 6" Newton mortar.	H.M.
	11.		Emptying of ammunition from boxes at ALBERTA RD position, & stacking same in a dry place. Remainder of Battery at REST BILLET, instruction in 6" mortar.	H.M.
	12.		Roofing up of frames at ALBERTA RD POSITION. Instruction of 6" mortar, at REST BILLET.	H.M.
	13.		Parts of trench rebuilt & revetted, owing to fall caused by wet weather. Roofing up of frames. Instruction of 6" mortar at REST BILLET.	H.M.

(A7092). Wt. W12859/M1293 750,000. 1/17. D. D. & L., Ltd. Forms/C.2118/14.

Instructions regarding War Diaries and Intelligence Summaries are contained in F. S. Regs., Part II. and the Staff Manual respectively. Title pages will be prepared in manuscript.

WAR DIARY
or
INTELLIGENCE SUMMARY.
(Erase heading not required.)

Army Form C. 2118.

Y 31. M.T.M. Bty Vol 22

Month ending 31st Octo 1917.

Place	Date 1917	Hour	Summary of Events and Information	Remarks and references to Appendices
In the field	14 Oct.		Alberta Road. Revetting parts of trench fallen in owing to weather. Continued boarding up frames. Preparing to re-camouflage pits & remove all surplus timber. Billet. Instruction in 6" Trench Mortar.	G.K.
	15th		Alberta Road. Continued boarding frames, revetting trench, stacking ammunition and re-camouflaging pits and trench. Owing to destructive shoot of the enemy on position & trenches round about, the work was considerably interfered with. Billet. Constructing 6" beds etc on range. ANZIN.	G.K.
	16.		Alberta Road. Continued work boarding frames & removing ammunition boxes, also work on camouflage destroyed by enemy bombardment. Billet. Work on camouflage, Signalling class, & demonstration shoot with 6" mortars.	G.K.
	17.		ALBERTA RD. Boarding of frames, revetting of trench & cleaning of ammunition. Shoot for 6" [illegible] mortars, at [illegible].	H.M.

(A7092) Wt. W12839/M1293 750,000. 1/17. D. D. & L., Ltd. Forms/C.2118/14.

Instructions regarding War Diaries and Intelligence Summaries are contained in F. S. Regs., Part II. and the Staff Manual respectively. Title pages will be prepared in manuscript.

Army Form C. 2118.

WAR DIARY
or
INTELLIGENCE SUMMARY.
(Erase heading not required.)

Place	Date 1917	Hour	Summary of Events and Information	Remarks and references to Appendices
[illegible]	18.	[illegible]	Completion of [illegible] frames at ALBERTA RD. position. Removal of guns, beds etc from position of [illegible] Shoot.	H.M.
	19	"	2. 6" Newton Mortars, taken over at Rest Billet, & cleaned.	H.M.
	20.	"	2. 6" mortars & beds carried from SASKATCHEWAN RD. to ALBERTA RD POSITION. Work on camouflage at Rest Billet.	H.M.
	21	"	1 - 6" mortar mounted & 59 rounds fired on wire in front of TORTOISE TRENCH.	H.M.
	22	"	No. 1 pit in ALBERTA RD. cleared of earth, thrown by bursting of enemy shell, site [illegible], camouflage repaired & replaced, 6" mortar put in action.	H.M.
	23.	"	60 rounds of ammunition carried to position (ALBERTA RD), all useless timber cleared from position.	H.M.
	24	"	41 rounds 6" ammunition fired on T.M. emplacement, map ref. T.24 b. 95.95.	H.M.
	25	"	36 rounds 6" ammunition fired on wire, map ref. T.24 d. 40 30.	H.M.

(A7092). Wt. W12839/M1293. 750,000. 1/17. D. D. & L., Ltd. Forms/C.2118/14.

Instructions regarding War Diaries and Intelligence Summaries are contained in F. S. Regs., Part II. and the Staff Manual respectively. Title pages will be prepared in manuscript.

WAR DIARY
or
INTELLIGENCE SUMMARY.
(Erase heading not required.)

Army Form C. 2118.

Y31 M T M Bty
VOL #22

Place	Date 1917.	Hour	Summary of Events and Information	Remarks and references to Appendices
[illegible] Field	26.	0815(?)	Commenced excavating No. 3 pit at position in ALBERTA RD.	H.H.(?)
	27.	"	17 rounds 6" ammunition fired at T.M. Emplacement, map ref. T.24.b.94.61(?)	H.H.(?)
	28.	"	1 temporary bed (2") pit in ALBERTA RD. constructed(?). Fired 30 - 2" bombs at wire, map ref. T.24.d.35.65. " 25 - 6" " " " " T.24.d.35.30. 2" Gd(?) taken up.	H.H.(?)
	29.	"	45. 6" ammunition fired on wire, map ref. T.24.d.35.30, T.24.d.35.15. Carried 2" guns & beds from position to SASKATCHEWAN RD.	H.H.(?)
	30.	"	45. 6" bombs fired on wire map ref. T.24.d.35.35, T.24.d.37.70. 150 - 6" bombs taken to ALBERTA RD.	H.H.(?)
	31.	"	135 - 6" bombs fired on wire, map ref. T.24.d.33.6[illegible], T.24.d.35.80. 150 - 6" bombs carried to ALBERTA RD.	H.H.(?)

H. Hill(?)
Lt. R.F.A.
O/c Y/31 T.M. Bty.

31.10.17.

(A7092). Wt. W12539/M1293. 750,000. 1/17. D. D. & L., Ltd. Forms/C.2118/14.

Instructions regarding War Diaries and Intelligence Summaries are contained in F. S. Regs., Part II. and the Staff Manual respectively. Title pages will be prepared in manuscript.

WAR DIARY
or
INTELLIGENCE SUMMARY.
(Erase heading not required.)

Army Form C. 2118.

Vol 16

Place	Date	Hour	Summary of Events and Information	Remarks and references to Appendices

C O N F I D E N T I A L.

W A R D I A R Y

O F

X/31 MEDIUM TRENCH MORTAR BATTERY.

From 1st October to 31st October, 1917.

V O L U M E XXII

A5834 Wt. W4973 M687 750,000 8/16 D. D. & L. Ltd. Forms/C.2118/13.

Army Form C. 2118.

WAR DIARY
or
INTELLIGENCE SUMMARY.
(Erase heading not required.)

Instructions regarding War Diaries and Intelligence Summaries are contained in F. S. Regs., Part II. and the Staff Manual respectively. Title pages will be prepared in manuscript.

X31 Med: T. M. Bty

October 1st to 31st 1917 VOL 22.

Place	Date	Hour	Summary of Events and Information	Remarks and references to Appendices
ARLEUX WOOD	1.10.17 to 12.10.17		Work continued with on positions in ARLEUX WOOD. [illegible]	
"	13.10.17		All men withdrawn from the line with the exception of 3 O.R. for drill on 6" Newton Trench Mortar. [illegible]	
	14.10.17		All available men at Rest Billet proceeded to range at ANZIN to lay platforms etc for Exhibition Shoot with 6" Newton Trench Mortars. [illegible]	
	15.10.17		work continued with on range. [illegible]	
	16.10.17		Exhibition Shoot carried out on range with very satisfactory results 180 rounds were fired. [illegible]	
	17.10.17 – 18.10.17		All available men proceeded to range to remove all beds and timber to Rest Billet. [illegible]	
	19.10.17		Half the battery proceeded to the line to continue work on positions. [illegible]	
	20.10.17		2 × 6" Newton trench mortars complete placed in position at B.6 central ready for action [illegible]	
	21.10.17 to 24.10.17		Work continued with on positions. [illegible]	

A5834 Wt. W4973/M687 750,000 8/16 D. D. & L. Ltd. Forms/C.2118/13.

Army Form C. 2118.

WAR DIARY
or
INTELLIGENCE SUMMARY.
(*Erase heading not required.*)

Instructions regarding War Diaries and Intelligence Summaries are contained in F. S. Regs., Part II. and the Staff Manual respectively. Title pages will be prepared in manuscript.

X31 Med: T. M. Bty.
Oct: 1st to 31st VOL 22 (continued)

Place	Date	Hour	Summary of Events and Information	Remarks and references to Appendices
ARLEUX WOOD	25.10.17	2-30pm to 4-0pm	Firing commenced with 6" Newton Trench Mortars 36 rounds fired on enemy front line from T30d. 60.88 to U.25.C.00.00. Several direct hits obtained on Trench. Enemy retaliated with M/T and 10. cm. about 90 rounds were fired into ARLEUX WOOD + CRUCIFIX CORNER. [initialled]	
"	26.10.17		Half Battery relief took place	
"	27.10.17	12-30pm to 4-0pm	65 Rounds 6" Newton fired on Enemy wire at C.1.a.15.35. no observation of this wire was possible. Enemy retaliated with about 200 rounds 10.5 cm. on three sunken roads joining at B.5.d. and 20 L.T.Ms on Brittania Trench + Sunken road. [initialled]	
"	28.10.17	2.0pm to 3.0pm	30 Rounds 2" Medium fired on Enemy wire a C.1.C 30.65. satisfactory results obtained. Enemy retaliated with 10-15 cm. on Sunken Road B.6.d. 2-2" Mortars returned to Rest Billet. [initialled]	
"	29.10.17		Remainder of Battery at Rest Billet proceeded to line to commence work on new positions at B.6. Central [initialled]	
	30.10.17	2-30pm to 3-0pm	40 Rounds 6" Newton fired on Enemy wire from C.1.a.20.45 C.1.a.30.55 good results obtained [initialled]	
	31.10.17	3-0pm to 4-0pm	Enemy attempted to locate Bty Position. He fired 25 - 10.5 cm Hows. into Arleux Wood No Damage done. [initialled]	[signature] 2/Lt R.F.A. for O/C X31 Med. T.M. Bty

A5834 Wt. W4973/M687 750,000 8/16 D. D. & L. Ltd. Forms/C.2118/13.

Army Form C. 2118.

Instructions regarding War Diaries and Intelligence Summaries are contained in F. S. Regs., Part II. and the Staff Manual respectively. Title pages will be prepared in manuscript.

WAR DIARY
or
INTELLIGENCE SUMMARY.
(Erase heading not required.)

Place	Date	Hour	Summary of Events and Information	Remarks and references to Appendices
			C O N F I D E N T I A L. W A R D I A R Y. O F V/31 HEAVY TRENCH MORTAR BATTERY. From 1st October to 31st October, 1917. V O L U M E XXII	

A5834 Wt. W4973/M687 750,000 8/16 D. D. & L. Ltd. Forms/C.2118/13.

Army Form C. 2118.

Instructions regarding War Diaries and Intelligence Summaries are contained in F. S. Regs., Part II. and the Staff Manual respectively. Title Pages will be prepared in manuscript.

1st Oct 17 to 31st Oct 17

WAR DIARY or ~~INTELLIGENCE SUMMARY~~

(Erase heading not required.)

V31. Heavy Trench Mortar Battery

Vol. 22

Vol. 16

Place	Date	Hour	Summary of Events and Information	Remarks and references to Appendices
	1917 October			
ARLEUX	1st		Work on two gun positions and dugouts at B5.d.60.60 continued. Ca.	
	2nd		Received 1 Heavy Mortar (Russian Gun) from Ordnance.	
			Continued work on positions. Ca.	
	3rd		Conveyed 60 rounds Ammunition to positions. Work Continued. Ca.	
	4th		Mortar complete conveyed to position. Work on dugout continued. Ca.	
	5th		Sub. bed laid in pit at 55° T. Mortar placed in action. Ca.	
	6th		Rivetting of pit and work on dugouts. Ca.	
	7th		Rivetting and sapping continued	
			A further 30 rounds conveyed to positions. Ca.	
	8th		Rivetting and sapping continued. Ca.	
	9th		Loading trench to pit completed	
			Sapping of dugout continued. Ca.	
	10th		Sapping continued. Back of pit rivetted. Ca.	
	11th		Trench boarded and sumped. Sapping continued. Ca.	
	12th		Trench rivetted. Loading shelter constructed. Sapping continued. Ca.	
	13th		Sapping continued. Ca.	
	14th		Gun mounted and cleaned	
			An enemy shell hit tree at back of pit, slightly damaging the pit and mounting of mortar. 1 O.R. seriously wounded. Sapping continued. Ca.	

2449 Wt. W14957/M90 750,000 1/16 J.B.C. & A. Forms/C.2118/12.

Army Form C. 2118.

Instructions regarding War Diaries and Intelligence Summaries are contained in F. S. Regs., Part II. and the Staff Manual respectively. Title pages will be prepared in manuscript.

WAR DIARY

~~or~~

~~INTELLIGENCE SUMMARY.~~

(Erase heading not required.)

V31 Heavy Trench Mortar Battery

Vol 16. Continued

Place	Date	Hour	Summary of Events and Information	Remarks and references to Appendices
ARLEUX	1917 October 15		Mortar dismounted. Steel platform repaired but mounting returned for repair.	
			Sapping of dugout continued. Ch.	
	16th		Gun pit repaired and rivetted. Sapping of dugout continued. Ch.	
	17th		Two entrances of dugout joined up and completed.	
			Gun mounting at workshop for repairs.	
			Part of Battery Personnel assisted Medium Batteries in demonstration of 6" Newton mortars	
	18th		Continued work on dugout. Mounting taken back to position. Ch.	
	19th		Sapping of Recess started. Timber salved from Bailleul. N.L.	
	20th		Sapping continued. Camouflage frame fitted. Loading shelter completed.	N.L.
	21st		Sapping continued. Gun mounted cleaned and dismounted.	N.L.
			30 shells prepared for firing.	
	22nd		Sapping continued.	N.L.
	23rd		— " —	N.L.
	24		— " — 29 Rounds H.E. fired on U25.b.6.0 – U25.c.15.42 (?).	
			Short (?) firing from 2 pm to 4-30 pm. No retaliation on gun. N.L.	
	25th		Work continued on dugouts	
	26th		Work continued in dugouts. Two telephone lines laid and Wireless Aerial fixed.	[illegible]
	27th		Work on dugout. 7 Rounds H.E. fired on Trench and Road junction at T30.c.65.85. (Heavy retaliation)	N.A.
	28		Second 9.45 T.M. (French Gun) conveyed to position. N.A.	

A7092 Wt. W125 9/M1293 750,000. 1/17. D. D & L. Ltd. Forms C2118/14.

Instructions regarding War Diaries and Intelligence Summaries are contained in F. S. Regs., Part II. and the Staff Manual respectively. Title pages will be prepared in manuscript.

WAR DIARY
or
~~INTELLIGENCE~~ SUMMARY.
(Erase heading not required.)

V31. Heavy Trench Mortar Battery

Vol 22 (Continued).

Army Form C. 2118.

Place	Date	Hour	Summary of Events and Information	Remarks and references to Appendices
Arleux	1917 October			
	28		Work on emplt. continued. R.H.B.	
	29		Work on emplt. Gas blankets fitted. 31 Rounds H.E. fired. Aeroplane observation used. Two targets registered.	R.H.B.
			Commenced to lay sub-bed of second Mortar	
	30		Work on emplt. continued. Sub-bed laid. New Camouflage fitted on No 2 Gunpit.	R.H.B.
	31st		Commenced work on 5 Mortar Gunpits for Z31. TM Battery. R.H.B. (3 gun pits at T23 a 80.60. 2 gun pits at T29 b 85.85)	

R.H. [illegible] Lt. R.G.A.
for Capt. R.G.A.
O.C. V31 Hy. T.M. Bty.

A7092 Wt. W125 9/M1293 750,000. 1/17. D. D. & L. Ltd. Forms/C2118/14.

Instructions regarding War Diaries and Intelligence Summaries are contained in F. S. Regs., Part II. and the Staff Manual respectively. Title pages will be prepared in manuscript.

WAR DIARY
or
INTELLIGENCE SUMMARY.
(Erase heading not required.)

231 Medium Trench Mortar Battery

Army Form C. 2118.

VOL XXII

Place	Date	Hour	Summary of Events and Information	Remarks and references to Appendices
ROCLINCOURT.	1/10/17 to 8/10/17		Work continued on 6" Newton positions. by HART ST:	L. D
	8/10/17		2 6" Newton Trench Mortars and 4 beds delivered to this Battery	L. D
	8/10/17 to 19/10/17		Work continued on 6" Newton positions	L. D
	19/10/17		2 6" Newton Trench Mortars and 4 beds delivered to this Bty:	L. D
	19/10/17 to 25/10/17		Work continued on 6" Newton positions and 2 guns mounted.	L. D
	25/10/17		Battery returned to rest billet for training of the 6" Newton.	L. D
	26/10/17 to 29/10/17		Battery engaged in training on 6" Newton	L. D
	29/10/17		Battery returned to the line, and started work on two new positions at T30 C 5.5.	L. D
	30/10/17 to 31/10/17		Work continued on these two positions.	L. D

L. Dancocks. 2Lt
O.C. Z/13 T.M.B.

A7092 Wt. W128 9/M1293 750,000. 1/17. D. D & L Ltd. Forms/C2118/14.

Army Form C. 2118.

WAR DIARY
or
INTELLIGENCE SUMMARY.
(Erase heading not required.)

Instructions regarding War Diaries and Intelligence Summaries are contained in F. S. Regs., Part II. and the Staff Manual respectively. Title pages will be prepared in manuscript.

Place	Date	Hour	Summary of Events and Information	Remarks and references to Appendices

C O N F I D E N T I A L.

W A R   D I A R Y

O F

Y/31 MEDIUM TRENCH MORTAR BATTERY.

From 1st November to 30th November, 1917.

V O L U M E   XXIII.

A5834 Wt. W4973 M687 750,000 8/16 D. D. & L. Ltd. Forms/C.2118/13.

1st - 30th Nov. 1917

Instructions regarding War Diaries and Intelligence Summaries are contained in F. S. Regs., Part II. and the Staff Manual respectively. Title pages will be prepared in manuscript.

WAR DIARY or INTELLIGENCE SUMMARY.

(Erase heading not required.)

Army Form C. 2118.

Y. 31. Medium Trench Mortar Battery

Vol XXIII

Place	Date	Hour	Summary of Events and Information	Remarks and references to Appendices
	Nov.		1917.	
Indefield	1.		104. 6" bombs fired on enemy wire, map ref. T. 24. d. 35.58. 150. 6" " taken to ALBERTA Rd. POSITION.	H.M.
	2.		150. 6" bombs fired on enemy wire, map ref. T. 24. d. 3255 to 34.65. 330. 6" " taken to ALBERTA Rd. POSITION.	H.M.
	3.		Excavated No. 3 pit at ALBERTA Rd. mounted 6" mortar. 205. 6" bombs fired on enemy wire, map ref. T. 24. d. 3268 to 30.80. 255. 6" " taken to ALBERTA Rd. POSITION.	H.M.
	4.		Excavated No. 4 pit at ALBERTA Rd. mounted 6" mortar. 195. 6" bombs fired on enemy wire, map ref. T. 24. d. 27.95 to 2090. 300. 6" " taken to ALBERTA Rd. POSITION.	H.M.
	5.		5. 6" bombs fired on enemy wire, map ref. T. 24. d. 40.35. 250. 6" " taken to ALBERTA Rd. POSITION.	H.M.
	6.		50. 6" bombs fired on enemy wire T. 24. d. 35.22.	H.M.
	7.		50. 6" bombs fired on enemy wire, map ref. T. 24. d. 33.30 to 35.10. 111. 6" " taken to ALBERTA Rd. POSITION.	H.M.
	8.		185. 6" fired in connection with raid operations. Nos. 1. 2. 3. 4 pits blown in by enemy fire.	H.M.

(A7092). Wt. [illegible]839/M1293. 750,000. 1/17. D. D. & L., Ltd. Forms/C.2118/14.

Instructions regarding War Diaries and Intelligence Summaries are contained in F. S. Regs., Part II. and the Staff Manual respectively. Title pages will be prepared in manuscript.

WAR DIARY
or
INTELLIGENCE SUMMARY.
(Erase heading not required.)

Army Form C. 2118.

Place	Date	Hour	Summary of Events and Information	Remarks and references to Appendices
	December 1917			
In the field	9.		H.Q. Battery personnel returned from line to REST BILLET.	H.M.
	10.		ALBERTA RD: POSITION shelled. work on clearing [illegible] commenced.	H.M.
	11.		Fired 20 - 6" Bombs on enemy M.G. Emplacement. [illegible] to ALBERTA RD position, [illegible] by hostile shelling.	H.M.
	12.		Fired 20. 6" Bombs, on enemy M.G. emplacement.	H.M.
	13.		Fired 20 - 6" Bombs on enemy M.G. emplacement. Work commenced on Ammunit Recess in WINNIPEG RD. K.	H.M.
	14.		Fired 22 - 6" Bombs on enemy M.G. emplacement. 1 - 6" Mortar carried from ALBERTA to WINNIPEG RD.	H.M.
	15.		Work continued on position in ALBERTA RD. Excavation completed for frame for Ammunit Recess. Gun 971 brought to Rest Billet, for repair.	H.M.
	16.		Attached men from V.31, handed to O/c. Z.31. All work stopped in ALBERTA & WINNIPEG RDS.	H.M.

(A7092). Wt. W12839/M1293 750,000. 1/17. D. D. & L., Ltd. Forms/C.2118/14.

Instructions regarding War Diaries and Intelligence Summaries are contained in F. S. Regs., Part II. and the Staff Manual respectively. Title pages will be prepared in manuscript.

WAR DIARY
or
INTELLIGENCE SUMMARY.
(Erase heading not required.)

Army Form C. 2118.

Place	Date November	Hour 1917	Summary of Events and Information	Remarks and references to Appendices
[illegible]	17.		N.C.O.s & men working at HART ST., for O.C. 2.31	[illegible]
do	18		N.C.O.s & men at Hart Street working for O.C. Z. 1 N.C.O. working for O.C. X Rear billet. [illegible] working on Nissen hut.	G.K.
do	19		N.C.O.s & men at Hart St. working for O.C. Z. 1 N.C.O. working for O.C. X Rear billet. men working on Nissen hut.	G.K.
do	20		Hart. St. N.C.O. & men attached to O.C. Z. 1 N.C.O. working for O.C. X Rear. billet. N.C.O.s & men constructing Nissen hut.	G.K.
do	21		Hart St. Taking up beds at Alberta Rd. & Winnipeg Rd. N. & carrying same to junction of Winnipeg Rd. & Hudson Tr. Rear. billet. Continued work on Nissen Hut.	G.K.
do	22.		Hart. St. Ammunition at Winnipeg Rd. N. cleaned & placed in sandbags. 3 Guns 7 beds taken from junction of W. Rd. N. & Hudson. Tr. to Sapper. Dump. Rear. billet. Continued work on Nissen Hut.	G.K.
"	23.		3 guns & 7 6" [illegible] beds, brought to REST BILLET, from SAPPER DUMP. ALBERTA & WINNIPEG Rd. the positions, handed over to 4th Canadian Div.	[illegible]

(A7092). Wt. W12859/M1293 750,000. 1/17. D. D. & L., Ltd. Forms/C.2118/14.

Instructions regarding War Diaries and Intelligence Summaries are contained in F. S. Regs., Part II. and the Staff Manual respectively. Title pages will be prepared in manuscript.

WAR DIARY
or
INTELLIGENCE SUMMARY.
(Erase heading not required.)

Army Form C. 2118.

Place	Date	Hour	Summary of Events and Information	Remarks and references to Appendices
	March	1917		
In the Field	24.		NCO's & men withdrawn from line to REST BILLET. Placed one 2 6" Newton positions in KING ST.	H.M.
	25.		Handed position in KING ST, to V.31 for work. Took over 3 6" Newton positions, OPPY WOOD, BLUE ALLEY, OLD KENT RD. " " 4. 6" Newton Mortars, 7 - 6" Newton beds from R.A. HQ. 21st Div. Handed to R.A. HQ. 21st Div, 4. 6" Newton Mortars & 7 - 6" Newton beds from REST BILLET. Half of Battery personnel living at dug-out in VISCOUNT TRENCH.	H.M.
	26.		Working on positions in BLUE ALLEY, & OPPY WOOD. 1 - 6" bed carried from OLD KENT RD. to BLUE ALLEY.	H.M.
	27.		60. 6" Newton smoke bombs, taken to OPPY WOOD & BLUE ALLEY positions. Work continued on these positions.	H.M.
	28.		40. 6" Newton smoke bombs, taken OPPY WOOD & BLUE ALLEY positions. Fired 90 - 6" Newton smoke bombs, in operations with "CHINESE" RAID.	H.M.

(A7092). Wt. W12839/M1293. 750,000. 1/17. D. D. & L., Ltd. Forms/C.2118/14.

Instructions regarding War Diaries and Intelligence Summaries are contained in F. S. Regs., Part II. and the Staff Manual respectively. Title pages will be prepared in manuscript.

WAR DIARY
or
INTELLIGENCE SUMMARY.
(Erase heading not required.)

Army Form C. 2118.

Place	Date 1917	Hour	Summary of Events and Information	Remarks and references to Appendices
In the field	28.		4 - 2" mortars complete, handed over to 48. Div. Artillery	H.M.
	29.		Working on OPPY WOOD position, trench.	H.M.
	30.		Working during day in BLUE ALLEY, relaying bed for No. 2 gun. " " night, on trench at OPPY WOOD position.	H.M.

H. [illegible] Lieut. R.F.A.
O/C. Y. 31. Trench Bty.

(A7092). Wt. W12839/M1293. 750,000. 1/17. D. D. & L., Ltd. Forms/C.2118/14.

Instructions regarding War Diaries and Intelligence Summaries are contained in F. S. Regs., Part II. and the Staff Manual respectively. Title pages will be prepared in manuscript.

WAR DIARY
or
INTELLIGENCE SUMMARY.
(Erase heading not required.)

Army Form C. 2118.

Vol 17

Place	Date	Hour	Summary of Events and Information	Remarks and references to Appendices

C O N F I D E N T I A L.

W A R   D I A R Y

O F

X/31 MEDIUM TRENCH MORTAR BATTERY.

From 1st November to 30th November, 1917.

V O L U M E XXIII

A5834 Wt. W4973 M687 750,000 8/16 D. D. & L. Ltd. Forms/C.2118/13.

Instructions regarding War Diaries and Intelligence Summaries are contained in F. S. Regs., Part II. and the Staff Manual respectively. Title pages will be prepared in manuscript.

WAR DIARY
or
INTELLIGENCE SUMMARY.
(Erase heading not required.)

Army Form C. 2118.

X31 Med: T. M. Bty
Nov: 1st to 30th 1917. VOL 23.
(1)

Place	Date	Hour	Summary of Events and Information	Remarks and references to Appendices
ARLEUX WOOD	1.11.17	2·40pm to 3·15pm	40 rounds, 6" Newton fired on Enemy wire from C.1.a.25.70. to C.1.a.35.82. Satisfactory results obtained. Enemy retaliated with 3. M.T.M. + 20-15cm How: into ARLEUX WOOD. R.A.F.	
"	2.11.17	2·40pm to 3.15pm	40 rounds 6" Newton fired on Enemy wire from C.1.a.20.45. to C.1.a.30.55 Good results obtained in spite of Cross-wind. Enemy retaliated with about 20.15cm How: at B.6.d. central. R.A.F.	
"	3.11.17	3·0pm to 4·0pm	100 rounds 6" Newton fired on Enemy wire from C.1.a.35.62 to C.1.a.20.90. Satisfactory results much damage done. no retaliation from Enemy. R.A.F.	
"	4.11.17	4·39pm to 4·55pm	90 rounds 6" Newton fired on Enemy wire from C.1.a.0.2. to C.1.a.0.7. Impossible to observe as shoot was during a bombardment. Enemy put up a barrage along the Divisional Front. R.A.F.	
"	5.11.17	3·0pm to 4·18pm	64 rounds 6" Newton fired on Enemy wire from C.1.a.0.5 to T.30.d.90.10 48 " " " " " " " " C.1.a.0.2. to C.1.a.0.7. Satisfactory results obtained no retaliation from the Enemy. R.A.F.	
"	6.11.17	2·45pm to 4·20pm	100 rounds 6" Newton fired on Enemy wire from C.1.a.0.5 to T.30.d.90.10 satisfactory results obtained. Enemy retaliation very weak 4-10.5cm. fired into ARLEUX WOOD. R.A.F.	
"	7.11.17	10·20am to 4·20pm	100 rounds 6" Newton fired on Enemy wire from C.1.a.0.5. to T.30.d.90.10 and from C.1.a.0.2 to C.1.a.0.7. satisfactory results obtained. Enemy retaliated with 20.15cm. and 40.10cm into ARLEUX WOOD + VILLAGE. R.A.F.	

(A7092). Wt. W12839/M1293 750,000. 1/17. D. D. & L., Ltd. Forms/C.2118/14.

Army Form C. 2118.

Instructions regarding War Diaries and Intelligence Summaries are contained in F. S. Regs., Part II. and the Staff Manual respectively. Title pages will be prepared in manuscript.

WAR DIARY
or
INTELLIGENCE SUMMARY.
(Erase heading not required.)

X31. Med: T. M. Bty.
Nov. 1st to 30th 1917. VOL 23 (continued) (2)

Place	Date	Hour	Summary of Events and Information	Remarks and references to Appendices
ARLEUX WOOD	8.11.17	9·20am to 10·30am	60 rounds 6" Newton fired on Enemy wire from C1.a.0.5 to T.30.d.90.10 (wire cutting) previous to special raid. Enemy retaliated with 30 - 10.5 cm. on positions in ARLEUX WOOD.	
"	"	12·0p to 12·45p	280 rounds 6" Newton fired on Enemy Trenches from T.30.d.95.10 to T.30.d.60.75. Enemy retaliated with all calibres along the Divisional front and about 30. 15 cm into ARLEUX WOOD + Sunken Road. KAT	
"	9.11.17		No firing work proceeded with in renovating Gun Pits and trenches to Pits also cleaning Dug-Out KAT	
"	10.11.17	2·0p to 2·1pm	14 rounds 6" Newton fired on Pill Box at U25.C12.82 1 minute hurricane bombardment. No retaliation from enemy. KAT	
"	11.11.17	10·0am to 10·1am	6 rounds 6" Newton fired on Pill Box at U25.C12.82 Enemy retaliated with about 20 10.5 cm into Sunken Road B.5.d.76. KAT	
"	12.11.17		work proceeded with in revetting Sub-Beds and cleaning trenches to Pits also cleaning Dug-Out, Ammunition recesses etc. KAT	
"	13.11.17	2·40pm to 3·45pm	30 rounds 6" Newton fired on Enemy wire from B.6.b.9.1 to B6.d.90.95. no observation of wire was possible stakes and pieces of wire were observed flying in the air. no retaliation from enemy. KAT	
"	14.11.17	3·15pm to 4pm	86 rounds 6" Newton fired on Enemy wire from B.6.d.95.90. to B.6.c.95.10. very satisfactory results obtained. Enemy retaliated with about 50 15 cm into ARLEUX WOOD. KAT	
"	15.11.17	2·0p to 2·2p	16 rounds 6" Newton fired on trench Junction at U25.d.15.40. two minutes hurricane bombardment satisfactory results obtained. Hostile retaliation nil	KAT
	16.11.17		No firing. Revetting of Pits + cleaning Trenches to Pits KAT	

A5834 Wt. W4973/M687 750,000 8/16 D. D. & L. Ltd. Forms/C.2118/13.

Instructions regarding War Diaries and Intelligence Summaries are contained in F. S. Regs., Part II. and the Staff Manual respectively. Title pages will be prepared in manuscript.

WAR DIARY
or
INTELLIGENCE SUMMARY.
(*Erase heading not required.*)

Army Form C. 2118.

X31. Med: T. M. Bty.
Nov 1st to 30th 1917 VOL23 (Continued) (3)

Place	Date	Hour	Summary of Events and Information	Remarks and references to Appendices
ARLEUX WOOD	17.11.17	11-0am to 11-3am	24 rounds 6" Newton fired T. M. position at V.25.c.25.30. as per programme satisfactory results obtained.	
"	"	3-0pm to 3-3pm	24 rounds 6" Newton fired into Fresnoy Park as per programme good results, enemy retaliation very slight, 2. 15cm into Sunken Road B.5.d.6.7 and 2.15cm into Arleux Wood. RAT	
"	18.11.17	6-30am to 6-32am	16 rounds 6" Newton fired on Trench junction V.25.d.15.40. very satisfactory results obtained.	
"	"	7-0am to 7-2am	16 rounds 6" Newton fired on Trench junction C.1.b.6.4. very satisfactory results obtained	
"	"	2-50pm to 4-0pm	25 rounds 6" Newton fired on Enemy wire at C.1.c.1.7. and B.6.b.9.2. satisfactory results obtained several O.Ks. Enemy retaliation slight.	RAT
"	19.11.17		No firing. Revetting of pits and cleaning of trenches + Dug-Out.	RAT
"	20.11.17		Collecting Ammunition from Dump and taking to positions and preparing same for Shoot. Half the men in the line returned to rest billet.	RAT
"	21.11.17		Erecting of Bomb Dug-Out at SAPPER DUMP. RAT	
"	22.11.17	2-30pm to 4-15pm	80 rounds 6" Newton fired on Enemy wire from T30.d.90.20 to T.30.d.75.30 owing to mist Observation very difficult. Erecting of Bomb Dug-Out at Sapper Dump completed. RAT All 2" Mortar equipment handed over to the 8th Div.	
"	23.11.17	2-0pm to 4-0pm	85 rounds 6" Newton fired on Enemy wire from T.30.d.75.30. to T.30.d.65.45 satisfactory results wire very badly damaged. Damaged trench to No1 Pit repaired. Improvements to Bomb Shelter at Sapper Dump.	RAT

(A7092) Wt W12839/M1293 750,000. 1/17. D. D. & L., Ltd. Forms/C.2118/14.

Instructions regarding War Diaries and Intelligence Summaries are contained in F. S. Regs., Part II. and the Staff Manual respectively. Title pages will be prepared in manuscript.

Army Form C. 2118.

WAR DIARY
or
INTELLIGENCE SUMMARY.
(Erase heading not required.)

X31 Med: T. M. Bty. Nov 1st to 30th 1917. VOL 23 (continued) (4).

Place	Date	Hour	Summary of Events and Information	Remarks and references to Appendices
ARLEUX WOOD	24.11.17	1-0pm to 2-15pm	46 rounds 6" Newton fired on enemy wire in front of FRESNOY PARK. shooting erratic owing to strong wind. From 11-0am to 11-30am 24 rounds fired into FRESNOY. 3 minutes intense bombardment.	
"	25.11.17		Cleaning up of Gun Pits etc, ammunition carried up to Positions.	
"	26.11.17	3.0pm to 3.3pm	12 rounds 6" Newton fired on village + unfil trenches 3 minutes bombardment. beds + billet thoroughly cleaned.	
"	27.11.17	1-0pm to 2-0pm	50 rounds 6" Newton fired on enemy wire from T30.d.68.48. to T.30.d.65.55 satisfactory results, wire badly damaged, enemy put up intermittent bombardment of ARLEUX WOOD in retaliation.	
"	28.11.17	1-0pm to 2.0pm	48 rounds 6" Newton fired on enemy wire from T.30.d.75.50 to T.30.d.70.60 Enemy continually shelled ARLEUX WOOD and VILLAGE. Men in Rest Billet proceeded to line to take over positions vacated by Z31 M.T.M. BTY.	
"	29.11.17		Continual bombardment of ARLEUX WOOD and VILLAGE by the enemy with 10.5 + 15. cm Hows. owing to this it was impossible to do much work on Pits.	
"	30.11.17	2.0pm to 2.30pm	30 rounds 6" Newton fired on Enemy wire north of HENIN LISTARD road. a fire was caused in enemy front line. Small explosions like hand grenades were heard.	
"	"	2.30pm to 3.0pm	6 rounds 6" Newton fired on Enemy wire at T.30.d.90.20. Wire registered in anticipation of probable shoot.	

[signature] 2nd Lt R.F.A.
for O/C X31. Med: T. M. Bty

(A7092). Wt W12839/M1293 750,000. 1/17. D. D. & L., Ltd. Forms/C.2118/14.

Army Form C.2118.

Instructions regarding War Diaries and Intelligence Summaries are contained in F. S. Regs., Part II. and the Staff Manual respectively. Title pages will be prepared in manuscript.

WAR DIARY
or
INTELLIGENCE SUMMARY.
(Erase heading not required.)

Place	Date	Hour	Summary of Events and Information	Remarks and references to Appendices
			C O N F I D E N T I A L.	
			W A R D I A R Y	
			O F	
			V/31 HEAVY TRENCH MORTAR BATTERY.	
			From 1st November to 30th November, 1917.	
			V O L U M E XXIII	

A5834 Wt. W4973 M687 750,000 8/16 D. D. & L. Ltd. Forms/C.2118/13.

Instructions regarding War Diaries and Intelligence Summaries are contained in F. S. Regs., Part II, and the Staff Manual respectively. Title pages will be prepared in manuscript.

1st – 30th Nov 17

WAR DIARY
or
~~INTELLIGENCE SUMMARY.~~
(Erase heading not required.)

Army Form C. 2118.

V31. Heavy Trench Mortar Battery

VOL. XXIII

Place	Date	Hour	Summary of Events and Information	Remarks and references to Appendices
ARLEUX	Nov. 1917			
	1st	1-0pm	Work continued on dugout. 18 Rounds H.E. fired – Targets U25c & C.1.a. Sweeping. Satisfactory	Ck
	2nd	1-40pm 4-15	30 Rounds fired – Targets – U.25.c & C.1.a. Satisfactory. 50 Rounds carried to position	Ck
	3rd	2-40pm	20 Rounds fired. Target – Pill Box at T.30.b.7.7 Work continued on Dugout } Ck	
	4th	2-15pm	30 Rounds fired. – Targets – Pill Box at U25.a.1.8. – FRESNOY. (Sweeping fire) Ck	
	5th	4-30pm 3-30pm	21 Rounds fired – Targets. Pill Box at U25.a.1 8. 3 fired into Fresnoy at 4-15pm Work continued on Dugout. Ck	
	6th	3.0pm	20 Rounds fired into Fresnoy & district. Trench from Ammunition Recess to gun pit dug. Ck	
	7th	4-20pm	5 Rounds fired into Fresnoy. Trench from Recess to gunpit completed & Camouflaged. No 2. Gun mounted Ck	
	8th	12 noon	54 Rounds fired. Targets – U25.a. 2.2 U25.a.5.3. U25.c.4 1. U25 c.5.5 Ck	
	9th		30 Rounds carried to Pit & converted to take Russian Charges. Billets improved Ck	
	10th	3.0pm	3 Rounds fired. Target – Pill Box at U25.a.12 82. Ck	
	11th		2 Sump holes dug. RRB	
	12th	10 am	4 Rounds fired. Target – U 25.a.12.82. 3.0pm 4 Rounds fired same Target; 3-15 1 – do –; 3-30 4 – do – } RRB. Relief carried out. RRB	
	13th		Fatigues. RRB	
	14th	11-0am	4 Rounds fired on U25. a 12 82. RRB.	
	15th	2pm	8 Rounds fired into Fresnoy RRB.	
	16th		Fatigues RRB	

A7092 Wt. W12S 9/M1293 750,000 1/17. D. D & L Ltd. Forms/C2118/14.

Instructions regarding War Diaries and Intelligence Summaries are contained in F. S. Regs., Part II. and the Staff Manual respectively. Title pages will be prepared in manuscript.

Army Form C. 2118.

WAR DIARY
or
~~INTELLIGENCE SUMMARY.~~ V31. Heavy Trench Mortar Battery

(*Erase heading not required.*)

Vol. XXIII (Continued)

Place	Date	Hour	Summary of Events and Information	Remarks and references to Appendices
ARLEUX	1917 Nov. 17th	11-0 AM	8 Rounds H.E. fired on T.M. Fresnoy Village. RPB.	
		3-0pm	8 Rounds H.E fired into FRESNOY. RPB.	
	18th	6.30am	6 Rounds. Delay fired. Target - Trench Junction at U.25. d. 15. 40. RPB.	
	-	7.0.am	6 Rounds. Delay fired. Target. Trench Junction at C.1. b. 6.4. RPB.	
	19th		2 feet of sapping done. RPB.	
	20th		4 feet of sapping done. Bunks fitted in mens dugout. RPB.	
	21st		50 Rounds carried to Position, cleaned & prepared. RPB.	
	22nd		Fatigues. - Laying of Trench boards in Sunken Road. Work on No 2 Gunpit RPB.	
	23rd		Trench to No 2. Gunpit widened & revetted. Barricade raised & strengthened RPB	
	24th	9-0am	8 Rounds, Delay, fired on Junction of Foot Alley & Village Trenches } C.S.	
		6 0pm.	8 Rounds, Delay, fired. Targets - U25.a. 05. 20. and U25.c. 55.65. }	
			Barricade built North of No 1 Gun Pit. } C.S.	
	25th	11-0am	8 Rounds Delay fired into Fresnoy Village }	
			Commenced work on 2 Pits in King Street. C.S.	
	26th		Continued work on Pits. Commenced work on Ammunition Recesses.	
			Pits Camouflaged. C.S.	
	27th		Work continued until noon. C.S.	
	28th		Work impossible owing to heavy Hostile fire. C.S.	
	29th		Work continued on Pits. Considerable Hostile Fire in the vicinity. Ca.	
	30th		Work continued on Pits. Ca.	

Carter Capt. RFA
O.C. V31. Heavy T.M. Battery

A7092 Wt. W125 9/M1293 750,000. 1/17. D. D & L. Ltd. Forms/C2118/14.

Army Form C. 2118.

Instructions regarding War Diaries and Intelligence Summaries are contained in F. S. Regs., Part II. and the Staff Manual respectively. Title pages will be prepared in manuscript.

WAR DIARY
or
INTELLIGENCE SUMMARY.

(Erase heading not required.)

Place	Date	Hour	Summary of Events and Information	Remarks and references to Appendices
			CONFIDENTIAL.	
			WAR DIARY	
			OF	
			Z/31 MEDIUM TRENCH MORTAR BATTERY.	
			From 1st November to 30th November, 1917.	
			VOLUME XXIII.	

A5834 Wt. W4973 M687 750,000 8/16 D. D. & L. Ltd. Forms/C.2118/13.

Instructions regarding War Diaries and Intelligence Summaries are contained in F. S. Regs., Part II. and the Staff Manual respectively. Title pages will be prepared in manuscript.

1st – 30th Nov 17.

WAR DIARY or INTELLIGENCE SUMMARY.

(Erase heading not required.)

Army Form C. 2118.

VOL XXIII

Place	Date	Hour	Summary of Events and Information	Remarks and references to Appendices
ROCLINCOURT	1/11/17 & 7/11/17		Work continued on positions in BRITTANIA TR: at T30 C 5.3	L.D
	8/11/17		140 Rounds 6" fired on selected targets in support of raid.	L.D
	9/11/17		Half the Battery returned to the Rest Billet at ROCLINCOURT.	L.D
	10/11/17 & 11/11/17		Work commenced on new dug-out in WINNIPEG RD. south of HUDSON TRENCH.	L.D
	12/11/17		Battery moved into dug-out in HART ST. Dug-out at junction of MANITOBA ROAD and OAK ALLEY handed over to Y31. Took over 2 positions south of HUDSON TR: in WINNIPEG ROAD. Handed over 3 positions north of HUDSON TRENCH in WINNIPEG ROAD to Y31.	L.D
	13/11/17 & 14/11/17		2 frames placed in position in new dug-out at WINNIPEG RD. Trench which had tumbled in cleaned. Beds and sub-beds in HART ST: taken up.	L.D L.D
	15/11/17		Fired 24 rounds 6" into FRESNOY PARK (eastern to western edge taking in view). All targets were successfully engaged.	L.D

A7092 Wt. W128 9/M1293 750,000. 1/17. D. D & L. Ltd. Forms/C2118/14.

Instructions regarding War Diaries and Intelligence Summaries are contained in F. S. Regs., Part II. and the Staff Manual respectively. Title pages will be prepared in manuscript.

II

WAR DIARY
or
INTELLIGENCE SUMMARY.
(Erase heading not required.)

Z. 31 TRENCH MORTAR BATTERY.

Army Form C. 2118.

VOL XXIII

Place	Date	Hour	Summary of Events and Information	Remarks and references to Appendices
ROCLINCOURT	16/11/17 to 19/11/17		Battery engaged in renovating pits in HART ST. carrying material, guides for carrying parties etc.	G.D
	20/11/17		50 Rounds 6" fired into enemy wire from T30 D5.9 to T30 D6.8 Wire considerably damaged, wire + stakes thrown into the air.	G.D
	21/11/17		45 Rounds 6" fired into enemy wire from T30 D5.9 to T30 D6.8. Observation was difficult owing rain and mist. There is now, practically no wire between these two points	G.D
	22/11/17		59 Rounds 6" inst: fired into enemy wire just south of HENIN-LIETARD road in front of FRESNOY PARK from T30 D 55.80. to T30 D 62.74. Observation extremely dificult. The wire was searched on previous registration.	[illegible]
	23/11/17		84 rounds 6" inst: fired into enemy wire in front of FRESNOY PARK from T30 D 6.8 to. T30 D 7.6. Wire very badly damaged between these two points.	[illegible]

A7092 Wt. W125.9/M1293 750,000. 1/17. D. D & L. Ltd. Forms/C2118/14.

Instructions regarding War Diaries and Intelligence Summaries are contained in F. S. Regs., Part II. and the Staff Manual respectively. Title pages will be prepared in manuscript.

WAR DIARY
or
INTELLIGENCE SUMMARY.
(Erase heading not required.)

Z. 31 TRENCH MORTAR BATTERY.

Army Form C. 2118.

Vol XXIII

Place	Date	Hour	Summary of Events and Information	Remarks and references to Appendices
ROCLINCOURT.	24/11/17		51 rounds 6" inst: fired into enemy wire south of HENIN-LIETARD road, in front of FRESNOY PARK, about T30D 62. 74. to 30 yards south of this point. Firing was erratic on account of a gusty wind, the wire was badly damaged, although no actual gap was cut.	[illegible]
	25/11/17	11.0am to 11.30am	24 rounds 6" delay. fired into FRESNOY.	
		2.15pm to 3.30pm	86 rounds 6" inst: fired into enemy wire in front of FRESNOY PARK from T30D 50, 95 to T30D 57 80. Shooting was erratic owing to wind. A quantity of wire and stakes were thrown into the air, especially at point T30D 50 90.	[illegible]
	26/11/17		No firing took place on this date.	[illegible]
	27/11/17		108. rounds 6" inst. fired into enemy wire between TUB TR. & HENIN-LIETARD Road. Wire very greatly damaged.	[illegible]
	28/11/17		Work carried on in pits, guns and all stores handed over to X31. M.T.M.B.	[illegible]

A7092 Wt. W128 g/M1293 750,000. 1/17. D. D & L Ltd. Forms/C2118/14.

Instructions regarding War Diaries and Intelligence Summaries are contained in F. S. Regs., Part II. and the Staff Manual respectively. Title pages will be prepared in manuscript.

WAR DIARY
or
INTELLIGENCE SUMMARY.
(Erase heading not required.)

Z. 31 TRENCH MORTAR BATTERY.

Army Form C. 2118.

VOL XXIII

Place	Date	Hour	Summary of Events and Information	Remarks and references to Appendices
ROCLINCOURT.	29/11/17		Battery withdrawn to rest billet at ROCLINCOURT. 1 Officer and 6 men proceeded to line to take over guns and positions from 31st Division	[illegible]
	30/11/17		Battery moved into new positions at GAVRELLE.	[illegible]

[illegible] Lt
for OC Z31 M.T.M.B

A7092 Wt. W12S.9/M1293 750,000. 1/17. D. D & L. Ltd. Forms/C2118/14.

Instructions regarding War Diaries and Intelligence Summaries are contained in F. S. Regs., Part II. and the Staff Manual respectively. Title Pages will be prepared in manuscript.

WAR DIARY
or
INTELLIGENCE SUMMARY
(Erase heading not required.)

Army Form C. 2118

Place	Date	Hour	Summary of Events and Information	Remarks and references to Appendices

CONFIDENTIAL.

WAR DIARY

OF

Y/31st MEDIUM TRENCH MORTAR BATTERY.

From 1st December to 31st December 1917.

VOLUME XXIV.

1875 Wt. W593/826 1,000,000 4/15 J.B.C. & A. A.D.S.S./Forms/C. 2118.

1st – 31st Dec 1917

WAR DIARY
or
INTELLIGENCE SUMMARY.
(Erase heading not required.)

/31 M. G. B
Vol XXIV

Army Form C. 2118.

Instructions regarding War Diaries and Intelligence Summaries are contained in F. S. Regs., Part II. and the Staff Manual respectively. Title pages will be prepared in manuscript.

Place	Date	Hour	Summary of Events and Information	Remarks and references to Appendices
1917	Decem.			
In the field	1.		Work during day at position in BLUE ALLEY. " " nights on trench, OPPY WOOD POSITION.	H.M.
	2.		Trench 200 yds in length, running from OPPY WOOD position to BLUE ALLEY, completed during the night.	H.M.
	3		Commenced work on [illegible] at OPPY WOOD position. Instructions received to stop all new work, guns, beds + ammunition thoroughly cleaned.	H.M.
	4.		Blue Alley: Thoroughly cleaned dug out preparatory to handing over same. Made frames for sub beds. Ammunition + guns cleaned. Rest Billet: No. 2 Sub. men continued work on Nissen hut.	G.K.
	5.		All 4 [illegible] beds in the line completed with [illegible], + [illegible] [illegible] by means of 2 [illegible] [illegible]. All guns withdrawn to REST BILLET, with exception of 1 NCO. + 5 O.Rs.	H.M.
	6.		Guns, beds etc in line, kept clean. Nissen hut at REST BILLET completed.	H.M.
	7		Guns, beds etc in line kept clean + kit inspection; list of deficiencies taken. Kit inspection of men in REST Billets, list of deficiencies taken + general fatigues.	G.K.

(A7092). Wt. W12839/M1293 750,000. 1/17. D. D. & L., Ltd. Forms/C.2118/14.

Instructions regarding War Diaries and Intelligence Summaries are contained in F. S. Regs., Part II. and the Staff Manual respectively. Title pages will be prepared in manuscript.

WAR DIARY
or
INTELLIGENCE SUMMARY.
(Erase heading not required.)

Army Form C. 2118.

Place	Date	Hour	Summary of Events and Information	Remarks and references to Appendices
In the field	1917 Dec 8		Ammunition, gun sheds in the line kept clean. Inspection of ammunition at Royne Dump: found same destroyed by shell fire. Rear billet. General fatigues and Rifle Drill by N.C.O's & men.	G.K.
	9		Ammunition, gun sheds in the line kept clean. Rear billet. General fatigues.	G.K.
	10		Ammunition, gun sheds in the line re-cleaned. Trenches that had fallen in cleaned up. Rear billet. General fatigues & Rifle drill.	G.K.
	11.		Commenced [illegible] [illegible] for BRADFORD TRENCH. REAR BILLET. [illegible] Rifle drill & [illegible] [illegible]	H.[illegible]
	12.		Work continued on new position, BRADFORD TRENCH. Camouflage for new position taken to forward billet. Guns & [illegible] cleaned at REST BILLET.	H.[illegible]
	13.		Work continued on new position BRADFORD TRENCH. REST BILLET, work on gun hut & men's huts.	H.[illegible]

(A7092). Wt. W12839/M1293. 750,000. 1/17. D. D. & L., Ltd. Forms/C.2118/14.

Instructions regarding War Diaries and Intelligence Summaries are contained in F. S. Regs., Part II. and the Staff Manual respectively. Title pages will be prepared in manuscript.

WAR DIARY
or
INTELLIGENCE SUMMARY.
(Erase heading not required.)

Army Form C. 2118.

Place	Date 1917	Hour	Summary of Events and Information	Remarks and references to Appendices
[illegible]	14		BLUE ALLEY position camouflaged. Cable laid & fitted with our own attachments.	H.M.
	15.		Deepened trench, 1 pit, BLUE ALLEY position. No 2 pit, dug out again (due to frosty ground & thaw), revetted sides of pit. [illegible]. Full working order inspection, loading material at R.E. dump.	H.M.
	16.		Found 36 complete rounds 6" Newton Ammunit., carried same to BLUE ALLEY position, cleaned & stacked same. Completed camouflaging of BLUE ALLEY position. Relief of Battery personnel in line carried out. 1 gun bed for No. 2 pit, OPPY WOOD position, sent into the line.	H.M.
	17.		Gun bed for No 2 pit, OPPY WOOD position, completed. Commenced camouflaging OPPY WOOD position. Revetting continued at BLUE ALLEY position.	H.M.
	18.		Work of revetting pits & trenches, continued at BLUE ALLEY position.	H.M.

(A7092). Wt. W12839/M1293 75,000. 1/17. D. D. & L., Ltd. Forms/C.2118/14.

Instructions regarding War Diaries and Intelligence Summaries are contained in F. S. Regs., Part II. and the Staff Manual respectively. Title pages will be prepared in manuscript.

WAR DIARY
or
INTELLIGENCE SUMMARY.
(Erase heading not required.)

Army Form C. 2118.

Place	Date	Hour	Summary of Events and Information	Remarks and references to Appendices
Decem	1917			
	19		Completed reversing of BLUE ALLEY position. Commenced reversing of trenches OPPY WOOD position.	G.M.
	20		Guns, ammunition etc, prepared for handing over in OPPY sector. 2 guns complete, 460 rounds ammunit. taken out from First Canadian Division.	G.M.
	21		Guns, beds & ammunition at BLUE ALLEY & OPPY WOOD handed over to 56th Division. Occupied position taken over from 2nd Canadian Division	G.K.
	22		Stores, material etc removed from dugout in NEW BRUNSWICK to dug out "BULFORD" in MONTREAL. Rear billet. General fatigues baths for N.C.O's & men.	G.K.
	23		Bombs taken from Infantry bomb dump to WINNIPEG ROAD SOUTH position; detonators & fuzes removed from ammunition found there. Guns & beds cleaned & oiled. ALBERTA RD. position cleaned & components squared up. REAR BILLET. General fatigues.	G.K.
	24		Preparations for shoot from WINNIPEG Rd. STH. Rear billet. Fatigues	G.K.
	25		Fired 25 rounds from WINNIPEG RD position. Men in line relieved by those at Rear billet.	G.K.

(A7092). Wt. W12839/M1293. 750,000. 1/17. D. D. & L., Ltd. Forms/C.2118/14.

Army Form C. 2118.

WAR DIARY
or
INTELLIGENCE SUMMARY.
(*Erase heading not required.*)

Instructions regarding War Diaries and Intelligence Summaries are contained in F. S. Regs., Part II. and the Staff Manual respectively. Title pages will be prepared in manuscript.

Place	Date	Hour	Summary of Events and Information	Remarks and references to Appendices
1917	December			
	26.		All ammunition checked at all positions. Bombs unfused etc at WINNIPEG Rd. S. position.	H.M.
	27.		New beds completed in forward dug-out. Material for tunnelling (at position in HUDSON TRENCH), carried in line.	H.M.
	28.		Commenced work on defensive position in HUDSON TRENCH.	H.M.
	29.		Trench camouflaged at ALBERTA Rd. position. Our attachments for beds put in at WINNIPEG Rd. SOUTH. Continued work on position in HUDSON TRENCH.	H.M.
	30		Work continued on position in HUDSON TRENCH.	H.M.
	31.		2. 6" Newton Mortars taken to ALBERTA Rd. position. Work continued on position in HUDSON TRENCH.	H.M.

H. Mills. Lt R.F.A.
O/c. Y 31. Tr. Mortar Bty.
1.1.18.

(A7092) Wt. W12839/M1293 750,000. 1/17. D. D. & L., Ltd. Forms/C.2118/14.

Instructions regarding War Diaries and Intelligence Summaries are contained in F. S. Regs., Part II. and the Staff Manual respectively. Title pages will be prepared in manuscript.

WAR DIARY
or
INTELLIGENCE SUMMARY.
(Erase heading not required.)

Army Form C. 2118.

X31 Medium Trench Mortar Bty
December 1st to 31st 1917. VOL XXIV (1)

Place	Date	Hour	Summary of Events and Information	Remarks and references to Appendices
ARLEUX WOOD	1.12.17		No firing. No 2 Pit prepared in order to fire on new target. Work done for Y/31 M.T.M. Bty at OPPY WOOD as per instructions by D.T.M.O. Enemy very active on positions in HART St. position badly damaged 1 Gun buried. R.a.F.	
"	2.12.17		Work commenced with in digging out Gun & removing beds from pits also repairing ammunition recess. R.a.F.	
"	3.12.17		Work continued with on Gun pits, and ammunition recess in HART St R.a.F.	
"	4.12.17		Work continued with on Gun pits. 1 Gun carried to SAPPER DUMP. 2 Beds & 1 Gun carried to positions in HART St. R.a.F.	
"	5.12.17		2 Guns made ready for action in HART St. Half personnel returned to Rest Billet. R.a.F	
"	6.12.17		Cleaning and building up pits in HART St. R.a.F.	
"	7.12.17		Work continued with on positions in HART St. R.a.F.	
"	8.12.17		Work continued with on positions in HART St. Cleaning Trench & Dug Out. R.a.F.	
"	9.12.17		Men withdrawn from HART St. Work commenced on positions & Trench in ARLEUX WOOD. R.a.F.	
"	10.12.17		All personnel at Rest Billet returned to line to work on positions in ARLEUX WOOD. R.a.F.	
"	11.12.17		Work continued with on positions in ARLEUX WOOD. R.a.F.	
"	12.12.17		Work continued with on positions in ARLEUX WOOD. Revetting of Trench from No 2 pit to No 3 pit. R.a.F.	
"	13.12.17		Work continued with on positions. Trench from BRITTANIA TRENCH to SUNKEN RD cleared out and camouflaged. R.a.F.	

(A7092). Wt. W12839/M1293 75,000. 1/17. D. D. & L., Ltd. Forms/C.2118/14.

WAR DIARY
or
INTELLIGENCE SUMMARY.
(Erase heading not required.)

Army Form C. 2118.

Instructions regarding War Diaries and Intelligence Summaries are contained in F. S. Regs., Part II. and the Staff Manual respectively. Title pages will be prepared in manuscript.

X31 Medium Trench Mortar Bty.
December 1st to 31st 1917. VOL XXIV continued (2)

Place	Date	Hour	Summary of Events and Information	Remarks and references to Appendices
ARLEUX WOOD	14.12.17		Work continued with on trench from No 2 pit to No 3 pit. Trench from BRITTANIA to SUNKEN Rd deepened. R.A.T.	
"	15.12.17		Work continued on pits in ARLEUX WOOD. Ammunition recess completed revetting completed in No 2 pit. R.A.T.	
"	16.12.17 to 18.12.17		Making ammunition recess for No 2 pit. cleaning of staircase and passage of Dug-Out. R.A.T.	
"	19.12.17		Ammunition recess for No 2 Pit completed. R.A.T.	
"	20.12.17 to 23.12.17		Revetting of Trenches to pits and ammunition recess R.A.T. 2-6" Newton Mortars complete, positions + Dug Out at HART St handed over to Z31 M.T.M. Bty.	
"	24.12.17		Beds screwed down ready for shoot at ARLEUX WOOD Positions R.A.T.	
"	25.12.17	12 noon 12.15pm	120 rounds 6" Newton fired on T. M. Position and Company H. Q as per D.T.M.O. programme satisfactory results obtained Enemy retaliated rather heavily on ARLEUX WOOD + VILLAGE. Work carried on at positions in SUNKEN Rd. Half personnel in line withdrawn to Rest Billets	R.A.T.
"	26.12.17 to 27.12.17		Work continued with on positions at SUNKEN Rd. R.A.T.	
"	28.12.17		Work commenced on new defensive positions in SUNKEN Rd + OLD KENT Rd.	R.A.T.
"	29.12.17		2-6" Newton Mortars complete sent to line to be placed in positions at KING St R.A.T.	
"	30.12.17		Work continued with on defensive positions in SUNKEN Rd + OLD KENT Rd.	R.A.T.

(A7092). Wt W12839/M1293 75,000. 1/17. D. D. & L., Ltd. Forms/C.2118/14.

Instructions regarding War Diaries and Intelligence Summaries are contained in F. S. Regs., Part II. and the Staff Manual respectively. Title pages will be prepared in manuscript.

WAR DIARY
or
INTELLIGENCE SUMMARY.
(Erase heading not required.)

Army Form C. 2118.

X31 Medium Trench Mortar Bty.
December 1st to 31st VOL XXIV (continued) (3)

Place	Date	Hour	Summary of Events and Information	Remarks and references to Appendices
ARLEUX WOOD	31.12.17.		Work continued with on defensive positions in SUNKEN Rd. 1 Bed placed in position at KING St. RAF	

R. A. Fraser
Lt. E. Yorks Regt.
1.1.18. O.C. X31. Med: T. M. Bty.

(A7092). Wt. W12839/M1293 75,0.0. 1/17. D. D. & L., Ltd. Forms/C.2118/14.

Instructions regarding War Diaries and Intelligence Summaries are contained in F. S. Regs., Part II. and the Staff Manual respectively. Title Pages will be prepared in manuscript.

WAR DIARY
or
INTELLIGENCE SUMMARY
(Erase heading not required.)

Army Form C. 2118

Vol 18

Place	Date	Hour	Summary of Events and Information	Remarks and references to Appendices

C O N F I D E N T I A L.

W A R D I A R Y

O F

V/31st HEAVY TRENCH MORTAR BATTERY.

From 1st December to 31st December 1917.

VOLUME XXIV.

1875 Wt. W593/826 1,000,000 4/15 J.B.C. & A. A.D.S.S./Forms/C. 2118.

Instructions regarding War Diaries and Intelligence Summaries are contained in F. S. Regs., Part II. and the Staff Manual respectively. Title pages will be prepared in manuscript.

1st – 31st Dec 17

WAR DIARY
or
~~INTELLIGENCE SUMMARY.~~

(Erase heading not required.)

Army Form C. 2118.

VOL XVIII

V31. Heavy Trench Mortar Battery

HEADQUARTERS … JAN 1918

VOL. XXIV

Place	Date	Hour	Summary of Events and Information	Remarks and references to Appendices
ARLEUX	1917 Dec. 1st		Working Party supplied to X31. M. T. M. Battery – Digging out Positions in ARLEUX WOOD. Cla	
	2nd		Working Party supplied to Y31 M.T.M. BATTERY. – Trench dug through OPPY WOOD. Cla	
	3rd		Trench dug in OPPY WOOD for Y31. M.T.M. BATTERY. Cla	
	4th		Guns and Beds cleaned, and Stores checked. Cla	
	5th		Ammunition cleaned & checked } Cla	
	6th		Dugouts cleaned. }	
	7th		Positions improved & cleaned. Cla	
	8th		Continued improvements on Gunpits. Cla	
	9th		Work on Gunpits continued. Cla	
	10th		Reconnoitred & commenced work on Medium T. M. Positions in King Street Cla	
	11th		Worked on new Medium T. M. Position at King Street. Cla	
	12th		Work continued on Medium Positions at King Street. Cla	
	13th		Work on Medium Positions continued. Ammunition Recess commenced. Cla	
	14th		Work on Medium Pits continued Cla	
	15th		Digging of Pits completed. Revetting commenced Cla	
	16th		Work on Medium Positions carried out. Bomb store constructed. Cla	

A7092 Wt. W125 9/M1293 750,000. 1/17. D. D & L. Ltd. Forms/C2118/14.

Instructions regarding War Diaries and Intelligence Summaries are contained in F. S. Regs., Part II. and the Staff Manual respectively. Title pages will be prepared in manuscript.

WAR DIARY

~~or~~ ~~INTELLIGENCE SUMMARY.~~

(Erase heading not required.)

Army Form C. 2118.

V31 Heavy Trench Mortar Battery

VOL. XXIV (CONTINUED)

Place	Date	Hour	Summary of Events and Information	Remarks and references to Appendices
ARLEUX	1917 Dec. 17		Ammunition Recess completed. Sub bed commenced. CC	
	18		One sub bed completed, also second Ammunition rack. CC	
	19		Second sub bed commenced. Trench further revetted. CC	
	20		Position cleared up. Relief carried out. CC	
	21		Sub bed for second pit completed. CC Handed over 1 Heavy Mortar (Mk III) as Reserve to 56th Division. CC	
	22		Work delayed by hostile shelling on Z Trench. CC	
	23		Ammunition rack revetted. Sides of pits sloped for revetting. CC	
	24		Positions completed ready for firing. GS	
	25		21 Rounds fired. Targets – U.5.c.7.3. [illegible] & T.30.a.7.7. GS	
	26		Guns, beds & billets cleaned. GS	
	27		Guns, beds & billets cleaned. GS	
			50 Rounds T.M.K carried from train to position. GS	
	28		Working party to X and to Z. Batteries. GS	
	29		Working party to X and to Z. Batteries. – Trenches cleared. GS	
	30		Working party to X and Z. Batteries. Guns & beds cleaned. GS	
	31		Working party to X and Z Batteries. GS	

Gilbert [illegible] Lieut. R.F.A.
O.C. V31. Heavy T. M. Battery

A7092 Wt. W125 9/M1293 750,000. 1/17. D. D & L. Ltd. Forms/C2118/14.

Army Form C. 2118

Instructions regarding War Diaries and Intelligence Summaries are contained in F. S. Regs., Part II. and the Staff Manual respectively. Title Pages will be prepared in manuscript.

WAR DIARY
or
INTELLIGENCE SUMMARY
(Erase heading not required.)

Place	Date	Hour	Summary of Events and Information	Remarks and references to Appendices

C O N F I D E N T I A L.

W A R   D I A R Y

O F

Z/31st MEDIUM TRENCH MORTAR BATTERY.

From 1st December to 31st December 1917.

VOLUME XXIV.

1875 Wt. W593/826 1,000,000 4/15 J.B.C. & A. A.D.S.S./Forms/C. 2118.

1st – 31st Dec 1917

Instructions regarding War Diaries and Intelligence Summaries are contained in F. S. Regs., Part II. and the Staff Manual respectively. Title pages will be prepared in manuscript.

WAR DIARY
or
~~INTELLIGENCE SUMMARY.~~
(*Erase heading not required.*)

Army Form C. 2118.

Z31. Medium Trench Mortar Battery

VOL. XXIV

Place	Date	Hour	Summary of Events and Information	Remarks and references to Appendices
ROELINCOURT	1-12-17		The Battery continues with work in the line. 6" T M positions at Sunken Rd. renovated. All damaged guns & [illegible] withdrawn from line	
	2-12-17		Sites reconnoitred for new positions. Ammunition recess rebuilt & positions cleaned up.	
	3-12-17		Work ~~carried~~ [done] on positions	
	4-12-17		Sub-bed at TOWY No1 completed.	
	5-12-17		Work carried on on positions.	
	6-12-17		Position at No1 TOWY completed ready for action.	
	7-12-17		Ammunition at positions cleaned – all component parts redistributed	
	8-12-17		Positions at Sunken Rd completed [RHB.]	
	9-12-17		~~Work carried on on positions~~ [RHB.] New position at RAILWAY T^R commenced.	
	10-12-17		Work carried on in new positions.	
	11-12-17		Work continued on RAILWAY TRENCH positions. Camouflage fitted.	RHB

A7092 Wt. W125 9/M1293 750,000. 1/17. D. D & L. Ltd. Forms/C2118/14.

2.

WAR DIARY
or
INTELLIGENCE SUMMARY.
(Erase heading not required.)

Instructions regarding War Diaries and Intelligence Summaries are contained in F. S. Regs., Part II. and the Staff Manual respectively. Title pages will be prepared in manuscript.

Army Form C. 2118.

231. Medium Trench Mortar Battery

VOL. XXIV

Place	Date	Hour	Summary of Events and Information	Remarks and references to Appendices
ROCLINCOURT	12-12-17		Work on Railway trench positions continued. Ammunition recess at NAVAL TRENCH DUMP improved	R.H.B.
	13/12/17		do	R.H.B.
	14/12/17		do One ammunition recess completed.	R.H.B.
	15/12/17		do .	R.H.B.
	16/12/17		do .	R.H.B.
	17/12/17		do .	R.H.B.
	18/12/17		do .	R.H.B.
	19/12/17		do .	R.H.B.
	20/12/17		do . No 2 Pit revetted, & made ready to receive sub. bed. No 1 Pit made ready to receive revetting	R.H.B.
	21/12/17		The battery returned to Rest Billet. Handed over guns, ammunition positions dug-outs etc to 2/56 M.T.M.Bty	R.H.B.
	22/12/17		At Rest Billet. Guns & beds taken over from X bty cleaned & stored.	R.H.B.
	23/12/17		Half the battery proceeded to the line to take over positions at HART ST from X 31 M.T.M.B	R.H.B.
	24/12/17		Eight bunks fitted up in dug-out. Telephone line to L.S.4 repaired and renewed in places.	R.H.B.
	25/12/17		61 Rds M.T.M. bombs fired at Hostile T.M. at T 30 d 7. 9. Relief carried out.	R.H.B.

A 7092 Wt. W 728-9/M1293 750,000. 1/17. D. D & L. Ltd. Forms/C2118/14.

3.

WAR DIARY
or
INTELLIGENCE SUMMARY.
(*Erase heading not required.*)

Instructions regarding War Diaries and Intelligence Summaries are contained in F. S. Regs., Part II. and the Staff Manual respectively. Title pages will be prepared in manuscript.

Army Form C. 2118.

Z/31 Medium Trench Mortar Battery

VOL XXIV

Place	Date	Hour	Summary of Events and Information	Remarks and references to Appendices
Rodincourt	26/12/17		4 more bunks fitted up for telephonists.	R.P.B.
	27/12/17		Work commenced on defensive positions north of ARLEUX.	R.P.B.
	28/12/17		ditto	R.P.B.
	29/12/17		ditto	R.P.B.
	30/12/17		ditto	R.P.B.
	31/12/17		Camouflage fitted on above positions. Guns & beds at HART St. cleaned and oiled, & pits cleared.	R.P.B. R.P.B.

R. P. Bloor
Lt. R.F.A.
O.C. Z/31 M.T.M. Bty.

A7092 Wt. W1258/M1293 750,000. 1/17. D. D & L. Ltd. Forms/C2118/14.

Instructions regarding War Diaries and Intelligence Summaries are contained in F. S. Regs., Part II. and the Staff Manual respectively. Title pages will be prepared in manuscript.

WAR DIARY
or
INTELLIGENCE SUMMARY.
(Erase heading not required.)

Army Form C. 2118.

Place	Date	Hour	Summary of Events and Information	Remarks and references to Appendices
			C O N F I D E N T I A L.	
			W A R D I A R Y	
			O F	
			V/31 MEDIUM TRENCH MORTAR BATTERY.	
			From 1st January to 31st January, 1918.	
			V O L U M E XXV.	

A5834 Wt. W4973/M687 750,000 8/16 D. D. & L. Ltd. Forms/C.2118/13.

Y/31 Med. T. M. Battery. January 1918. Vol XXV

WAR DIARY
or
~~INTELLIGENCE SUMMARY.~~
(Erase heading not required.)

Army Form C. 2118.

Instructions regarding War Diaries and Intelligence Summaries are contained in F. S. Regs., Part II, and the Staff Manual respectively. Title pages will be prepared in manuscript.

Place	Date	Hour	Summary of Events and Information	Remarks and references to Appendices
1918. In the field	January 1		Work continued on defensive position, HUDSON TRENCH.	H.M.
	2		Work continued on defensive position HUDSON TR.	G.K.
	3		Work continued on positions in HUDSON TR. Guns placed ALBERTA RD and ready for firing. Rear billets fatigues.	G.K.
	4		Continued work on defensive position HUDSON TR & laying wire from dug out to Batt. H.Qrs & from there to ALBERTA RD. Rear billets. Fatigues & baths.	G.K.
	5		Fired 50 rounds from ALBERTA RD. position. Continued work on defensive position in HUDSON TR.	G.K.
	6		Fired 50 rounds retaliation from ALBERTA RD. Completed tunnel in HUDSON TRENCH & commenced excavating trench. Rear billets. Baths & fatigues.	G.K.
	7		Construction of new pits ALBERTA RD. Ammunition & component parts WINNIPEG. RD. N. stacked ready for infantry carrying party. No. 2. pit WINNIPEG. RD. S. cleaned up after being knocked in.	G.K.
	8		[illegible] ALBERTA RD. [illegible] on position in HUDSON TRENCH.	H.M.
	9		Work continued on [illegible] at ALBERTA RD, & defensive position, HUDSON TR.	H.M.

(A7092). Wt. W12839/M1293. 750,000. 1/17. D. D. & L., Ltd. Forms/C.2118/14.

WAR DIARY
or
INTELLIGENCE SUMMARY.
(Erase heading not required.)

Army Form C. 2118.

Instructions regarding War Diaries and Intelligence Summaries are contained in F. S. Regs., Part II. and the Staff Manual respectively. Title pages will be prepared in manuscript.

Place	Date	~~Hour~~	Summary of Events and Information	Remarks and references to Appendices
1918	January			
In the Field	10.		Fired 98 rounds on enemy front line wire, map refs T.24.b.2.1 to T.24.b.3.9, with aeroplane observation.	H.M.
	11		Fired 88 rounds & worked on defensive position in HUDSON TRENCH	R.K.
	12		Fired 54 rounds & carrying ammunition from WINNIPEG RD to ALBERTA RD.	R.K.
	13.		Fired 57 rounds cleaned up MONTREAL TRENCH & sent up party at night to SAPPER DUMP for ammunition	R.K.
	14		Fired 64 rounds & carrying ammunition at night	R.K.
	15		Fired 50 rounds digging out position at WINNIPEG RD Carrying ammunition at night	R.K.
	16		Cleaning up puts & trench at ALBERTA RD fallen in owing to the weather	R.K.
	17		Cleaning up puts & trench at ALBERTA RD fallen in owing to the weather	R.K.

(A7092). Wt. W12839/M1293. 750,000. 1/17. D. D. & L., Ltd. Forms/C.2118/14.

Instructions regarding War Diaries and Intelligence Summaries are contained in F. S. Regs., Part II. and the Staff Manual respectively. Title pages will be prepared in manuscript.

WAR DIARY

or

~~INTELLIGENCE~~ SUMMARY.

(Erase heading not required.)

Army Form C. 2118.

Place	Date	~~Hour~~	Summary of Events and Information	Remarks and references to Appendices
In the Field	January	18	All Men cleaning & revetting & re-camouflaging trench & positions at ALBERTA RD	G.K.
		19	All Men cleaning & revetting & re-camouflaging trench & positions at ALBERTA RD.	G.K.
		20	All Men cleaning & revetting & re-camouflaging trench & positions at ALBERTA RD	G.K.
		21	All Men cleaning & revetting & re-camouflaging trench & positions at ALBERTA RD	G.K.
		22	All Men cleaning & revetting & re-camouflaging trench & positions at ALBERTA RD.	[illegible]
		23	All Men cleaning & revetting & re-camouflaging trench & positions at ALBERTA RD	
		24	Continued work on ALBERTA RD positions & also worked on WINNIPEG RD S. position laying new sub beds and rebuilding pits	
		25	Continued work on ALBERTA RD positions & also worked on WINNIPEG RD S. positions laying new sub beds and rebuilding pits	G.K.

(A7092). Wt. W12839/M1293. 750,000. 1/17. D. D. & L., Ltd. Forms/C.2118/14.

Army Form C. 2118.

Instructions regarding War Diaries and Intelligence Summaries are contained in F. S. Regs., Part II. and the Staff Manual respectively. Title pages will be prepared in manuscript.

WAR DIARY
or
~~INTELLIGENCE~~ SUMMARY.
(Erase heading not required.)

Place	Date 1918	~~Hour~~	Summary of Events and Information	Remarks and references to Appendices
In the Field	January 26		Continued work on ALBERTA RD. positions & also worked on WINNIPEG. RD. S. positions laying new sub beds & rebuilding pits.	G.K.
	27		Continued work on ALBERTA. RD. positions & also worked on WINNIPEG. RD. S. positions laying new sub beds & rebuilding pits	G.K.
	28		Continued work on ALBERTA. RD. positions & also worked on WINNIPEG. RD. S positions laying new sub beds & rebuilding pits	G.K.
	29		Continued work on defensive position HUDSON. TR also work on WINNIPEG. RD. S. positions	G.K.
	30		Preparing to fire with aeroplane observation; Continued work on defensive positions HUDSON. TR	G.K.
	31		Continued with defensive positions HUDSON. TR made slight Alterations to WINNIPEG. RD. S. positions. Signallers salvaging wire	G.K.

G. K[illegible] 2nd Lt.
Y. 31. M. T. M. B.

(A7092). Wt. W12839/M1293. 750,000. 1/17. D. D. & L., Ltd. Forms/C.2118/14.

Army Form C. 2118.

Instructions regarding War Diaries and Intelligence Summaries are contained in F. S. Regs., Part II. and the Staff Manual respectively. Title pages will be prepared in manuscript.

WAR DIARY
or
INTELLIGENCE SUMMARY.

(Erase heading not required.)

Place	Date	Hour	Summary of Events and Information	Remarks and references to Appendices

Vol 19

C O N F I D E N T I A L.

W A R D I A R Y

O F

V/31 HEAVY TRENCH MORTAR BATTERY.

From 1st January to 31st January, 1918.

V O L U M E XXV.

A5834 Wt. W4973/M687 750,000 8/16 D. D. & L. Ltd. Forms/C.2118/13.

Army Form C. 2118.

Instructions regarding War Diaries and Intelligence Summaries are contained in F. S. Regs., Part II. and the Staff Manual respectively. Title pages will be prepared in manuscript.

WAR DIARY
~~or~~ ~~INTELLIGENCE SUMMARY.~~
(Erase heading not required.)

V31 Heavy Trench Mortar Battery

VOL. XXV.

Place	Date	Hour	Summary of Events and Information	Remarks and references to Appendices
ARLEUX	1918 Jan. 1st		Working party supplied to X and Z Batteries.	
	2nd		-do-	
	3rd		-do-	
	4th		25 Rounds fired on T30.a.90.96. (T.M.) successful. Working parties supplied to X and Z Batteries	
	5th		28 Rounds fired on C1.a.45.65. successful	
	6th		Working parties supplied to X and Z Batteries.	
	7th		-do-	
			Site dug out in new 9.45. H.T.M. Position.	
	8th		Working parties supplied to X & Z Batteries. Beams removed etc.	
	9th		Working party supplied to X Battery. 50 Bombs carried to position.	
	10th		Working party to X Battery. 25 bombs stocked in recess & cleaned.	
	11th		-do- Worked on new 9.45. pit	
	12th		Work continued on new 9.45 position. Working party supplied to X Battery	
	13th		Fired 19 rounds with aeroplane observation at Company Headquarters – C1.c.55.80	
			Working party to X Battery. Work done on new 9.45 position	
	14th		Supplied working parties to X & Y Batteries. Conveyed new 9.45 (mark III) mortar to new Position. Continued work on this position.	
	15th		Working party supplied to Y Battery. 12 Rounds fired at C1.b.1.1 at request of Infantry.	

A7092 Wt. W123,9/M1293 750,000. 1/17. D. D & L. Ltd. Forms/C2118/14.

Army Form C. 2118.

WAR DIARY

~~or~~

~~INTELLIGENCE SUMMARY.~~ V/31. Heavy Trench Mortar Battery

(Erase heading not required.)

Instructions regarding War Diaries and Intelligence Summaries are contained in F. S. Regs., Part II. and the Staff Manual respectively. Title pages will be prepared in manuscript.

Place	Date	Hour	Summary of Events and Information VOL. XXV (continued)	Remarks and references to Appendices
ARLEUX	1918 Jany. 16th		Relief carried out. Bad weather conditions prevented work. C.C.	
	17th		Ammunition recesses completed at new position. Old positions renovated. C.C.	
	18th		Water pumped out in new pit, & work continued. C.C.	
	19th		Subbed laid in new position, & mortar mounted. C.C.	
	20th		No. 3. Gun pit improved. Working party supplied to Y Battery. C.C.	
	21st		Further work done on No 3 position. Working party to Y Battery. C.C.	
	22nd		No 3. Pit rivetted. Working party to Y Battery. C.C.	
	23rd		No 3 Pit sandbagged at sides.	
	24th		6 Rounds fired at U.25.c.45.60. (Hostile T.M).	
			Roof strengthened at No 3 Pit & sandbagging at back of pit continued. C.C.	
	25th		Sandbagging continued at No 3 Pit. Working party to Y/31. Batty. C.C.	
	26th		Sandbagging completed at No. 3 Position. — do — C.C.	
	27th		No. 3. Position. – Roof taken off and remade. – Gun cleaned ready for action. C.C.	
	28th		All guns & beds cleaned. Work done on Officers dugout. C.C.	
	29th		No 1 Pit re-sandbagged & improved. C.C.	
	30th		50 rounds T.M.K cleaned & stacked at No 1 & 2 Pits } C.C. 50 rounds T.M.K unloaded & carried to No 3. Pit. }	
	31st		Ammunition & Guns cleaned. Relief carried out. C.C.	

C. Carter Capt. R.F.A.

O.C. V/31. Heavy T. M. Battery

(A7092). Wt. W12839/M1293. 750,000. 1/17. D. D. & L., Ltd. Forms/C.2118/14.

Army Form C. 2118.

Instructions regarding War Diaries and Intelligence Summaries are contained in F. S. Regs., Part II. and the Staff Manual respectively. Title pages will be prepared in manuscript.

WAR DIARY
or
INTELLIGENCE SUMMARY.

(Erase heading not required.)

Place	Date	Hour	Summary of Events and Information	Remarks and references to Appendices

C O N F I D E N T I A L.

W A R D I A R Y

O F

X/31 MEDIUM TRENCH MORTAR BATTERY.

From 1st January to 31st January, 1918.

V O L U M E XXV.

A5834 Wt. W4973/M687 750,000 8/16 D. D. & L. Ltd. Forms/C.2118/13.

Army Form C. 2118.

WAR DIARY
or
INTELLIGENCE SUMMARY.
(*Erase heading not required.*)

Instructions regarding War Diaries and Intelligence Summaries are contained in F. S. Regs., Part II. and the Staff Manual respectively. Title pages will be prepared in manuscript.

X31 Medium Trench Mortar Bty
January 1st to 31st 1918. VOL 25 (1)

Place	Date	Hour	Summary of Events and Information	Remarks and references to Appendices
ARLEUX WOOD	1.1.18		Work continued on Defensive Position at SUNKEN Rd. R.a.T	
	2.1.18		Work continued on Defensive Positions at SUNKEN Rd. Sub-bed placed in position at KING St. R.a.T.	
"	3.1.18		Work continued with on Defensive Position at SUNKEN Rd R.a.T.	
"	4.1.18		Work continued on Defensive Position at Sunken Rd. Ammunition Recess completed. Work commenced on Defensive Position at OLD KENT Rd 2 Pit + Ammunition recess commenced R.a.T.	
"	5.1.18 to 8.1.18		Work continued on Defensive Positions at SUNKEN Rd R.a.T. OLD KENT Rd + KING St R.a.T.	
"	9.1.18		Work continued on Defensive Position	
		12-30p to 12-35p	3 Rounds 6" Newton fired on Enemy wire at C.1.c.1.8. R.a.T.	
"	10.1.18	10-30am to 12-0pm	36 Rounds 6" Newton fired on Enemy wire at C.1.a 30.65 from KING St position wire badly damaged. R.a.T.	
"	11.1.18	10-30am to 12 Noon	145 Rounds fired from ARLEUX WOOD on to Enemy wire at C1.a.c.1.8 and B.6.d.95.20. no observation. R.a.T.	
		3-0pm to 3-15p	23 Rounds fired from King St on to enemy wire at C.1.a.30.65. Observation very difficult owing to mist. R.a.T.	

(A7092) Wt W12839/M1293 75,000. 1/17. D. D. & L., Ltd. Forms/C.2118/14.

Instructions regarding War Diaries and Intelligence Summaries are contained in F. S. Regs., Part II. and the Staff Manual respectively. Title pages will be prepared in manuscript.

WAR DIARY
or
INTELLIGENCE SUMMARY.
(*Erase heading not required.*)

Army Form C. 2118.

X31. Medium Trench Mortar Bty
January 1st to 31st 1918 VOL 25 continued.

Place	Date	Hour	Summary of Events and Information	Remarks and references to Appendices
ARLEUX WOOD	12.1.18	1-30pm to 3-0pm	100 Rounds fired from ARLEUX WOOD on to Enemy wire at C.1.a.1.8 and B.6.d.95.20. satisfactory results obtained K.a.F.	
"	13.1.18	10-30am to 11-0am	15 Rounds fired from KING ST on to Enemy wire at C.7.a.30.55. Wire damaged	K.a.F.
"	"	3-30pm to 4-15pm	191 Rounds fired from ARLEUX WOOD on to Enemy wire at C.1.a.8 and B.6.b.9.1. Aroplane Observation	K.a.F.
"	14.1.18	10-30am to 11.0am	23 Rounds fired from KING ST on to Enemy wire at C.7.a.3.6. wire badly damaged.	K.a.F.
"	"	3.0pm to 4.0pm	102 Rounds fired from ARLEUX WOOD on to Enemy wire at C.1.a.8. and B.6.d.95.20. no observation.	K.a.F.
"	15.1.18	11-0am to 11-45am	50 Rounds fired from ARLEUX WOOD on to Enemy wire at C.1.c.1.8. no observation	K.a.F.
"	16.1.18		No firing Pits and Trenches to Pits cleared, ammunition recess repaired.	K.a.F.
"	17.1.18		No firing Dug Out cleaned also Trenches + Pits. K.a.F.	
"	18.1.18		No firing Trenches + Pits Cleaned. K.a.F.	
"	19.1.18		No firing Trenches + Pits Cleaned. K.a.F.	
"	20.1.18		No firing Trenches + Pits Cleaned. K.a.F.	
"	21.1.18	7.0am to 7.2am	16 Rounds fired on to Enemy Wire at C.1.a.0.0 + U25.c.0.0.15 2 minutes hurricane bombardment. Cleaning of Trenches + Pits K.a.F.	
"	22.1.18		No firing Trenches + Pits cleaned, commenced revetting of trenches	K.a.F.
"	23.1.18		Revetting of Trenches continued. K.a.F.	
"	24.1.18	8/0am to 8/2am	30 Rounds fired on to Enemy Wire at C.1.a.0.0 + U25.c.0.0.15 2 minutes hurricane bombardment. Revetting of trenches continued K.a.F.	

(A7092). Wt. W12839/M1293 75,000. 1/17. D. D. & L., Ltd. Forms/C.2118/14.

Instructions regarding War Diaries and Intelligence Summaries are contained in F. S. Regs., Part II. and the Staff Manual respectively. Title pages will be prepared in manuscript.

WAR DIARY
or
INTELLIGENCE SUMMARY.
(Erase heading not required.)

Army Form C. 2118.

X31. Medium Trench Mortar Battery
January 1st to 31st VOL 25 (continued).

Place	Date	Hour	Summary of Events and Information	Remarks and references to Appendices
ARLEUX WOOD.	25.1.18		Re Revetting of Trenches. constructing new ammunition recess. R.A.F.	
	26.1.18	6-0am to 6-2am	16 Rounds fired on U.25.C.7/1. Hurricane Bombardment. Clearing of Trenches continued. R.A.F.	
"	27.1.18		Clearing of Trenches + Pits continued. R.A.F.	
"	28.1.18		Clearing of Trenches + Pits continued. R.A.F.	
	29.1.18		Clearing of Trenches + Pits continued. R.A.F.	
"	30.1.18	11-30am to 11-32am	16 Rounds fired on U.25.C.7/1. Hurricane Bombardment. Clearing + revetting of Trenches continued. R.A.F.	
"	31.1.18		Clearing + Revetting of Trenches continued. R.A.F.	

R. A. Fraser
Lt. E. Yorks Rgt.
O/C X31 M.T.M. Bty.

(A7092) Wt W12839/M1293 750,000 1/17. D. D. & L., Ltd. Forms/C.2118/14.

Instructions regarding War Diaries and Intelligence Summaries are contained in F. S. Regs., Part II. and the Staff Manual respectively. Title pages will be prepared in manuscript.

WAR DIARY
or
INTELLIGENCE SUMMARY.
(Erase heading not required.)

Army Form C. 2118.

Place	Date	Hour	Summary of Events and Information	Remarks and references to Appendices

CONFIDENTIAL.

WAR DIARY

OF

7/31 MEDIUM TRENCH MORTAR BATTERY.

From 1st January to 31st January, 1918.

VOLUME XXV.

A5834 Wt. W4973/M687 750,000 8/16 D. D. & L. Ltd. Forms/C.2118/13.

Army Form C. 2118.

WAR DIARY
or
INTELLIGENCE SUMMARY.
(Erase heading not required.)

January 1918

D 31. Medium Trench Mortar Battery

Vol ~~XXIV~~ XXV

Instructions regarding War Diaries and Intelligence Summaries are contained in F. S. Regs., Part II. and the Staff Manual respectively. Title pages will be prepared in manuscript.

Place	Date	Hour	Summary of Events and Information	Remarks and references to Appendices
ROCLINCOURT.	1/1/18		Work continued on defensive positions near ARLEUX. Ammunition recess commenced, & four frames placed in position.	R.A.B.
	2/1/18.		Work on positions north of ARLEUX continued. Relief carried out.	R.A.B.
	3/1/18.		——— ditto ———.	R.A.B.
	4/1/18.		——— ditto ———. Second ammunition recess commenced.	R.A.B.
	5/1/18.		Work on positions north of ARLEUX continued. One ammunition recess finished.	R.A.B.
	6/1/18		——— ditto ———. Timber for [illegible] received.	R.A.B.
	7/1/18.		55 [illegible] expended. 23 [illegible] fired on Enemy WIRE WEST of FRESNOY PARK. Relief carried out. 96 bombs received by infantry carrying party.	R.A.B.
	8/1/18		Work on positions north of ARLEUX continued. 50 bombs fired on ENEMY WIRE W of FRESNOY PARK.	R.A.B.
	9/1/18		——— ditto ———. 65 bombs fired on Enemy WIRE WEST OF FRESNOY PARK.	
	10/1/18		Work on positions north of ARLEUX continued. 50 rounds fired at Enemy wire, T30 d 65. 70 to T30 d 70.35 (FRESNOY PARK).	R.A.B.
	11/1/18		Work on HART St positions. Revetted trench to ammunition recess. Cleared pits of fallen earth etc. Fired 3 rounds at enemy wire at T30 d 75 30. Received 77 rounds by infantry carrying party.	R.A.B.

A7092 Wt. W128 9/M1293 750,000 1/17. D. D & L. Ltd. Forms/C2118/14.

Instructions regarding War Diaries and Intelligence Summaries are contained in F. S. Regs., Part II. and the Staff Manual respectively. Title pages will be prepared in manuscript.

WAR DIARY or INTELLIGENCE SUMMARY.

(Erase heading not required.)

Army Form C. 2118.

Z 31. Medium Trench Mortar Battery

VOL XXV

Place	Date	Hour	Summary of Events and Information	Remarks and references to Appendices
ROCLINCOURT	12/1/18		Relaid No 2 bed at HART St. Fired 26 rounds at enemy wire West of FRESNOY PARK, T 30 d, 75 30. Both guns went out of action. Guns put in action again. 40 rounds received by infantry carrying party. Relief carried out.	R.H.B.
	13/1/18		Work on HART St positions continued. Bed surrounds improved and strengthened.	R.H.B.
	14/1/18		121 Rounds fired on enemy wire WEST of FRESNOY PARK. One large truck of ammunition unloaded at SAPPER DUMP. 50 rounds received by infantry carrying party.	R.H.B.
	15/1/18		Work on gun beds done at HART St. 50 rounds fired on wire WEST of FRESNOY PARK. Work done on positions north of ARLEUX. 180 rounds got as far as HUDSON CT. Carrying party exhausted and [illegible] were unable to carry the ammunition to HART St.	R.H.B.
	16/1/18		Thaw set in. Trench leading from OAK ALLEY to ammunition recess collapsed, work on trench done. Sump [illegible] between pits.	R.H.B.
	17/1/18		Ammunition carried from HUDSON CT to WINNIPEG Rd SOUTH position. 60 rounds carried from HUDSON CT to WINNIPEG Rd SOUTH positions. Relief carried out.	R.H.B.
	18/1/18		Trench between dugout entrances cleared of fallen earth etc.	R.H.B.
	19/1/18		DITTO	R.H.B.

A7092 Wt. W12S:9/M1293 750,000. 1/17. D. D & I. Ltd. Forms/C2118/14.

Instructions regarding War Diaries and Intelligence Summaries are contained in F. S. Regs., Part II. and the Staff Manual respectively. Title pages will be prepared in manuscript.

WAR DIARY or INTELLIGENCE SUMMARY.

(Erase heading not required.)

Army Form C. 2118.

Z 31. Medium Trench Mortar Battery

VOL. XXV

Place	Date	Hour	Summary of Events and Information	Remarks and references to Appendices
ROCLINCOURT	20/1/18		Work done on dug-out at Junction of HART ST and OAK ALLEY for accommodation of party from Y battery. Relief carried out.	RAB.
	21/1/18		Guns, beds stages, & gun pits cleaned, 2 [illegible] Entrances to dug-out cleaned. Party sent for night work on ALBERTA Rd positions under OC Y battery.	RAB.
	22/1/18		Dug out & positions at HART St cleaned up generally. Party sent to work under OC Y battery. Work continued at ALBERTA Rd.	RAB
	23/1/18		Work on ammunition recess at positions near ARLEUX continued. Party sent to work for Y Battery.	RAB.
	24/1/18		Bombs fired as per instructions received. TARGET T30 d 6.9 Party sent to work for Y Bty	RAB
	25/1/18		[illegible] ammunition continued at HART St. —— ditto ——	RAB.
	26/1/18		—— ditto —— . —— ditto ——	RAB.
	27/1/18		—— ditto —— . —— ditto ——	RAB.
	28/1/18		[illegible] beds & guns complete carried to WINNIPEG ROAD SOUTH position. Ammunition [illegible] and returned to SAPPER DUMP. Work on Reserve positions near ARLEUX continued.	

A7092 Wt. W12859/M1293 750,000. 1/17. D. D & L. Ltd. Forms/C2118/14.

Instructions regarding War Diaries and Intelligence Summaries are contained in F. S. Regs., Part II. and the Staff Manual respectively. Title pages will be prepared in manuscript.

~~WAR~~ DIARY or INTELLIGENCE SUMMARY.

(Erase heading not required.)

Army Form C. 2118.

Z 31. Medium Trench Mortar Battery

VOL XXV

Place	Date	Hour	Summary of Events and Information	Remarks and references to Appendices
ROCLINCOURT	29/1/18		Work carried on at Reserve positions near ARLEUX. Ammunition cleaned at HART St. 2 guns & RE material conveyed from SAPPER DUMP to HART St.	R.R.B.
	30/1/18		Work continued on Reserve positions near ARLEUX	R.R.B.
	31/1/18		——— ditto ——— . Bed of No 2 pit HART St relaid.	R.R.B.

R.R. Bevan
Lt RFA
OC Z/31 M.T.M. Bty.

Army Form C. 2118.

WAR DIARY
or
INTELLIGENCE SUMMARY.
(Erase heading not required.)

Instructions regarding War Diaries and Intelligence Summaries are contained in F. S. Regs., Part II. and the Staff Manual respectively. Title pages will be prepared in manuscript.

Place	Date	Hour	Summary of Events and Information	Remarks and references to Appendices
			C O N F I D E N T I A L.	
			W A R D I A R Y	
			O F	
			Z/31 MEDIUM TRENCH MORTAR BATTERY.	
			From 1st February to 28th February, 1918.	
			V O L U M E XXVI	

2353 Wt. W2544/1454 700,000 5/15 D. D. & L. A.D.S.S./Forms/C. 2118.

Army Form C. 2118.

Z 31. Medium Trench Mortar Battery

WAR DIARY
or
~~INTELLIGENCE SUMMARY.~~
(Erase heading not required.)

VOL XXVI

Instructions regarding War Diaries and Intelligence Summaries are contained in F. S. Regs., Part II. and the Staff Manual respectively. Title pages will be prepared in manuscript.

Place	Date	Hour	Summary of Events and Information	Remarks and references to Appendices
ROCLINCOURT.	1·2·18		Work carried on in reserve positions near ARLEUX. Bed in N°2 pit HART ST: relaid	
	2·2·18		Work carried on in reserve positions near ARLEUX.	
	3·2·18		Work begun at reserve positions at MANITOBA ROAD.	
	4·2·18		Work continued on reserve positions at MANITOBA ROAD. Camouflage carried from SAPPER DUMP.	
	5·2·18		Work continued in reserve positions in MANITOBA ROAD.	
	6·2·18		Work carried on in reserve positions in MANITOBA ROAD. 50 rounds 6" (Delay) fired at Enemy T.M. at T30 B.70.65. and junction of TUB and FRISK trenches. 65 rounds carried from WINNIPEG. SOUTH. to HART ST:	
	7·2·18		Work carried on in reserve positions MANITOBA ROAD. Two trucks of bombs met at ANTELOPE and pushed up to WINNIPEG–HUDSON railhead.	

A7092 Wt. W128.9/M1203 750,000. 1/17. D. D & L. Ltd. Forms/C2118/14.

Army Form C. 2118.

Instructions regarding War Diaries and Intelligence Summaries are contained in F. S. Regs., Part II. and the Staff Manual respectively. Title pages will be prepared in manuscript.

WAR DIARY

or

~~INTELLIGENCE SUMMARY.~~

(Erase heading not required.)

Z 31 Medium Trench Mortar Battery

VOL XXVI

Place	Date	Hour	Summary of Events and Information	Remarks and references to Appendices
ROCLINCOURT.	8.2.18		Work continued on defensive positions at MANITOBA ROAD	H.R.S
	9.2.18		Work carried on at MANITOBA ROAD.	H.R.S
	10.2.18		Work carried on in reserve positions at MANITOBA ROAD and ARLEUX. Beds cleaned at HART ST.	H.R.S
	11.2.18		Work continued on reserve positions in MANITOBA ROAD.	H.R.S
	12.2.18		Work carried on in reserve positions in MANITOBA ROAD and ARLEUX.	H.R.S
	13.2.18		Work on No 2 pit HART ST:	H.R.S
			Closed.	
			The whole of the personnel being transfered to X 31 M.T.M.B over the reorganisation of 6" Trench Mortar batteries Authority 1st Army No 1569 (G) OB/166 d/20-1-18.	

H. Robson Smith
Lt. R.F.A
O.C. Z 31. M.T.M. Bty

A7092 Wt. W128 9/M1293 750,000. 1/17. D. D & L. Ltd. Forms/C2118/14.

Army Form C. 2118.

Instructions regarding War Diaries and Intelligence Summaries are contained in F. S. Regs., Part II. and the Staff Manual respectively. Title pages will be prepared in manuscript.

WAR DIARY
or
INTELLIGENCE SUMMARY.
(Erase heading not required.)

Vol 20

Place	Date	Hour	Summary of Events and Information	Remarks and references to Appendices

C O N F I D E N T I A L.

W A R D I A R Y

O F

X/31 MEDIUM TRENCH MORTAR BATTERY.

From 1st February to 28th February, 1918.

V O L U M E XXVI

2353 Wt. W2544/1454 700,000 5/15 D. D. & L. A.D.S.S./Forms/C. 2118.

Army Form C. 2118.

Instructions regarding War Diaries and Intelligence Summaries are contained in F. S. Regs., Part II. and the Staff Manual respectively. Title pages will be prepared in manuscript.

WAR DIARY
or
INTELLIGENCE SUMMARY.

(*Erase heading not required.*)

X31 Medium Trench Mortar Battery
February 1st to 28th VOL XXVI

Place	Date	Hour	Summary of Events and Information	Remarks and references to Appendices
ARLEUX WOOD	1.2.18		Revetting of Trenches + Pits at ARLEUX WOOD, KING St, OLD KENT Rd continued. Work on reserve positions at SUNKEN Rd commenced.	
"	2.2.18		Revetting of Trenches continued with.	
"	3.2.18		Revetting of Trenches continued with.	
"	4.2.18		Revetting of Trenches continued with.	
	5.2.18		Revetting of Trenches continued with.	
	6.2.18		Revetting of Trenches continued with. Excavation of Ammunition recess at OLD KENT Rd.	
	7.2.18		Excavation of Ammunition Recess continued with.	
	8.2.18		Work continued on Ammunition Recess and Trench connecting No 2 Pit with ammunition Recess OLD. KENT Rd	
	9.2.18		Ammunition Recess for No 2 Pit rebuilt at KING. St. Work continued on Ammunition Recess and Trench from same to No 2 Pit OLD. KENT. RD. Work continued on reserve positions on Sunken Rd.	
	10.2.18		King St / Revetting of trenches between pits. OLD. KENT. RD Revetting of No 2 Pit. Excavation of Ammunition Recess SUNKEN. RD. Work continued on Trench between Pits	
	11.2.18		King St. Revetting of Trench between Pits Old Kent Rd. Revetting of No 2 Pit	
	12.2.18		[illegible] Rounds ammunition carried from SAPPER DUMP to King St positions.	
	13.2.18		Took over HART ST. pits, [illegible] from Z Battery. Reserve positions in SUNKEN RD. camouflaged. 1 Bed carried from railway and stored in SUNKEN RD. Bombs prepared for carrying party. Work on No 2 pit HART. ST.	

(A7092) Wt W12839/M1293 750,000 1/17 D. D. & L., Ltd. Forms/C.2118/14.

Instructions regarding War Diaries and Intelligence Summaries are contained in F. S. Regs., Part II. and the Staff Manual respectively. Title pages will be prepared in manuscript.

WAR DIARY
or
~~INTELLIGENCE SUMMARY.~~

(Erase heading not required.)

Army Form C. 2118.

X. 31. Medium Trench Mortar Battery

Place	Date	Hour	Summary of Events and Information	Remarks and references to Appendices
In the field	14.4		Carrying party and am. 98 rounds carried to ARLEUX WOOD. An O.P. found in ARLEUX village and preparations for same. Wire laid to same O.P. Work started on No 2 pit HART ST. 13 rounds fired into enemy wire northern edge of FRESNOY PARK.	G.K.
	15.4		Carrying party and ammunition carried to ARLEUX WOOD. Fired 124 rounds from this position. Fired [illegible] rounds from HART ST and then continued work on No 2 pit.	G.K.
	16.4		Work continued on new positions in OLD KENT RD + SUNKEN RD. Tried out No 2 pits at HART ST [illegible]. Continued work on MANITOBA RD positions.	G.K.
	17.4		[illegible] ARLEUX village [illegible] (WATER TOWER) [illegible]. Ammunition [illegible] at HART ST, KING ST, ARLEUX + SAPPER DUMP. Work continued on positions in MANITOBA RD.	G.K.
	18.4		Continued work on defensive positions in OLD KENT RD + SUNKEN RD. Work continued on defensive positions in MANITOBA RD.	G.K.
	19.4		Work continued on Defensive Positions MANITOBA RD, OLD KENT RD and SUNKEN RD. Bombs recounted at SAPPER DUMP. R.E. material sent up and taken to Positions.	W.R.S.

A5834 Wt. W4973/M687 750,000 8/16 D. D. & L. Ltd. Forms/C.2118/13.

Army Form C. 2118.

Instructions regarding War Diaries and Intelligence Summaries are contained in F. S. Regs., Part II. and the Staff Manual respectively. Title pages will be prepared in manuscript.

WAR DIARY
or
INTELLIGENCE SUMMARY. 3

(*Erase heading not required.*)

X 31 Hv T. M. Bty

Place	Date	Hour	Summary of Events and Information	Remarks and references to Appendices
In the Field	20.2.18		Clearing HART ST. trench + positions and continued work on MANITOBA. R^D positions Clearing up BLACKBURN. R^D and preparations made for Men's billets etc. in 8" positions	HRS
	21.2.18		Clearing HART ST trench and positions and continued work on MANITOBA R^D positions Clearing up BLACKBURN. R^D and preparations made for Mens billets etc in 8" positions	HRS
	22.2.18		Work commenced on SUGAR. POST. defensive Positions	HRS
	23.2.18		Cleared up pits HART. ST. also cleaned and oiled guns + beds Work continued on defensive positions	HRS
	24.2.18		Work continued on Defensive positions also preparations made for men to occupy dug-out near SAPPER DUMP	HRS
	25.2.18		Work continued on Defensive position at SUGAR POST	HRS
	26.2.18		Work continued on Defensive position at SUGAR. POST	HRS

A5834 Wt. W4973/M687 750,000 8/16 D. D. & L. Ltd. Forms/C.2118/13.

Army Form C. 2118.

Instructions regarding War Diaries and Intelligence Summaries are contained in F. S. Regs., Part II. and the Staff Manual respectively. Title pages will be prepared in manuscript.

WAR DIARY
or
INTELLIGENCE SUMMARY.
(Erase heading not required.)

X 31 M T M Bty

Place	Date	Hour	Summary of Events and Information	Remarks and references to Appendices
In the Field	27.2.18		Work continued on Defensive position at SUGAR POST also work on ammunition recess at SAPPER DUMP	H.R.S
	28.2.18		Work continued on Defensive position at SUGAR POST	H.R.S

H Robson Smith
Capt R F A
O/C X 31 M T M Bty

Instructions regarding War Diaries and Intelligence Summaries are contained in F. S. Regs., Part II. and the Staff Manual respectively. Title pages will be prepared in manuscript.

WAR DIARY
or
INTELLIGENCE SUMMARY.
(Erase heading not required.)

Army Form C. 2118.

Place	Date	Hour	Summary of Events and Information	Remarks and references to Appendices
			C O N F I D E N T I A L.	
			W A R D I A R Y	
			O F	
			Y/31 MEDIUM TRENCH MORTAR BATTERY.	
			From 1st February to 28th February, 1918.	
			V O L U M E XXVI	

2353 Wt. W2544/1454 700,000 5/15 D. D. & L. A.D.S.S./Forms/C. 2118.

Instructions regarding War Diaries and Intelligence Summaries are contained in F. S. Regs., Part II. and the Staff Manual respectively. Title pages will be prepared in manuscript.

WAR DIARY
or
INTELLIGENCE SUMMARY.
(Erase heading not required.)

Army Form C. 2118.

VOL XXVI

Y. 31 Medium Trench Mortar Batt.

Place	Date	Hour	Summary of Events and Information	Remarks and references to Appendices
In the Line	1918 Feby 1		New pit proof put in No 1 pit ALBERTA RD to replace one damaged. Trench at defensive position HUDSON C.T. dug out & partly revetted; work proceeding on No 2 pit and trench leading to the pit.	G.K.
do	2		Carried out shoot with aeroplane observation. Successfully registered on targets C 2, 3, 4, 5 & 6. Fired 41 rounds. Also continued work on defensive position in HUDSON C.T.	G.K.
do	3		Continued work on defensive position HUDSON C.T. Detachment at ALBERTA RD for work on pit bed damaged by hostile fire & for retaliatory shoot if necessary.	G.K.
do	4		Continued work on defensive position HUDSON C.T. 1 N.C.O. + 3 men at ALBERTA RD for work on trench & bed No. 1 pit & for retaliatory shoot if necessary	G.K.
do	5		Continued work on defensive position HUDSON C.T. 1 N.C.O. + 2 men at ALBERTA RD for retaliatory shoot if necessary. Fired 46 rounds between 11 & 12 pm on Target T.R. 2 75.70	G.K.
do	6.		Work continued on defensive position, HUDSON TRENCH. 100 rounds Ammunition carried to ALBERTA RD. position. Damaged elevating arc replaced on gun bed. (No 4. ALBERTA RD).	H.M.

(A7092). Wt. W12839/M1293. 750,000. 1/17. D. D. & L., Ltd. Forms/C.2118/14.

Instructions regarding War Diaries and Intelligence Summaries are contained in F. S. Regs., Part II. and the Staff Manual respectively. Title pages will be prepared in manuscript.

WAR DIARY
or
INTELLIGENCE SUMMARY.
(Erase heading not required.)

Army Form C. 2118.

Place	Date	Hour	Summary of Events and Information	Remarks and references to Appendices
	February			
In the Field	Feb 6		Work on HUDSON positions. detachment at ALBERTA RD. Stay (damaged) taken from No 4 Bed, bed replaced with good stay + relaid	altered twice in error G.K.
	7		Work continued on HUDSON TRENCH position. 1 Roll of Camouflage carried from WINNIPEG RD to position in HUDSON TRENCH. No 1 sub-bed (ALBERTA RD) completed, new elevating stay on bed gun now ready for action 1 detachment at ALBERTA RD during day. 3 detachments gone down at dusk for scheme	G.K.
	8		Work continued on position in HUDSON TRENCH deepening + revetting of trench, excavating gun pit Usual detachment at ALBERTA RD for retaliation purposes. Three detachments standing by at ALBERTA RD. position. from 5-30 Pm to 6 am, as per instructions for scheme	G.K.
	9		Work continued at HUDSON TRENCH position, excavating pit + revetting trench side. Fired 100 rounds on hostile T.M. with Aeroplane observation, Map ref T24 b 73.12.	G.K.
	10		Work continued on position, HUDSON TRENCH. One detachment on duty at ALBERTA RD position during day light for retaliation purposes. Fired 100 rounds on hostile T.M. Map Ref T24 b 75.95. with aeroplane observation.	G.K.
	11		One detachment on duty at ALBERTA RD during day light for retaliation purposes. Work continued at position in HUDSON TRENCH. Prepared + fired 60 rounds from ALBERTA RD position, on hostile T.M'S, Map references - T.18 d. 93. 26 T.18 d. 94. 20, T.18 d. 87. 17. 100 rounds ammunition taken to ALBERTA RD. position	G.K.

(A7092). Wt. W12839/M1293 750,000. 1/17. D. D. & L., Ltd. Forms/C.2118/14.

Instructions regarding War Diaries and Intelligence Summaries are contained in F. S. Regs., Part II. and the Staff Manual respectively. Title pages will be prepared in manuscript.

WAR DIARY
or
INTELLIGENCE SUMMARY.
(Erase heading not required.)

Army Form C. 2118.

Place	Date February	Hour	Summary of Events and Information	Remarks and references to Appendices
In the Field	12		20 rounds of ammunition carried from WINNIPEG RD to ALBERTA RD position. No 2 bed ALBERTA RD taken up, new elevating stay complete put in bed, bed relaid. Gun now in action. Work continued on position HUDSON TRENCH	H.M.
	13		Sub. bed laid in No 1 pit, back put in No 2 pit HUDSON TRENCH position. Work on excavating No 2 pit, widening & revetting of trenches (HUDSON position). Usual detachment on duty at ALBERTA RD, during daylight, for retaliation purposes	H.M.
	14		Work continued on No 2 pit & trenches HUDSON TRENCH position. Fired 50 rounds on enemy wire, map Ref T 24 d. 3. 8	H.M.
	15		Fired 100 rounds on enemy wire, Map Refs. T24. d. 4. 4. Work continued in HUDSON TRENCH position. 150 rounds ammunition, taken to ALBERTA RD position	H.M.
	16		Work continued on HUDSON TRENCH position. 100 rounds carried to ALBERTA RD position.	H.M.
	17.		Work continued on defensive position, HUDSON TRENCH.	H.M.
	18.		Work continued on defensive position, HUDSON TRENCH.	H.M.
	19.		Work continued on defensive position, HUDSON TRENCH.	H.M.

(A7092). Wt. W12839/M1293. 750,000. 1/17. D. D. & L., Ltd. Forms/C.2118/14.

Instructions regarding War Diaries and Intelligence Summaries are contained in F. S. Regs., Part II. and the Staff Manual respectively. Title pages will be prepared in manuscript.

WAR DIARY
or
INTELLIGENCE SUMMARY.

(Erase heading not required.)

Army Form C. 2118.

Place	Date	Hour	Summary of Events and Information	Remarks and references to Appendices
1918				
Feby.	20.		Work continued on defensive position HUDSON TRENCH. Reconnoitred position on RED LINE, WILLERVAL SOUTH.	H.M.
	21.		Work stopped on defensive position, HUDSON TRENCH. Work commenced on new defensive position, RED LINE, WILLERVAL NORTH.	H.M.
	22.		Work continued on new defensive position, RED LINE.	H.M.
	23.		Work continued on new defensive position, RED LINE.	H.M.
	24.		Fired 25 rounds, retaliation. Work continued on defensive position, RED LINE	H.M.
	25.		2 guns brought out of line to billets. Work continued on defensive position, RED LINE.	H.M.
	26.		Work continued on defensive position RED LINE. Detachment on duty at ALBERTA Rd. during day light.	H.M.
	27.		Work continued on defensive position, RED LINE. Detachment on duty at ALBERTA Rd., during day light.	H.M.

(A7092). Wt. W12839/M1293. 750,000. 1/17. D. D. & L., Ltd. Forms/C.2118/14.

Army Form C. 2118.

Instructions regarding War Diaries and Intelligence Summaries are contained in F. S. Regs., Part II. and the Staff Manual respectively. Title pages will be prepared in manuscript.

WAR DIARY
or
INTELLIGENCE SUMMARY.
(Erase heading not required.)

Place	Date	Hour	Summary of Events and Information	Remarks and references to Appendices
1917.				
Feb.	28.		Work continued on defensive position RED LINE. Detachment on duty at HOBEKTA Rd. during day light for [illegible] purposes. All guns manned, SOS lines, standing by from 5.30. to 9 am. Fired 5 rounds on H.T.M., retaliation, map ref T.18 d. 97.66. Fired 2 rounds from HOBEKTA Rd. position, test for [illegible].	

H Wills
Capt RFA
O/C "Y" [illegible]

(A7092). Wt. W12839/M1293. 750,000. 1/17. D. D. & L., Ltd. Forms/C.2118/14.

C O N F I D E N T I A L.

W A R   D I A R Y

O F

Y /31 MEDIUM TRENCH MORTAR BATTERY

From 1st March 1918 to 31st March 1918.

V O L U M E   XXVII

Instructions regarding War Diaries and Intelligence Summaries are contained in F. S. Regs., Part II. and the Staff Manual respectively. Title pages will be prepared in manuscript.

WAR DIARY
or
INTELLIGENCE SUMMARY. Y/31. 31st Div. Artillery

(*Erase heading not required.*)

Army Form C. 2118.

MARCH 1st to 31st VOL XXVII

Place	Date	Hour	Summary of Events and Information	Remarks and references to Appendices
In the Field March	1918.			
	1st		Work continued on defensive positions, HUDSON TRENCH, MANITOBA ROAD, + RED LINE, (WILLERVAL NORTH).	HM
	2nd		Work continued on defensive positions, RED LINE.	HM
	3rd + 4th		All Guns, Beds + Positions handed over to 62nd Divnl T. Ms. All Men withdrawn from line to Rest Billet	HM
	5th		Battery moved by Motor Lorry to CAMBLIGNEUL.	HM
	6th to 21st		Physical + Recreational Training carried out according to D.T.M.O. instructions.	HM
	22nd		Battery moved by Motor Lorry to BAVINCOURT.	HM
	23rd 24th		Physical Training continued.	HM
	25th		Battery moved by Motor Lorry to DOUCHY-LES-AYETTE thence by hand carts to MONCHY-AU-BOIS.	HM
	26th to 31st x		x 1 Officer + 34 O.Rs attached to Divisional Ammunition Dump for Duty. Remainder of Battery + Stores moved by hand carts to GAUDIEMPRE.	HM

[signature]
Capt. R.G.A.
O/C Y/31. M.T.M. Bty.

CONFIDENTIAL.

Vol 21

WAR DIARY

OF

X/31 MEDIUM TRENCH MORTAR BATTERY

From 1st March 1918 to 31st March 1918.

VOLUME XXVII

Instructions regarding War Diaries and Intelligence Summaries are contained in F. S. Regs., Part II. and the Staff Manual respectively. Title pages will be prepared in manuscript.

WAR DIARY
or
~~INTELLIGENCE SUMMARY.~~
(Erase heading not required.)

Army Form C. 2118.

X 31 Medium Trench Mortar Battery

VOL XXVII

Place	Date	Hour	Summary of Events and Information	Remarks and references to Appendices
ROCLINCOURT	1.3.18		Work carried on defensive positions at SUGAR POST.	A.R.S
	2.3.18		Work carried on at SUGAR POST. Frame put on at No 1 pit	A.R.S
	3.3.18		Handed over guns, beds and positions to X 62 M.T.M. Bty	A.R.S
	4.3.18		Personnel withdrew to rest billet at ROCLINCOURT.	A.R.S
	5.3.18		Battery moved by motor lorry to CAMBLIGNEUL.	A.R.S.
CAMBLIGNEUL	6.3.18 to 21.3.18		Battery engaged in re-drilling, and training etc.	A.R.S
	22.3.18		Battery moved by motor lorry to BAVINCOURT	A.R.S
BAVINCOURT	23.3.18 to 24.3.18		Awaiting orders. Re-drilling etc continued	A.R.S
	25.3.18		Moved by motor lorry to DOUCHY LES AYETTE.	A.R.S
	26.3.18		Battery moved by road to MONCHY-AU-BOIS. 1 Officer and 24 ORs attached to 31st A.R.P. for duty	A.R.S

A7092 Wt. W1258/M1293 750,000. 1/17. D. D & L. Ltd. Forms/C2118/14.

Instructions regarding War Diaries and Intelligence Summaries are contained in F. S. Regs., Part II. and the Staff Manual respectively. Title pages will be prepared in manuscript.

2/

WAR DIARY
or
INTELLIGENCE SUMMARY.

(*Erase heading not required.*)

Army Form C. 2118.

X 31 Medium Trench Mortar Battery.

31 VOL XXVII

Place	Date	Hour	Summary of Events and Information	Remarks and references to Appendices
GAUDIEMPRE	27.3.18 to 31.3.18		Remainder of personnel moved stores etc: by hand-cart to GAUDIEMPRE	W.R.S

W. Robins Smith

Capt: R.F.A

O.C. X 31. M. T. M. Bty

A7092 Wt. W128 9/M1293 750,000. 1/17. D. D & L. Ltd. Forms/C2118/14.

C O N F I D E N T I A L.

W A R D I A R Y

O F

Y/31 MEDIUM TRENCH MORTAR BATTERY

From 1st April to 30th April, 1918.

V O L U M E XXVIII

Instructions regarding War Diaries and Intelligence Summaries are contained in F. S. Regs., Part II. and the Staff Manual respectively. Title pages will be prepared in manuscript.

Army Form C. 2118.

WAR DIARY
or
~~INTELLIGENCE~~ SUMMARY.
(Erase heading not required.)

Y/31. Medium Trench Mortar Bty
April 1st to 30th 1918. VOL XXVIII

Place	Date	Hour	Summary of Events and Information	Remarks and references to Appendices
GAUDIEMPRE	1.4.18		Part Personnel still attached to 31st A. R. P. for Duty	HM
	2.4.18		Do	HM
	3.4.18		Do	HM
	4.4.18		Do	HM
	5.4.18		Do	HM
	6.4.18			HM
	7.4.18		1 Officer and 11. O.R. attached to 165th Bde R.F.A for Duty	HM
	8.4.18		Do	
	"		Part personnel still attached to 31st A R P.	HM
	9.4.18		Do	
	10.4.18		Personnel withdrawn from 165th Bde.	HM
	11.4.18		Part personnel still attached to 31st A.R.P.	HM
	"		1 Signaller attached to 165th Bde + 4 Signallers attached to 170th Bde.	HM
	12.4.18		Do	HM
	13.4.18		14 O.R withdrawn from A.R.P. replaced by 14. O.R. of X31. M.T.M. Bty.	HM
	"		2 Signallers returned from 170th Bde.	HM
	14.4.18		11. O.R. still attached to 31st A.R.P. 2 Signallers still attached to 170th Bde +1 Sig: still attached to 165 Bde. 16. O.R. proceeded to 165th Bde for Duty	HM
	15.4.18		11. O.R still attached to 31st A.R.P. 2 Signallers still attached to 170th Bde 17 O.R still attached to 165th Bde.	HM
	16.4.18 to 30.4.18		Do.	HM

H. Mills.
Capt: R.F.A.
O/C Y/31. Med: T.M. Bty

(A7091) Wt. W12839/M1293 750,000 1/17. D. D. & L., Ltd. Forms/C.2118/14

31st Division

X/31 Medium Trench Mortar Battery

APRIL 1918

Vol 22

C O N F I D E N T I A L.

W A R D I A R Y

O F

X/31 MEDIUM TRENCH MORTAR BATTERY

From 1st April to 30th April, 1918.

V O L U M E XXVIII

Army Form C. 2118.

WAR DIARY
or
INTELLIGENCE SUMMARY.
(Erase heading not required.)

X31. Medium Trench Mortar Battery

VOL XXVIII

Instructions regarding War Diaries and Intelligence Summaries are contained in F. S. Regs., Part II. and the Staff Manual respectively. Title pages will be prepared in manuscript.

Place	Date	Hour	Summary of Events and Information	Remarks and references to Appendices
GAUDIEMPRE.	Apl 1 to Apl 6		Personnel still attached to 31st ARP for duty.	HRS.
	Apl 7.		1 Officer and 11 ORs attached to 170 Bde RFA for salvage work. remainder of personnel still at 31st ARP.	HRS.
	Apl 8 & Apl 9.		ditto	
	Apl 10.		Personnel from 170 Bde. returned, attached to 31st ARP.	HRS.
	Apl 11.		5 Signallers attached to 165 Bde: for duty.	HRS.
	Apl 12 & Apl 13.		Remainder of personnel still attached to 31st ARP.	HRS.
	Apl 14.		14 ORs withdrawn from 31st ARP and attached to 165 Bde RFA for duty.	HRS.
	Apl 15 to Apl 30.		14 ORs still attached to 165 Bde. RFA. remainder of personnel to 31st ARP for duty.	HRS.

M. Robins Smith
Capt. RFA
OC. X 31. M.T.M.B.

A7092 Wt. W125/9/M1293 750,000. 1/17. D. D & L. Ltd. Forms/C2118/14.

C O N F I D E N T I A L.

W A R   D I A R Y

O F

Y/31 MEDIUM TRENCH MORTAR BATTERY.

From 1st May to 31st May, 1918.

V O L U M E ~~XXIII.~~ XXIX.

Instructions regarding War Diaries and Intelligence Summaries are contained in F. S. Regs., Part II. and the Staff Manual respectively. Title pages will be prepared in manuscript.

WAR DIARY
or
INTELLIGENCE SUMMARY.
(Erase heading not required.)

Army Form C. 2118.

Y31 Med: T. M. Bty.

May 1st to 31st VOL XXIII

Place	Date	Hour	Summary of Events and Information	Remarks and references to Appendices
GAUDIEMPRE	1.5.18 to 4.5.18		Personnel still attached to 165 Bde R.F.A and 31st A. R. P. for duty. Usual parades, training etc at Rest Billet.	H. M.
	5.5.18		17 O.Rs posted to this battery from X40. T. M. Bty. Six 6" Newton Trench Mortars & 12 Beds drawn from 3rd Army Gun Park.	H. M.
	6.5.18 to 10.5.18		Personnel still attached to 165 Bde R.F.A and 31st A R.P. for duty. Usual parades, training etc at Rest Billet.	H. M.
	11.5.18		5 O.Rs (First Army T. M. School personnel) Posted to 1st Army Reinforcement camp.	H. M.
	12.5.18 to 25.5.18		Personnel still attached to 165 Bde R.F.A and 31st A. R. P. for duty. Usual parades, training etc at Rest Billet	H. M.
	26.5.18		Personnel withdrawn from 165 Bde R.F.A.	H. M.
	27.5.18		1 Officer + 15. O.Rs with 2 6" Newton Mortars complete attached to 32nd Divisional Artillery for duty. Part Personnel still attached to 31st A. R. P. for duty. Usual parades, training etc at Rest Billet.	H. M.
	28.5.18 to 30.5.18		Part personnel still attached to 32nd Div: Arty: for duty. Part personnel still attached to 31st A. R. P. Usual parades etc at Rest Billet	H. M.
	31.5.18		Personnel withdrawn from 31st A R. P. Part personnel still attached to 32nd Div: Arty. Usual parades etc at Rest Billet	H. M.

H. Mills.
Capt: R.F.A
O/C Y31 M. T. M. Bty.

(A7092). Wt. W12839/M1293. 750,000. 1/17. D. D. & L., Ltd. Forms/C.2118/14.

Vol 23

C O N F I D E N T I A L.

W A R   D I A R Y

O F

X/31 MEDIUM TRENCH MORTAR BATTERY.

From 1st May to 31st May, 1918.

V O L U M E ~~XXIII.~~ XX/X.

1st to 31st May 1918

Instructions regarding War Diaries and Intelligence Summaries are contained in F. S. Regs., Part II. and the Staff Manual respectively. Title pages will be prepared in manuscript.

WAR DIARY
or
~~INTELLIGENCE SUMMARY.~~
(Erase heading not required.)

Army Form C. 2118.

X31. Medium Trench Mortar Battery

VOL XXIII

Place	Date	Hour	Summary of Events and Information	Remarks and references to Appendices
GAUDIEMPRE.	1.5.18 to 4.5.18		Personnel still attached to 165 Bde. R.F.A and 31st ARP for duty.	W.R.S
	5.5.18		13. ORs posted from X/40 T.M.B to this Battery. Six 6" Newton Trench Mortars and 12 Beds drawn from 3rd Army Gun Park.	W.R.S.
	6.5.18 to 10.5.18		Personnel still attached to 165 Bde. R.F.A and 31st A.R.P for duty. Re-drilling reinforcements at Rest Billet	W.R.S.
	11.5.18		6 ORs (1st Army T.M. School) returned to 1st Army R.A. Reinforcement Camp.	W.R.S.
	12.5.18 to 25.5.18		Personnel still attached 165 Bde. R.F.A and 31st A.R.P for duty. personnel at Rest Billet engaged in re-drilling, training etc:	W.R.S
	26.5.18		16 ORs rejoined unit from 165 Bde. R.F.A	W.R.S.
	27.5.18		1 Section (1 Officer + 15 ORs) with 2 guns complete, attached to Guards. Div: Artillery for duty.	W.R.S.
	28.5.18 to 30.5.18		Re-drilling, training etc: at Rest Billet.	W.R.S.
	31.5.18		1 Officer and 14 ORs rejoined unit from 31st A.R.P.	

W Robin Smith
Capt. R.F.A
O/C X 31 M.T.M.B

C O N F I D E N T I A L.

W A R D I A R Y

O F

Y/31 MEDIUM TRENCH MORTAR BATTERY.

From 1st June to 30th June,1918.

V O L U M E ~~XXIV~~ XXX.

Instructions regarding War Diaries and Intelligence Summaries are contained in F. S. Regs., Part II. and the Staff Manual respectively. Title pages will be prepared in manuscript.

WAR DIARY
or
INTELLIGENCE SUMMARY.
(Erase heading not required.)

Army Form C. 2118.

V/31 Medium Trench Mortar Battery.
June 1st to 30th 1918. VOL XXX.

Place	Date	Hour	Summary of Events and Information	Remarks and references to Appendices
GAUDIEMPRE	1.6.18 to 5.6.18		Part personnel still attached to 32nd Div: Arty. Usual parades training etc at Rest Billet	H.M.
"	6.6.18 to 12.6.18		6 O.Rs attached to 31st Div: Arty for Signalling Course. Usual parades etc at Rest Billet	H.M.
"	13.6.18		1 Officer + 15 O.Rs with 2-6" Mortars complete rejoined from 32nd Div: Arty. 6 O.Rs rejoined from 31st Div: Arty.	H.M.
	14.6.18		Battery engaged in overhauling Mortars and Equipment prior to moving. and handing over to Guards T.M. Btys.	H.M.
MONCHY	15.6.18		Battery moved complete to MONCHY and relieved Y Guards Trench Mortar Bty. (1 Section proceeded to line and took over Mortars and positions at AYETTE. Reserve positions taken over at ESSARTS and QUESNOY FARM.	H.M.
	16.6.18 to 18.6.18		Work commenced in renovating Gun Pits and Dug-Outs at positions also on Dug-Out at ~~[illegible]~~ ESSARTS RESERVE.	H.M.
	19.6.18	10/40pm	Work continued at positions + Reserve positions. 20 Rounds fired on Enemy Trench from F.17.b.00.85. to F.11.d.50.40. at signal given by Infantry	H.M.
	20.6.18	10/30pm	Work continued at positions + Reserve positions. 10 Rounds fired on suspected T.M emplacement at F.12.c.9.3. 30 Rounds fired on Enemy Trench from F.17.b.00.85. to F.11.d.50.40.	H.M.
	21.6.18	12/Mid Night	Work continued with at positions + Reserve positions. 10 Rounds fired on T.M. emplacement at F.12.c.9.3. 30 Rounds fired on Enemy Trench from F.11.d.40.25. to F.11.d.90.55	H.M.
	22.6.18 to 23.6.18		Work continued with at positions + Reserve positions. 7 O.Rs. posted to 40th Divisional T.Ms.	H.M.

(A7092). Wt. W12839/M1293 750,000. 1/17. D. D. & L., Ltd. Forms/C.2118 14.

Instructions regarding War Diaries and Intelligence Summaries are contained in F. S. Regs., Part II. and the Staff Manual respectively. Title pages will be prepared in manuscript.

WAR DIARY
or
INTELLIGENCE SUMMARY.
(*Erase heading not required.*)

Army Form C. 2118.

Y/31. Medium Trench Mortar Bty

June 1st to 30th VOL XXX continued

Place	Date	Hour	Summary of Events and Information	Remarks and references to Appendices
MONCHY	24.6.18 to 25.6.18		Work continued on positions an reserve positions.	H.M.
	26.6.18		Positions in line, Reserve positions Guns, Beds etc handed over to 2nd Divisional Trench Mortars. Guns & Beds taken over from Y/2. M.T.M. Bty at St AMAND. All Ranks withdrawn from line, and Reserve positions. Battery moved complete by Motor Lorry to MONDECOURT.	H.M.
	27.6.18		Battery moved complete by Motor Lorry to LA BELLE HOTESSE	H.M.
	28.6.18 to 30.6.18		Battery engaged in overhauling Mortars and Beds taken over from Y/2 M.T.M. Bty Usual parades etc.	H.M.

H. Mills
Capt: R.F.A.
O/C Y/31 M.T.M. Bty
1.7.18.

(A7092). Wt. W12839/M1293. 750,000. 1/17. D. D. & L., Ltd. Forms/C.2118/14.

VR 24

C O N F I D E N T I A L.

W A R   D I A R Y

O F

X/31 MEDIUM TRENCH MORTAR BATTERY.

From 1st June to 30th June, 1918.

V O L U M E ~~XXIV~~ XXX.

1st – 30th June 1918

Army Form C. 2118.

Instructions regarding War Diaries and Intelligence Summaries are contained in F. S. Regs., Part II. and the Staff Manual respectively. Title pages will be prepared in manuscript.

WAR DIARY or ~~INTELLIGENCE SUMMARY.~~

(Erase heading not required.)

X 31st Medium Trench Mortar Battery

VOL. XXX

Place	Date	Hour	Summary of Events and Information	Remarks and references to Appendices
GAUDIEMPRE	1.6.18 to 2.6.18		1 Section with 2 guns complete attached to Guards DA. Remainder of personnel at Rest Billet engaged in re-drilling, training etc.	WRS
	3.6.18		6 ORs proceeded on signalling course at 31st Div. Artillery Signal School	WRS
	4.6.18 to 13.6.18		1 Section still attached to Guards D.A., retraining etc at Rest Billet	WRS
	14.6.18		6 ORs on signalling course rejoined unit.	WRS.
MONCHY.	15.6.18		Battery moved to MONCHY and relieved "X" Guards T.M. Bty. in the line. Section attached Guards DA. rejoined unit. One section moved into the line, one section in reserve positions, remainder occupied rest billet at BERLES.	WRS.
	16.6.18		Work commenced on dug out at positions near AYETTE	WRS.
	17.6.18 to 20.6.18		Work continued on dug-out at forward positions.	WRS
	20.6.18		41 rounds fired on F6c 60.40. and F6c 50.00 as per Infantry programme	WRS.
	21.6.18		Work continued on dug-out. 31 rounds fired as per Infantry programme.	WRS.
	22.6.18		Work continued on positions and dug-out near AYETTE.	WRS.
	23.6.18		4 ORs posted to 40th Divisional Trench Mortars.	WRS.

A7092 Wt. W12859/M1293 750,000. 1/17. D. D & L Ltd. Forms/C2118/14.

Army Form C. 2118.

Instructions regarding War Diaries and Intelligence Summaries are contained in F. S. Regs., Part II. and the Staff Manual respectively. Title pages will be prepared in manuscript.

WAR DIARY
or
~~INTELLIGENCE~~ SUMMARY. 2

VOL ~~XXIV~~ XXX

(*Erase heading not required.*) X 31. Medium Trench Mortar Battery

Place	Date	Hour	Summary of Events and Information	Remarks and references to Appendices
MONCHY.	23.6.18 to 26.6.18		Work continued on positions and dug out near AYETTE	HRS.
	26.6.18		Personnel withdrawn from the line to MONCHY on being relieved by 'X' 2. M.T.M.B. Battery complete moved by motor lorry to MONDICOURT.	HRS.
	27.6.18		Battery complete moved by motor lorry to LA BELLE HOTESSE	HRS.
LA BELLE HOTESSE.	28.6.18		Battery Commander, 2 Officers + 2 N.C.Os proceeded ~~to~~ to line to view positions etc.	HRS.
	29.6.18 + 30.6.18		Re-drilling, training, overhauling guns and stores etc	HRS.

H. Robson Smith
Capt. R.F.A.
O/C X 31 M.T.M.B.

A7092 Wt. W125.9/M1293 750,000. 1/17. D. D & L. Ltd. Forms/C2118/14.

1st - 31st July 1918

Army Form C. 2118.

Instructions regarding War Diaries and Intelligence Summaries are contained in F. S. Regs., Part II. and the Staff Manual respectively. Title pages will be prepared in manuscript.

WAR DIARY
or
INTELLIGENCE SUMMARY.
(Erase heading not required.)

Y31. Med: T. M. Bty
July 1st to 31st 1918
VOL XXXI

Place	Date	Hour	Summary of Events and Information	Remarks and references to Appendices
LA BELLE HATESSE	1.7.18 & 2.7.18		Battery engaged in overhauling Mortars and beds. Usual Parades, Training etc. 2 Mortars complete handed to Y29 Med: T.M. Bty	H.M.
	3.7.18		Battery moved complete by motor lorry to GRAND HAZARD. Took over from Y29. Med: T. M. Bty 2 Mortars complete, positions etc in the line. Also Reserve Positions	H.M.
GRAND HAZARD	4.7.18 to 7.7.18		Work commenced on positions forward and Reserve Positions & Billets. 6.7.18 27 rounds 6" Newton fired on Target E.17 b.35.42. In reply to S.O.S.	H.M.
	8.7.18	10.15 P.M.	17 rounds 6" Newton fired on TERN FARM. E17. b. 44. Good results obtained, a large number of coloured lights immediately went up, a dump of lights evidently hit. Work continued ~~with~~ on Positions etc	H.M.
	9.7.18	9.45 PM	32 rounds 6" Newton fired on TERN FARM. E. 17. b 44. in co-operation with infantry. Work continued ~~with~~ on Positions etc	H.M.
	10.7.18 to 13.7.18		Work continued ~~with~~ on Positions in Reserve	H.M.
	14.7.18		Mortars withdrawn from forward positions and placed in reserve Work continued ~~with~~ on Reserve positions etc	H.M.
	15.7.18 to 21.7.18		Work continued ~~with~~ on Reserve Positions etc.	H.M.

(A7092) Wt. W12839/M1293 750,000 1/17. D. D. & L., Ltd. Forms/C.2118/14.

Army Form C. 2118.

Instructions regarding War Diaries and Intelligence Summaries are contained in F. S. Regs., Part II. and the Staff Manual respectively. Title pages will be prepared in manuscript.

WAR DIARY
or
INTELLIGENCE SUMMARY.
(Erase heading not required.)

Y31. Medium T. M. Bty
July 1st to 31st 1918 VOL XXXI continued

Place	Date	Hour	Summary of Events and Information	Remarks and references to Appendices
	22.7.18		4 rounds 6" Newton fired on Target E.14. b. 6.1. for registration purposes. Work continued ~~with~~ on Reserve Position etc	H.M.
	23.7.18		Work continued ~~with~~ on Positions etc	H.M.
	24.7.18	12-35 am	96 rounds 6" Newton fired E.14. b. 6.1. in connection with Operations. Work continued ~~with~~ on Positions etc	H.M.
	25.7.18 to 29.7.18		Work continued on Positions etc	H.M.
	30.7.18	4 pm	51 rounds 6" Newton fired on Houses at E.14. b. 6.1. satisfactory results obtained. Enemy retaliation ~~slight~~ NIL. Work continued on Positions etc	H.M.
	31.7.18		Work continued on Positions etc	H.M.
	1.7.18 to 31.7.18		Section relief takes place every 7 days. Usual Parades, Training and ~~fatigues~~ working parties carried out at Rest Billet (GRAND HAZARD)	H.M.

H. M.
Capt: R.G.A.
O/C Y31 M. T. M. Bty

(A7092). Wt. W12839/M1293. 750,000. 1/17. D. D. & L., Ltd. Forms/C.2118/14.

CONFIDENTIAL.

WAR DIARY

OF

X/31 MEDIUM TRENCH MORTAR BATTERY.

From 1st July to 31st July, 1918.

VOLUME. XXXI

1st – 31st July 1918

WAR DIARY
or
~~INTELLIGENCE SUMMARY.~~
(Erase heading not required.)

Instructions regarding War Diaries and Intelligence Summaries are contained in F. S. Regs., Part II. and the Staff Manual respectively. Title pages will be prepared in manuscript.

Army Form C. 2118.

X/31 Medium Trench Mortar Battery

Vol. XXXI

Place	Date	Hour	Summary of Events and Information	Remarks and references to Appendices
LA BELLE	1.7.18		Training & re-drilling, all stores, guns, equipment overhauled	W.R.S.
HOTASSE	2.7.18			
	3.7.18		Battery moved by motor lorry to GRAND HAZARD, and relieved X.9th Medium Trench Mortars in the line.	W.R.S.
GRAND HAZARD	4.7.18		Work commenced on new encampment at E.27a.	W.R.S.
	5.7.18		Work commenced on Numbers 1 and 2 reserve positions at E.27d.	W.R.S.
	11.7.18		and work continued on new encampment.	
	12.7.18		Work commenced on Numbers 3 and 4 reserve positions at E.27a.	W.R.S.
	18.7.18			W.R.S.
	20.7.18		Work continued on reserve positions and encampment.	
	21.7.18		2 temporary emplacements made, guns placed in position in accordance with Infantry Programme, and 50 rounds fired into E.30.a.6.4.	W.R.S.
	22.7.18		2 emplacements made and 50 rounds 6" Newton fired into Enclosure in E.30.d.2.0 as per Infantry Programme.	W.R.S.

A7092 Wt. W128.9/M1293 750,000. 1/17. D. D & L. Ltd. Forms/C2118/14.

Instructions regarding War Diaries and Intelligence Summaries are contained in F. S. Regs., Part II, and the Staff Manual respectively. Title pages will be prepared in manuscript.

WAR DIARY
or
~~INTELLIGENCE SUMMARY.~~
(Erase heading not required.)

Army Form C. 2118.

"X" 31 Medium Trench Mortar Battery

VOL XXXI

Place	Date	Hour	Summary of Events and Information	Remarks and references to Appendices
GRAND [illegible]	23.7.18 and 24.7.18		Forward guns withdrawn, work continued on rear positions and new encampment.	W.R.S.
	25.7.18		2 guns placed in temporary emplacements in connection with raid.	W.R.S.
	26.7.18		Work continued on rear positions and encampment.	W.R.S.
	27.7.18 28.7.18		2 guns [illegible] in connection with raid removed to temporary positions and 60 rounds fired on enemy post at K.6.c.80.80.	W.R.S.
	29.7.18		70 rounds fired at enemy post at K.6.c.80.80.	W.R.S.
	30.7.18		Work on positions, guns and ammunition cleaned.	
	31.7.18	[illegible]	30 rounds [illegible] fired at enemy post at K.6.c.80.80	W.R.S.
		[illegible]	10 " " " " " "	
			Work on new positions.	W.R.S.

W. R[illegible] [illegible]
Capt. R.G.A.
O/C X 31. T.M.B.

A.6092 Wt. W12S 9/M1293 750,000. 1/17. D. D & L. Ltd. Forms/C2118/14.

CONFIDENTIAL.

WAR DIARY

OF

Y/31 MEDIUM TRENCH MORTAR BATTERY.

From 1st August to 31st August, 1918.

VOLUME XXXII.

Army Form C. 2118.

Instructions regarding War Diaries and Intelligence Summaries are contained in F. S. Regs., Part II. and the Staff Manual respectively. Title pages will be prepared in manuscript.

WAR DIARY
or
INTELLIGENCE SUMMARY.
(Erase heading not required.)

Y/31. Medium Trench Mortar Bty
August 1st to 31st 1918
VOL XXXII

Place	Date	Hour	Summary of Events and Information	Remarks and references to Appendices
NIEPPE FOREST	1.8.18		Work continued on Positions etc.	
"	2.8.18	2-30 am	13 rounds 6" Newton fired on E.17 d. 9.1. 12 rounds on E.17 d. 80.65. work continued on Positions etc	EMBL
"	3.8.18	12-5 to 12-20 am.	27 rounds 6" Newton fired on E.17.d.75.60. } In conjunction with 27 rounds 6" Newton fired on E.17 d. 9.8. } Infantry Operations. Work continued on Positions etc	EMBL
"	4.8.18 to 11.8.18		Work continued on Positions etc.	EMBL
	12.8.18 to 30.8.18		Work continued on Reserve Positions. Work commenced on two Reserve Positions at E.16.b.5.2.	EMBL
	31.8.18		1 Mobile Mortar taken forward to CUTLET CORNER at F21.a.6.4. Work continued on Reserve Positions.	EMBL
	1.8.18 to 31.8.18		Usual Parades and working parties carried out at Rest Billet GRAND HASARD D9.c.3.4.	EMBL

E.L. Gilbert Cooper 2/Lt R.F.A.
for Capt. R.F.A.
O/C Y/31. Med: T. M. Bty

(A7092). Wt. W12839/M1293. 750,000. 1/17. D. D. & L., Ltd. Forms/C.2118/14.

C O N F I D E N T I A L.

9826

W A R D I A R Y

O F

X/31 MEDIUM TRENCH MORTAR BATTERY.

From 1st August to 31st August,1918.

V O L U M E XXXII

Instructions regarding War Diaries and Intelligence Summaries are contained in F. S. Regs., Part II. and the Staff Manual respectively. Title pages will be prepared in manuscript.

1st–31st August 1918

WAR DIARY
or
INTELLIGENCE SUMMARY.
(Erase heading not required.)

Army Form C. 2118.

-2 SEP 1918

Vol. XXXII. X31 Medium Trench Mortar Bty.

Place	Date	Hour	Summary of Events and Information	Remarks and references to Appendices
GRAND HAZARD	1.8.18	12-10am	20 Rounds 6" N.H. fired at enemy post at K6c.75.80. Work continued on reserve positions	GW
		11-40pm	20 Rounds 6" N.H. fired at enemy post at K6c.75.80.	
	2.8.18		Work carried on at reserve positions Relief carried out.	GW
	3.8.18	6 am	30 rounds fired at enemy post at K6c.75.80. and 12 rounds at enclosure E30a.55.40. Enemy retaliation was rather heavy, causing 2 Casualties in one the Detachments. 1 Lorry load (120 rounds) [illegible] & guided up to positions and unloaded	GW
	4.8.18		Work carried on at positions, guns & ammunition etc. cleaned.	GW
	5.8.18		Work carried on at reserve positions and encampment	GW
	6.8.18		Work carried on at reserve positions	GW
	7.8.18		Work carried on at reserve positions and encampment. 120 rounds [illegible] unloaded from lorry and carried up to [illegible] Dump.	GW
	8.8.18		Work [illegible] reserve positions and [illegible]	GK

A7092 Wt. W128 9/M1293 750,000. 1/17. D. D. & L. Ltd. Forms/C2118/14.

Army Form C. 2118.

Instructions regarding War Diaries and Intelligence Summaries are contained in F. S. Regs., Part II. and the Staff Manual respectively. Title pages will be prepared in manuscript.

WAR DIARY
or
INTELLIGENCE SUMMARY.
(Erase heading not required.)

Vol XXVII X/31. Trench Mortar Bty.

Place	Date	Hour	Summary of Events and Information	Remarks and references to Appendices
LE GRAND HAZAR	9.8.18		Work carried on at [illegible] positions. Relief carried out.	G.K.
	10.8.18		Work carried on at positions, guns and ammunition cleaned	G.K.
	11.8.18		20 rounds fired on enclosure E.30.a.60.85. Work on positions	G.K.
	12.8.18	1.45am	24 rounds 6" T.M. fired in conjunction with Artillery on enclosure E.30.a.60.85	G.K.
		8.0am	21 rounds fired on enclosure E.30.a.60.85. Work on positions	
	13.8.18		Work carried on at positions. Guns and ammunition cleaned	G.K.
	14.8.18		Work carried on at positions	G.K.
	15.8.18		Work on positions, guns, ammunition [illegible] cleaned,	G.K.
	16.8.18		Work on reserve positions, forward positions [illegible] up and cleared of [illegible] etc.	G.K.
	17.8.18		90 rounds 6" T.M. fired on houses in E.24.C. & E.30	G.K.
	18.8.18		Work carried on at positions. [illegible] and [illegible] to WOOD Dump.	G.K.
	19.8.18		Work on positions and encampment.	G.K.

A7092 Wt. W128 9/M1293 750,000. 1/17. D. D & L. Ltd. Forms/C2118/14.

Army Form C. 2118.

WAR DIARY 3
or
INTELLIGENCE SUMMARY.
(*Erase heading not required.*) VOL XXVII X/31. Trench Mortar Bty.

Instructions regarding War Diaries and Intelligence Summaries are contained in F. S. Regs., Part II. and the Staff Manual respectively. Title pages will be prepared in manuscript.

Place	Date	Hour	Summary of Events and Information	Remarks and references to Appendices
GRAND HAZARD	20.8.18 to 25.8.18		Improvements carried out on reserve positions and encampment. All guns, ammunition &c at reserve and forward positions cleaned daily.	G.K.
	26.8.18 to 30.8.18		Work continued on ~~reserve~~ ~~position~~ reserve positions and encampment. Guns, ammunition, and forward pits cleaned daily.	G.K.

G. Kyes [illegible]
O/C. X.31. M.T.M.B.

A7092 Wt. W125 9/M1293 750,000. 1/17. D. D & L. Ltd. Forms/C2118/14.

CONFIDENTIAL.

WAR DIARY

OF

V/31 MEDIUM TRENCH MORTAR BATTERY.

From 1st September to 30th September, 1918.

VOLUME ~~XXXII~~ XXXIII

Army Form C. 2118.

Instructions regarding War Diaries and Intelligence Summaries are contained in F. S. Regs., Part II. and the Staff Manual respectively. Title pages will be prepared in manuscript.

WAR DIARY
or
~~INTELLIGENCE SUMMARY.~~
(Erase heading not required.)

Y31 Medium Trench Mortar Bty
September 1st to 30th 1918.

VOL XXXIII

Place	Date	Hour	Summary of Events and Information	Remarks and references to Appendices
NIEPPE FOREST	1.9.18		Work continued on Reserve Positions.	H.H.F.
	2.9.18		All Mortars, Beds, etc withdrawn from the line to Rear Billet GRAND HASARD.	H.H.F.
	3.9.18		Personnel engaged in overhauling Mortars etc.	H.H.F.
	4.9.18 to 7.9.18		1 Officer + 21. O.R. attached to No 2 Section 31st D.A.C. for Duty in Salvaging Ammunition in the evacuated area. Usual parades etc at Rest Billet GRAND HASARD.	H.H.F.
	8.9.18		1 Officer + 21 O.R. rejoined from 31st D.A.C.	H.H.F.
	9.9.18		Personnel engaged in overhauling Mortars etc.	H.H.F.
	10.9.18		Battery moved complete by Motor Lorries to field at A.4 a.4.6 Sheet 36 NW	H.H.F.
	11.9.18		Personnel engaged in making bivouacs etc.	H.H.F.
	12.9.18		1 Officer + 9 O.R. proceeded to 9th A.R.P. on METEREN – FLETRE Rd to take over.	H.H.F.
	13.9.18		5 O.R. proceeded to H.Q. 170th Bde R.F.A. for duty	H.H.F.
	14.9.18		5 O.R. proceeded to 9th A.R.P. for duty.	H.H.F.

(A7092). Wt. W12839/M1293. 750,000. 1/17. D. D. & L., Ltd. Forms/C.2118/14

Army Form C. 2118.

Instructions regarding War Diaries and Intelligence Summaries are contained in F. S. Regs., Part II. and the Staff Manual respectively. Title pages will be prepared in manuscript.

WAR DIARY
or
~~INTELLIGENCE SUMMARY.~~
(Erase heading not required.)

Y/31 Med: T. M. Bty.
Sept 1st to 30th 1918 Continued
VOL XXXIII

Place	Date	Hour	Summary of Events and Information	Remarks and references to Appendices
	15.9.18 to 18.9.18		Redrilling, training etc carried out. 5 O.R. Rejoined from 170th Bde on 17th.	HGF
	19.9.18		Battery moved complete by Motor Lorry to GODEWAERSVELDE and encamped for night. 1 Officer + 14 O.R picked up at 9th A.R.P.	HGF
	20.9.18		Battery awaited movement orders to proceed to II Corps Area.	HGF
	21.9.18		Battery moved complete by Motor Lorry to field near WOESTEN and encamped. Battery attached to 38th A.F.A. Bde.	HGF
	22.9.18		Personnel, 6 Sub. beds, 6 Gun Beds proceeded to forward Area at YPRES.	HGF
	23.9.18		Personnel engaged in constructing positions	HGF
	24.9.18 to 27.9.18		6 Mortars complete taken forward to be placed in positions. Parties detailed for carrying ammunition to positions.	HGF
	28.9.18		450 Rounds 6" Newton fired on Enemy Posts at C23b.90.00. & C29.b.55.85. in conjunction with operations with Belgian Army. Satisfactory results obtained.	HGF
	29.9.18		All Guns, Beds etc withdrawn from line to forward billet at YPRES	HGF
	30.9.18		Battery moved complete by Motor Lorry to field at A.4.a.4.6. Sheet 36 N.W. and encamped.	HGF

H G Fisher 2/Lt R.F.A.
for O/C Y/31. M.T. M. Bty.

(A7092). Wt. W12839/M1293. 750,000. 1/17. D. D. & L., Ltd. Forms/C.2118/14.

VR 27

C O N F I D E N T I A L.

W A R D I A R Y

O F

X/31 MEDIUM TRENCH MORTAR BATTERY.

From 1st September to 30th September, 1918.

V O L U M E ~~XXXII~~ XXXIII

Instructions regarding War Diaries and Intelligence Summaries are contained in F. S. Regs., Part II. and the Staff Manual respectively. Title pages will be prepared in manuscript.

WAR DIARY
or
INTELLIGENCE SUMMARY.
(Erase heading not required.)

Army Form C. 2118.

Volume XXXIII

VOL. XXVII X/31 Medium Trench Mortar By

Place	Date	Hour	Summary of Events and Information	Remarks and references to Appendices
NIEPPE FOREST.	1.9.18.		Work continued at positions.	NS.
	2.9.18		Battery withdrew from the line. All guns, beds, stores etc brought back to ALMOND HOUSE.	NS.
	3.9.18 to 6.9.18.		1 Officer and 20 OR's attached to 31st DAC for salvage work. All guns, beds, equipment and stores thoroughly over-hauled and cleaned.	NS.
	7.9.18		1 Officer and 5 OR's proceeded to new sector with 1 mobile gun complete.	NS.
	8.9.18.		14 rounds fired as per infantry programme.	NS.
	9.9.18 and 10.9.18		Re-training and drilling etc. Personnel rejoined from 31st DAC	NS.
	11.9.18		Battery moved by lorry and encamped in field at A[illegible] Mobile gun fired 25 rounds as per programme	NS.
	12.9.18		Work on encampment. Building of bivouacs and shelters etc.	NS.
	13.9.18		5 OR's proceeded to HQ 170 Bde. RFA for duty.	NS.

A7092 Wt. W12839/M1293. 750,000. 1/17. D. D & L. Ltd. Forms/C2118/14.

Army Form C. 2118.

Instructions regarding War Diaries and Intelligence Summaries are contained in F. S. Regs., Part II. and the Staff Manual respectively. Title pages will be prepared in manuscript.

WAR DIARY
or
INTELLIGENCE SUMMARY.

(Erase heading not required.) Vol. XXVII. X/31 Medium Trench Mortar Bty.

Place	Date	Hour	Summary of Events and Information	Remarks and references to Appendices
	14.9.18		5 [illegible] attached to 9th ARP	NS
	15.9.18 to 18.9.18		Re-fitting, training etc. and work on encampment.	NS
	19.9.18		Personnel rejoined from 40 Bde. and 9th ARP. Orders received to move into II Corps area. Battery moved by lorry and encamped for the night in fields near GODEWAERSVELDE	NS
WOESTEN.	20.9.18		Battery moved by motor lorry to WOESTEN.	NS
	21.9.18 to 27.9.18		Positions reconnoitred, personnel, mortars, beds stores etc taken to forward Billet near YPRES. Battery attached to 8th Belgian Division. Work on positions commenced and ammunition taken forward. Positions completed and 6 mortars ready for immediate action.	NS
	28.9.18		450 rounds 6" T.M. fired on enemy trench running from C29 c 63.53. to C29 c 99.01 and trench running through C29 central This was carried out in conjunction with the Belgian Army and most satisfactory results obtained.	NS

A7092 Wt. W123.9/M1293 750,000. 1/17. D. D. & L. Ltd. Forms C2118/14.

Instructions regarding War Diaries and Intelligence Summaries are contained in F. S. Regs., Part II. and the Staff Manual respectively. Title pages will be prepared in manuscript.

WAR DIARY
or
INTELLIGENCE SUMMARY.

(*Erase heading not required.*) VOL XXVII X/31 Medium Trench Mortar Battery.

Army Form C. 2118.

Place	Date	Hour	Summary of Events and Information	Remarks and references to Appendices
	29.9.18		All mortars withdrawn from the line to Forward Billet near YPRES	AS
BAILLEUL	30.9.18		Battery moved by motor lorry to field at A10 b 1.5 (Sheet 36. NW) and encamped.	AS

A Singleton 2/Lt R.F.A.
O/C X/31. M.T.M.B.

A7092 Wt. W128.9/M1293 750,000. 1/17. D. D & L. Ltd. Forms/C2118/14.

C O N F I D E N T I A L.

W A R   D I A R Y

O F

Y/31 MEDIUM TRENCH MORTAR BATTERY.

From 1st. October to 31st. October, 1918.

V O L U M E ~~XXVIII~~ XXXIV

Instructions regarding War Diaries and Intelligence Summaries are contained in F. S. Regs., Part II. and the Staff Manual respectively. Title pages will be prepared in manuscript.

WAR DIARY
or
INTELLIGENCE SUMMARY.
(Erase heading not required.)

Army Form C. 2118.

Y31 MED: T.M. BTY
October 1st to 31st 1918.
VOL XXVIII

Place	Date	Hour	Summary of Events and Information	Remarks and references to Appendices
	1.10.18		Battery still encamped in field at A.4.a.4.6.	
	2.10.18		Battery moved complete by Motor Lorry to CAESTRE.	
CAESTRE	3.10.18 to 6.10.18		Personnel engaged overhauling Guns, Beds etc, and renovating billets.	
"	4.10.18 to 10.10.18		Battery engaged in Redrilling, Training etc. 6. O.R attached from 31st D.A.C. for instruction on 6" Newton T.M.	
"	11.10.18		6. O.R. proceed to H.Q. 170th Bde R.F.A. for duty.	
"	12.10.18 to 18.10.18		Redrilling continued. 6. O.R. from D.A.C. returned to Unit (14.10.18.) 6. O.R. rejoined from H.Q. 170th Bde R.F.A. 18.2.18. 2 Officers attd: 31st D.A.C. for duty.	
"	19.10.18 to 26.10.18		Redrilling continued.	
	27/10.18		Battery moved complete by Motor Lorry to HEULE.	
	28.10.18		Personnel engaged cleaning Mortars etc. 2 Officers rejoined from D.A.C.	
	29.10.18		3. Officers & 15 O.R. proceeded to VICHTE to establish a rear billet.	
	30.10.18		3 Officers & 15 O.R. proceeded to line with 1 Mobile Mortar complete. Remainder of Battery moved from HEULE to VICHTE.	
	31.10.18		15 Rounds fired on FACTORY in OKKERVITK in conjunction with operations. Mortar taken with infantry to CASTER. One NCO & 9 men attached for duty to 165 Brigade R.F.A.	

W. B. Hawkes 2/Lt R.F.A.
for O/C Y/31 M.T.M. Bty

(A7092). Wt. W12839/M1293. 750,000. 1/17. D. D. & L., Ltd. Forms/C.2118/14.

Vol 28

C O N F I D E N T I A L.

W A R D I A R Y

O F

X/31 MEDIUM TRENCH MORTAR BATTERY

From 1st. October to 31st. October, 1918.

V O L U M E ~~XXVIII~~ XXXIV.

Instructions regarding War Diaries and Intelligence Summaries are contained in F. S. Regs., Part II. and the Staff Manual respectively. Title pages will be prepared in manuscript.

1st - 31st Oct 1918

WAR DIARY
or
INTELLIGENCE SUMMARY.

(Erase heading not required.)

Army Form C. 2118.

X/31. Medium Trench Mortar Battery

Vol XXVIII

Place	Date	Hour	Summary of Events and Information	Remarks and references to Appendices
BAILLEUL	1.10.18		Guns & stores cleaned. Work on encampment.	
	2.10.18		Battery moved by lorries to billets near CAESTRE	
CAESTRE	3.10.18		Guns, stores & equipment overhauled & cleaned.	
CAESTRE	3.10.18 to 26.10.18		Re-training & drilling etc	
	27.10.18		Battery moved by lorries to billets at HEULE	
HEULE	28.10.18		Guns & stores overhauled	
	29.10.18		[illegible] & detachment proceeded to position at P5A and Q1A9[illegible]	
			1 Officer & 1 man proceeded to 2nd Army TM School	
	30.10.18		Battery moved by [illegible] to billets at [illegible]	
[illegible]	[illegible]		One NCO and one man killed in action. One man wounded	
			One NCO & [illegible] men attached to [illegible] Brigade	
	~~31.10.18~~		~~Battery en~~	

H Singleton 2Lt R.F.A.
O/C X/31 M.T.M.B.

A7092 Wt. W128 9/M1293 750,000. 1/17. D. D & L. Ltd. Forms/C2118/14.

C O N F I D E N T I A L.

W A R D I A R Y

O F

Y/31 MEDIUM TRENCH MORTAR BATTERY.

From 1st November to 30th November, 1918.

V O L U M E ~~XXIX~~. XXXV.

Vol. XXIX.

Instructions regarding War Diaries and Intelligence Summaries are contained in F. S. Regs., Part II. and the Staff Manual respectively. Title pages will be prepared in manuscript.

WAR DIARY
or
INTELLIGENCE SUMMARY.
(Erase heading not required.)

Y/31 Med: T.M. Bty.
November 1st to 30th 1918.
VOL XXIX

Army Form C. 2118.

Place	Date	Hour	Summary of Events and Information	Remarks and references to Appendices
	1.11.18 & 2.11.18		Mobile Mortar withdrawn from line to Rear Billet VICHTE. Battery moved complete to HEULE.	[illegible]
	3.11.18		Battery moved complete by Motor Lorry from HEULE to BOUSBECQUE.	[illegible]
	4.11.18		Personnel engaged in Cleaning of Guns, Beds & Cleaning of Billets 10. O.R. rejoined from 165th Bde R.F.A.	[illegible]
	5.11.18 to 7.11.18		Redrilling etc, 4 Mortars & Equipment handed over to Ordnance Transport attached from ~~B~~ 31st D.A.C. (8 O.R + 16 Mules)	[illegible]
	8.11.18 to 11.11.18		Battery moved with Transport Wagons to RENAIX.	[illegible]
	12.11.18 to 15.11.18		Battery attached to 170th Bde R.F.A. Redrilling etc.	[illegible]
	16.11.18 & 17.11.18		Battery moved with Transport to GULLEGHEM. Personnel attached to No 2. Section 31st D.A.C. for duty	[illegible]
	18.11.18 to 25.11.18		Duty with No 2 Section 31st D.A.C.	[illegible]
	26.11.18 to 30.11.18.		Battery moved with Transport to HALLINES.	[illegible]

E.M. Gilbert Roper 2/Lt R.F.A.
O/C Y/31. Med: T.M. Bty

(A7092). Wt. W12839/M1293 750,000. 1/17. D. D. & L., Ltd. Forms/C.2118/14.

C O N F I D E N T I A L.

Vol 29

W A R D I A R Y

O F

X/31 MEDIUM TRENCH MORTAR BATTERY.

From 1st November to 30th November, 1918.

V O L U M E ~~XXIX~~. XXXV.

Vol. XXIX.

Army Form C. 2118.

Instructions regarding War Diaries and Intelligence Summaries are contained in F. S. Regs., Part II. and the Staff Manual respectively. Title pages will be prepared in manuscript.

WAR DIARY
or
INTELLIGENCE SUMMARY.

(Erase heading not required.)

Vol. XXIX X/31 Medium Trench Mortar Bty

Place	Date	Hour	Summary of Events and Information	Remarks and references to Appendices
VICHTE	1.11.18		Four O.R. attached to Dump	RMLC
	2.11.18		Battery moved by Lorries to Billets at HEULE	RMLC
HEULE	3.11.18		Battery moved by Lorries to Billets at BOUSBEQUE. Personnel rejoined from 165 Bde Dump	[illegible]
BOUSBEQUE	4.11.18		Guns and Beds overhauled and cleaned.	[illegible]
	5.11.18 to 7.11.18		Re-drilling etc. All stores, guns and equipment overhauled and cleaned. 4 Mortars and Equipment returned to D.A.D.O.S.	[illegible]
	8.11.18 to 11.11.18		Battery moved by road to RUSSEIGNIES	RMLC
	12.11.18 to 15.11.18		Battery attached to 165 Bde. R.F.A. Awaiting instructions	[illegible]
	16.11.18 to 17.11.18		Battery moved by road to GULLEGHEM	[illegible]
	17.11.18 to 31.11.18.		Battery personnel attached to 1st Section 31 D.A.C for all duties	

[illegible] Capt. R.F.A. for O.C. X.31 M.T.M. Bty

A7092 Wt. W128 9/M1293 750,000. 1/17. D. D & L. Ltd. Forms/C2118/14.

C O N F I D E N T I A L.

W A R   D I A R Y

O F

Y/31 MEDIUM TRENCH MORTAR BATTERY.

From 1st December to 31st December,1918.

V O L U M E XXX.VI.

Instructions regarding War Diaries and Intelligence Summaries are contained in F. S. Regs., Part II. and the Staff Manual respectively. Title pages will be prepared in manuscript.

WAR DIARY
or
INTELLIGENCE SUMMARY.
(Erase heading not required.)

Army Form C. 2118.

Y31 Medium Trench Mortar Bty.
December 1st to 31st 1918.
VOL XXIX XXXVI

Place	Date	Hour	Summary of Events and Information	Remarks and references to Appendices
In the Field	1.12.18 to 6.12.18		Battery still attached to No 2 Section 31st D.A.C. for duty	
"	7.12.18		Battery moved complete with No 2 Section D.A.C. from HALLINES to ESQUERDES.	
"	8.12.18 to 31.12.18		Duty with No 2 Section D.A.C. Transport + 6 Drivers returned to original unit (No 3 Section 31st D.A.C.) on 31.12.18.	

[illegible signature] 2/Lt R.G.A.
O/C Y31 Med: T.M. Bty.

(A7092). Wt. W12839/M1293. 750,000. 1/17. D. D. & L., Ltd. Forms/C2118/14.

Instructions regarding War Diaries and Intelligence Summaries are contained in F. S. Regs., Part II. and the Staff Manual respectively. Title pages will be prepared in manuscript.

WAR DIARY
or
INTELLIGENCE SUMMARY.
(Erase heading not required.)

Army Form C. 2118.

~~Vol XXX~~ Vol XXVI.

X/31. Medium ~~Trench~~ Mortar Bty.

Place	Date	Hour	Summary of Events and Information	Remarks and references to Appendices
In the field	1.12.18 to 6.12.18		Battery attached for duty to No. 1 Section 31 D.A.C	[initials]
	7.12.18		Battery moved from HALLINES to billets in ESQUERDES.	[initials]
	8.12.18 to 31.12.18		Battery attached to No. 1 Section 31st DAC for duty. Transport attached from No. 3 Section returned on 31.12.18.	[initials]

[signature]
2nd Lt for Capt. R.F.A.
o/c X/31. M.T.M. Bty.

A7092 Wt. W128 9/M1293 750,000. 1/17. D. D & L. Ltd. Forms/C2118/14.

31

Vol 31

CONFIDENTIAL.

WAR DIARY

OF

X/31 MEDIUM TRENCH MORTAR BATTERY.

From 1st January to 31st January, 1919.

VOLUME ~~XXXI~~. XXXVII

Instructions regarding War Diaries and Intelligence Summaries are contained in F. S. Regs., Part II. and the Staff Manual respectively. Title pages will be prepared in manuscript.

WAR DIARY
or
INTELLIGENCE SUMMARY.
(Erase heading not required.)

X 31 Medium Trench Mortar Battery

Vol. XXXVII

Army Form C. 2118.

Place	Date	Hour	Summary of Events and Information	Remarks and references to Appendices
Esquerdes	1.1.19 to 31.1.19		Attached to No 1 Section 31 DAC	A.M.
			A. Hicks Capt RFA OC X31 M T M Bty	

A5834 Wt. W4973/M687 750,000 8/16 D. D. & L. Ltd. Forms/C.2118/13.

C O N F I D E N T I A L.

W A R D I A R Y

O F

Y/31 MEDIUM TRENCH MORTAR BATTERY.

From 1st January to 31st January,1919.

V O L U M E XXXVII

Vol XXXVII

Army Form C. 2118.

Instructions regarding War Diaries and Intelligence Summaries are contained in F. S. Regs., Part II. and the Staff Manual respectively. Title pages will be prepared in manuscript.

Y 31 Tm B.

WAR DIARY
or
~~INTELLIGENCE SUMMARY.~~

(*Erase heading not required.*)

Jan. 1919.

Place	Date	Hour	Summary of Events and Information	Remarks and references to Appendices
Esquerdes	1st to 31st		Attached No. 2 Sect. 31st DAC	H M

H M [illegible]
Capt RFA
a/Adjt. 31st DAC

A5834 Wt. W4973/M687 750,000 8/16 D. D. & L. Ltd. Forms/C.2118/13.

C O N F I D E N T I A L.

Vol 32

W A R D I A R Y

O F

X/31 & Y/31 MEDIUM TRENCH MORTAR BATTERIES.

From 1st February to 28th February,1919.

V O L U M E XXXVIII

Vol. XXXVIII

Army Form C. 2118.

31st Div. Medm T.M.Bs. X/31 + Y/31 **WAR DIARY** ~~or~~ ~~INTELLIGENCE~~ ~~SUMMARY~~. Feb. 1919

(*Erase heading not required.*)

Instructions regarding War Diaries and Intelligence Summaries are contained in F. S. Regs., Part II, and the Staff Manual respectively. Title pages will be prepared in manuscript.

Place	Date	Hour	Summary of Events and Information	Remarks and references to Appendices
Esquerdes	1st to 28th		Attached 31st D.A.C.	
			28/19	
			[illegible] Capt. RGA Commdg. 31st DAC	

A5834 Wt. W4973/M687 750,000 8/16 D. D. & L. Ltd. Forms/C.2118/13.